MOB
STORIES OF DEATH AND BETRAYAL
FROM ORGANIZED CRIME

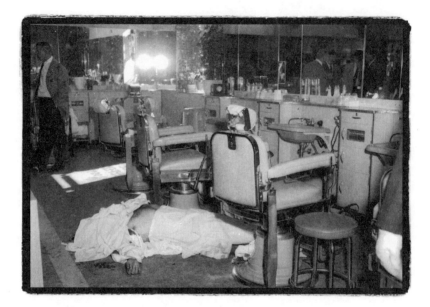

MOB

STORIES OF DEATH AND BETRAYAL
FROM ORGANIZED CRIME

EDITED BY CLINT WILLIS

Thunder's Mouth Press
New York

Adrenaline ® and the Adrenaline® logo are trademarks of
Avalon Publishing Group Incorporated, New York, NY.

An Adrenaline Book®

Published by
Thunder's Mouth Press
An Imprint of Avalon Publishing Group Incorporated
161 William Street, 16th floor
New York, NY 10038

A Balliett & Fitzgerald book

Distributed by Publishers Group West

Book design: Sue Canavan

frontispiece photo: © AP Photo Archive

Manufactured in the United States of America

ISBN: 1-56025-324-X

Library of Congress Cataloging-in-Publication Data is available.

For Mona and Oz

c o n t e n t s

p h o t o g r a p h s

introduction

W hen John Gotti, Sr., the notorious "Dapper Don", went to prison in 1992 for racketeering and murder, John Gotti, Jr. ran the Gambino crime family on his father's behalf. Gotti Jr. in 1999 sent *New York Times Magazine* reporter Jeffrey Goldberg a letter that included this passage:

> When I think of the American Indian I think of their courage, strength, pride, their respect and loyalty toward their brothers. I honor the reverence they share for tradition and life. These traits are hungered for in a society that is unfortunately plagued by those whose only values are self-centered and directed at others' expense…

Mobsters often fall back on words like honor, loyalty, respect and tradition to explain their appalling crimes. Government tapes and mafia memoirs often feature mobsters talking about their work in terms people reserve for the most sacred institutions in their lives—the Marine Corps, say, or the Catholic church.

Like those institutions, the mafia seems to promise authentic life—even a version of immortality—to its most faithful members. The institution in turn lives in its rituals and its language, which are embodied in the individual members. Gotti, Sr., in a typical outburst to confidants (recorded by an FBI bug at his favorite hangout) repeats the traditional Sicilian term *Cosa Nostra* (literal translation: "our thing") three times as he tries to make his point that the Gambino crime family will endure:

> And this is gonna be a *Cosa Nostra* till I die. Be it an hour from now, or be it tonight, or a hundred years from now when I'm in jail. It's gonna be a *Cosa Nostra* . . . It's gonna be the way I say it's gonna be, a *Cosa Nostra*.

That was back when Gotti Sr. was running the family; a job he got by ordering the murder of his predecessor, Paul Castellano, shot to death outside of Sparks Steakhouse in Manhattan on December 16, 1985. Castellano ten months before his death offered his own take on mob tradition. A couple of FBI agents arrested him at his Staten Island home on February 25, 1985, and the three men rode into Manhattan together. One of the agents remarked that their investigation had required them to trace Castellano's family back for five generations. The Don, age 69, responded with these words:

> Well, then you know. There are certain promises you make that are more sacred than anything that happens in a court of law . . . Some of the promises, it's true, you make too young, before you really have an understanding of what they mean. But once you've made those first promises, other promises are called for. And the thing is, you can't deny the new ones without betraying the old ones. The promises get bigger, there are more people to get hurt and disappointed if you don't live up to them...

Castellano and the Gottis worked hard to convince themselves that xi

their behavior reflected values worth preserving. Such self-deception is one reason that gangsters, like terrorists or serial killers, provoke a confusing mix of pity, disapproval and fear, all tinged with a sneaking fascination. We gaze with interest as well as loathing at the pathological gap between the gangster's self-image and the way he behaves in the world. The talk about tradition and honor and respect crops up among organized criminals of all stripes—Russian pornographers, Colombian drug lords, Italian arms dealers. Meanwhile, they all behave badly. Crime reporter George Anastasia's description of Philadelphia mobster Nicky Scarfo's mob during the early '80s (see Anastasia's 1991 book *Blood and Honor*) has a familiar ring to it:

> Life inside the Scarfo organization was a three-dimensional chess game. Plots and intrigue unfolded on several different levels and collisions occurred on various planes. So for months during the Rocibene war, protagonists would…socialize at weddings and funerals. If they happened to be in the same restaurant, they'd greet each other warmly and buy each other a round of drinks.

Even the gangsters get tired of it. Anastasia quotes Scarfo associate Nick Carmamandi:

> You heard of the double cross? In this business you gotta watch for the triple cross. You gotta always be alert. There's so much jealousy. Guys always trying to set you up, put you in traps. Trying to get ya killed. There was so much viciousness in this thing.

"Captains are greedy, just like everybody else," writes Joe Pistone, the FBI agent who spent six years as an undercover wiseguy under the name Donnie Brasco:

...so you never told anybody the whole story with money. If you made $100,000 on a score, you might tell your captain you came out with $80,000. That was the standard. It goes that way right up the line. That's why nobody totally trusts anybody.

And the penalty for such lies?

You might get whacked for $200—if it wasn't your first time skimming, or if the other guys needed to be shown a lesson, or if your captain or boss just felt like having you whacked . . . So the practice of skimming, from your own family, was common, and so was the result of getting whacked.

What motivates people to live that way? Henry Hill grew up during the late '50s in the Brownsville–East New York section of Brooklyn. His neighborhood was full of mobsters, as he explains in *Wiseguy*, the 1985 book he wrote with Nicholas Pileggi:

I used to watch them from my window, and I dreamed of being like them...to me, being a wiseguy was better than being President of the United States. It meant power among people who had no power. It meant perks in a working-class neighborhood that had no privileges. To be a wiseguy was to own the world...

Here is mob boss and future hit victim Paul Castellano again, explaining his point of view to the two FBI agents who arrested him:

We're not children here. The law is—how should I put it? A convenience. Or a convenience for some people, and an inconvenience for other people. Like, take the law that says you can't go into someone else's house...I have a house, so, hey, I like that law. The guy without a house—what's he think of it? *Stay out in the rain, schnook.* That's what the law means to him...

That kind of talk is self-serving, but that doesn't mean there's no truth to it.

Still, none of this explains how a value such as honor fits into a culture based on constant deception and casual brutality. Gangsters themselves seem confused about this, and no wonder: Their professional behavior is dishonorable by any definition that our broader culture endorses.

A gangster who wishes to model himself on some idealized version of a Native American—loyal, proud, reverent toward life—is in a fix. What's he supposed to do the next time he has to set up a friend? The gangster who asks himself what Crazy Horse would do might turn down the job—in which case he's liable to get whacked himself.

For gangsters like the Gottis or Castellano, who trace their corporate roots back to Sicily, the confusion derives in part from problems of translation. Pino Arlacchi created Italy's *Direzione Investigativa Antimafia* to fight organized crime in that country. His treatise on Sicily's mafiosi (*Mafia Business*, 1988) includes this passage:

> To behave as a mafioso was to behave honorably *(onorevole)*. It was to conform, in other words, to certain rules of cunning, courage and ferocity, of robbery and fraud...An honorable act is, in the last analysis, not much more than a successful act of aggression...

In short, behavior described as *onorevole* is violent, deceitful and successful—but entirely dishonorable by most standards.

Contemporary mafiosi in this country have used another word— *omerta*—to describe a code that governs a mobster once he is formally inducted into the *Cosa Nostra*. This version of *omerta* essentialy calls for the mafioso to keep his family's secrets. But the code of *omerta* in Sicily sanctioned a double moral standard with appalling aspects. Dealings with fellow mafiosi required

> ...'tact and fine manners...education, courtesy, kindness, and persuasion by argument and without compulsion.' But dealings with the common people and with one's enemies obeyed the opposite principle of false *omerta*...'false kindness, false condescension, false courtesy, which are snares concealing death to unsuspecting trouble-makers...and to the wicked and contemptible.'

Arlacchi goes on to stress the sheer difficulty and brutality of life in Sicily during the first half of the last century. Even family life was based not on intimacy but on subordination:

> The society into which the mafioso was born was a tragic and brutal world, sparing neither the weak nor the defenseless...Honor was connected less with justice than with domination and physical strength...In the carrying out of his day-to-day 'duties,' the mafioso did not follow any abstract ideal of morality and justice. He sought honor and power, and in pursuit of his goals he was quite ready to flout *any* established rule of conduct . . . When power was at stake, mafiosi had no hesitation in violating the most deep-rooted cultural and ethical norms.

Much of the literature of organized crime comes from the criminals themselves, in accounts that surprisingly often strike a note of happiness, of low-rent dreams fulfilled. It doesn't last. Things go wrong, and that's when wiseguys start trying to explain themselves in terms of the very notions that a mafioso must abandon to succeed: contemporary ideas of honor and respect, guilt and innocence. They may start talking about Native Americans or telling FBI agents about their childhoods. They may make excuses. Listen to Sammy

Gravano, the Gambino family hit man who betrayed John Gotti, Sr. to the FBI, and more recently was found guilty of drug trafficking with his son, age 24:

> In Bensonhurst, that was it, becomin' a made guy. It's all we kids ever talked about . . . I never saw the other side of it until I was in, and then it's too late and you just do your work . . .

The gangsters and their victims often are one and the same. There's Paul Castellano, his corpse sprawled on the sidewalk in front of Spark's. There's Gotti Sr., who arrived at the United States Penitentiary in Marion, Illinois, nine years ago to begin serving a life sentence. He took up residence in a six-by-eight-foot cell, with a radio, a 12-inch black-and-white television, a single cot, a basin and a toilet; he was to live in that space for 22 to 23 hours a day. There's Gravano, who went to see *The Godfather* when he was 27 years old. Years later, Gravano had this to say to prosecutor John Gleeson:

> I walked out (of the movie) feeling so good. That was my life. My life was honor and respect. Now, years go by, and the only thing I can love about my life is the movie.

A now-defunct financial magazine 15 years ago asked me to write a story on mob influence in the stock market. Financial regulators gave me the names of a half-dozen brokerage firms suspected of having some connection with organized crime. I called a few of the firms, introducing myself as a journalist interested in writing about their investment banking operations.

I arranged a meeting with the managers of a firm in New Jersey. That done, I hung up and spent the rest of the day in a state of mounting anxiety. I felt guilty about lying to my new acquaintances. I'd never before set out to harm anyone.

I began to imagine how angry they would be when my story ran. I didn't have any real enemies in the world; the idea that I might be making some dangerous ones scared me more than I like to admit even now.

I also disliked the prospect of telling lies to these people, and I didn't care if it was in a good cause. My worries about lying also circled back around to fear: If I told lies, I somehow lost my ability to defend myself from even the worst people. Who would believe me?

The truth is that I didn't want to believe that such bad guys existed, let alone help anyone prove it. I called the magazine editor and told him I couldn't finish the piece.

And now? I know that mafiosi and other gangsters exist, and so I think about why and what it means. It occurs to me that gangsters can't defend themselves: They have lied too often—to themselves, to each other, to the rest of us. They can only show us what can happen when we lie and hide; when we lose our capacity to acknowledge and live with the way things are. At some point, a real gangster cuts the ties that bind him to the rest of us and to the planet, and then gravity doesn't apply; he's spiraling off into the black, as alone as anyone can ever be.

I'm afraid of those people and they make me sad. I don't think if you're paying attention you can have the fear without the sorrow. And I'm interested: I read the stories. I want to know more—not because I think I can save them, but maybe because I'm interested in doing what I can to save myself.

—*Clint Willis*

from Underboss
by Peter Maas

Peter Maas' (born 1929) first mafia book was the 1968 best-seller The Valachi Papers, *about Mob turncoat Joe Valachi. Twenty-nine years later, Maas teamed up with Sam "Sammy the Bull" Gravano, former right-hand man to Gambino family crime boss John Gotti, Sr. Gravano's career as a wiseguy ended in 1992 when he testified against Gotti in federal court. Back in 1979, though, Sammy was still a rising star.*

A fter Sammy took over the Plaza Suite in Gravesend, just east of Bensonhurst, it became one of the most popular discotheques in Brooklyn.

The disco, housed in a building belonging to Sammy, was originally owned by four businessmen, who formed a corporation in 1979 called Enjoy Yourself, Inc., and obtained a liquor license. Two of them immediately had silent partners, a soldier in the Genovese family whose street name was Salty and a captain in the Colombo family, Vinnie Sicilian. Intimidated by this turn of events, the other two shareholders brought in Sammy for protection and support. This, in effect, granted him a fifty percent interest in the disco.

Unhappy with what he considered to be sloppy management, Sammy decided to take over the whole operation and got rid of the four original owners. "I just bullied my way in. I said I was going to make them an offer they couldn't refuse. I didn't have to explain. I imagine they all saw *The Godfather*. I had a sit-down with Vinnie

Sicilian and Salty. I told them that this doesn't do anything to their end. 'What you were getting, you will continue to get, but those other guys are out,' I said. They went along with it. All they cared about was their end. Matter of fact, they got more from me than what they got before. And everybody's happy. Every week I would send one of my guys to each of them with an envelope. They loved it."

Unlike his earlier club ventures, Sammy, now immersed in his construction projects, was not on the scene every night. "I got rid of the bouncers, who weren't doing their job, and put in guys with me, like Mike DeBatt and Tommy Carbonaro, known as Huck, who were also working my after-hours club, the 20/20. I have my own professional manager, Joe Skaggs. I bring in new bartenders and I hire good working neighborhood girls as waitresses. Everybody who was in there are people around me, or people who knew people who were close and loyal to me."

The Plaza Suite, located on the second floor, was more than 5,000 square feet. The decor was burgundy and gray. There was a long bar to the right as you came in. Banquettes surrounded the dance floor. In the rear there was a separate lounge area, a sort of VIP section.

Long lines curled around the block. The wait to enter was frequently an hour or more. Some nights it was simply impossible to get in. The music was basically deejay, but there were live performances as well. Sammy had "oldies" nights that featured, among others, Chubby Checker. On weekends, he would have first-rate attractions like The Four Tops, whose 1981 hit single, "When She Was the Girl," reached number one on the *Billboard* charts.

Sammy divided the ground floor of the building—2937 86th Street—in half. Part was devoted to his construction headquarters, with his private office and space for his brother-in-law, Eddie Garafola, and clerical help. The other part contained display space for a carpeting and hardwood flooring company he had started to complement his various construction bids.

"It was a sweet deal," Sammy said. "And then it all went crazy. It was incredible."

One day, in the late spring of 1982, Joe Skaggs came to Sammy and told him, "There's this guy. His name is Frank Fiala. He's been in here. He's a multimillionaire. He's got a Rolls-Royce. He's got private planes. A helicopter. A yacht. I don't know what else. He wants to rent the place for one night, an off night, on a Wednesday. He's giving himself a surprise birthday party."

"I forget what Joey said he'll pay. It was a lot. Around thirty, forty thousand, I believe. Something tells me this is very weird. The guy must be stark raving mad, throwing himself a surprise birthday party. What kind of person is that? But I said, 'Joey, you're the manager. I really don't care. Do what you think is best.'

"Joe must have been a little unsure himself. We've never done nothing like this before. He said, 'No, Sammy, I want you to be involved. I need your approval.' My brother-in-law, Eddie, and Louie Milito are with me in my office listening to this, and when they hear what the guy wants to pay to rent the joint, they're all for it."

Much of what Skaggs told Sammy was factual. Fiala was a millionaire several times over, who was then living in the Flatbush section of Brooklyn. His estranged wife resided in Virginia Beach. He owned two Cessna airplanes, one of which seated seven, and had two pilots on salary to fly them. He possessed a Mercedes, an Audi and a Cadillac limousine. And he did have a new Rolls-Royce, for which he paid $85,000. Since he desired immediate use of the Rolls-Royce, he threw in an extra $4,000 to have the showroom's front plate-glass window removed, so he could drive right out in it. Besides the cars, he had a 41-foot yacht. A familiar figure at Plato's Retreat, a fashionable sex club in Manhattan, he also was in the process of purchasing a helicopter he had been leasing on a trial basis.

Fiala, just short of his thirty-seventh birthday at the time, had arrived in the United States as a fourteen-year-old immigrant from Czechoslovakia. Ostensibly, his wealth stemmed from his ownership of a Brooklyn-based manufacturer of marine parts and supplies, where he had begun as an apprentice. What Sammy did not know was that Fiala had another source of income. He was a major cocaine trafficker. Eventually it would be discovered that in a feud with two rival Colombian dealers, Fiala not only had them murdered but their children as well.

Sammy saw Fiala at a meeting Skaggs set up. Milito and Garafola were present as well. Fiala did not know who Sammy was and addressed Skaggs. He reiterated how much he adored the Plaza Suite. No other place would do for his party, which he described in grandiose terms. There would be at least three hundred guests. He would take care of the catering himself. The surprise was that none of the guests would know in advance that it was his birthday. A feature of the party would be a raffle. Among the prizes would be a Rolls-Royce, a top-of-the-line Triumph motorcycle and a vacation trip on a luxury cruise ship through the Caribbean islands.

Fiala grew more expansive. He announced that he wanted to redecorate the Plaza Suite for the party. "He was telling Joey," Sammy said, "that he would put up another ten, twenty thousand, to do it for just this one night. He said he's going to rip this down and put that rip, paint this, whatever."

Sammy signaled Skaggs that he wanted to speak to him in private. Skaggs excused himself and Sammy followed him out of the office. Garafola and Milito tagged along. Sammy told Skaggs, "Joey, throw this bum out. Number one, he's nuts. Number two, he ain't touching this club. It's gorgeous. Forget about this. We don't need it.'

"But my brother-in-law's right in there saying to me, 'No, no, Sammy. This is found money. Let him have the party. Maybe we can rig the raffle, win the car and the motorcycle and the boat trip. We'll rig the whole thing.'

"So I finally go along with it. I said to Joey, 'Tell him he can have his party. He can have his raffle. But it's gonna be rigged. And absolutely no redecorating. He can't touch a thing.'

"Joey comes back and says, 'No problem. He has agreed to everything.'"

Preoccupied with his construction contracts, Sammy started hearing disturbing reports. Fiala was around the Plaza Suite all the time. He was taking Plaza Suite employees on airplane rides. He was in the disco constantly at night, doing cocaine himself, handing out bags of coke. "I hear he's like the Pied Piper," Sammy said. "In a week, he's got every-body and his mother following him around. I'm really starting to lose my patience with this guy, but Eddie and Louie are saying to go along with it. We got everything to gain, there's no downside. But I'm still get-ting more and more nervous. I hear that he's talking about how his party is the party to end all parties. It's going to be wild, all the weirdos and freaks that will show up.

"A night or two before the party, I sit down with my guys and I tell them, 'Listen, he's saying he's having three hundred people in there. If half of them are like this maniac, we could have a serious problem.'

"I said I wanted Stymie and my other main guy, Old Man Paruta, to be there. I told Mike DeBatt and Huck to get everybody together. They're there because they're the regular bouncers, but I want more of my people around. If there's three hundred of them at the party, I want at least twenty of us, my friends, there, too. That should make it even, if there's a problem."

Sammy decided to be on hand himself the night of the party. The first thing he noticed was that the only visible raffle prize was not a brand-new Triumph but a broken-down, filthy motorcycle of uncertain vintage, clearly not in working shape. And instead of the heralded three hundred guests, perhaps eighty at most had arrived. "I look at Eddie and Louie and I say, 'This is a scam. This guy scammed us. It's a joke.'

Then Joe Skaggs, the Plaza Suite manager, approached Sammy and informed him that the check Fiala wrote to rent the disco had bounced. Skaggs said that Fiala was claiming that it must have been a banking mistake. He promised he would take care of it.

"So I said to Eddie and Louie, 'See what we did? We let our greed override our brains. And I'm part of it. This is a total scam. As long as there's no more problems, don't worry about it. We got beat. We got roped in. It's not the first time and it won't be the last time. But let's use this as a good example for the future. Let's just get through the night.'"

Appalled, Sammy watched the highlight of the party: Fiala, seated in a chair in the middle of the dance floor, had his hair cut and his head shaved by two statuesque blondes. "I can't believe what I'm seeing," Sammy remembered. "They're shaving him bald while all these crazies are screaming and jumping up and down. Then the next thing I know, they've ordered in the food, Chinese food, a truckload of it. There are no utensils. People are eating with their hands. There's cartons all over. It's a mess. My stomach is literally turning. I'm in knots, but I'm trying to get through this night.

"Now Mike DeBatt comes over and says, 'Sammy, he's got a gun. He had it in an attaché case. He just took it out. He's got it in his belt.'

"Mike's a huge guy, huge, a college football player, and I said, 'Go over to him. Tell him very, very polite that we're not allowed to have guns in the place. Tell him to put the gun back in his case and let's just have a nice time.' Mike DeBatt does that and this Fiala puts it away. Then when he ain't looking, I send Stymie over to grab the case and put it in one of our cars outside.

"I send out for some guns for my guys. I tell Old Man Paruta, 'See them three guys around him? If there's a beef and they come out with anything, if they move in any way, shape or form to put their hands in their jackets or pants, anything like that, shoot them.'

"Who knows what could happen next? I've had it. My patience has gone. It's maybe two a.m. I have somebody call him over to the table I'm at and I say, 'Listen, Frank, you don't owe me nothing. But the party's over. Get rid of your friends.' I keep my voice very calm, very easy. I tell him again he don't owe me nothing.

"He starts taking medals out of his pocket, military medals. He starts talking about military things, what these medals are for. What the hell is this? He says, 'You insult me.'

"I told him, 'You can stick your medals up your ass. You want out of here with your life? Listen to me. Get your friends out *now*. You had your party. It's finished. I'm telling you, let's don't end it like a funeral.' He mutters a few more things, I forget what, but him and the rest of them are gone. I said to my guys, 'We learned a good lesson here.'"

Two days later Joe Skaggs approached Sammy and said that Fiala was so aggrieved that he wanted to buy the Plaza Suite and the building as well. The cost did not matter. It was the only way he could save face and live with himself.

Sammy replied, "Joey, tell him the place ain't for sale, OK?"

Skaggs then handed Sammy a bagful of cash from Fiala. It covered the amount of the bounced check. Skaggs reported that Fiala had said the mistake was made by his accountant, his bank, "or something." At any rate, Fiala was now fully paid up.

"Good," Sammy said. "The place is still not for sale."

The following day Skaggs returned with the news that Fiala was unwilling to take no for an answer. He was offering a million dollars. The property by itself, considering its location, was worth less than $200,000, if that. The Plaza Suite, of course, was a success, with a considerable cash flow easily hidden from the Internal Revenue Service. But a million dollars was a million dollars.

Despite his misgivings, Sammy said, "I have to admit that it rang my greed bell when I heard that million-dollar figure. A million was always a magical number for me. And when my brother-in-law heard it, he said, 'Sammy, you got to be crazy not to sell. Give it to this maniac. What do we care. You can always open up another disco.'

"I have my lawyer, who is also my accountant, check this Fiala out. He told me, 'Sammy, he's a nut, but he's for real. He's negotiating to buy a radio station. He's a multimillionaire. He's Czechoslovakian. He does have a yacht, planes, a Rolls-Royce, a couple of other major cars.'

"So I meet with him. He still don't really know who I am. I guess he figures I'm connected, but just how he isn't sure. Probably he doesn't care. I'm starting to think maybe he's putting too much of his product up his nose."

Fiala proposed to Sammy that he write a check for $100,000 as a down payment to be held in escrow. He would then pay $650,000 under the table in cash. At the closing, he would hand over a check for another $250,000, which together with the escrow check would be recorded as the sales price for tax purposes.

"He writes out the escrow check. Now we got to deal with the six fifty under the table. First off, he wants to give it to me in gold. He wants me to fly to Czechoslovakia or Yugoslavia, wherever the fuck he's from. I feel he's looking to whack me. I definitely ain't going to no Communist country, for shit sure. So that's out. Next, he wants to meet me at some private airfield in Jersey. I'll pull up in a limo and he'll have an armored truck there to give it to me. Sounds like James Bond shit to me. He's still talking gold. What am I going to do with six fifty in gold? I told him I won't do that, either. Then he says, all right, he'll have me go to this bank he has accounts in and I'll get it in green. To show you what numbnuts we are, me and my brother-in-law go down there with suitcases. But it turns out we have to sign for the money. We walk away. The suitcases are still empty."

Sammy finally devised a way to resolve the problem. He had a friend, Joe Ingrassia—Joe the Checkcasher—who ran the Bensonhurst Check Cashing Service. Ingrassia had many contacts in the money transfer business. One of them was an armored car service he used that carried large cash payrolls. A certified bank check for $650,000 from Fiala went to a dummy account Sammy set up. The check was subsequently deposited in the account of the armored car company. Ingrassia next went to the company and picked up the cash—in hundred-dollar bills—for Sammy. The transaction was completed on Friday June 25, 1982.

Even before this occurred, as soon as the escrow down payment by check had been made, Fiala, to Sammy's intense annoyance, had started acting as if he already owned the Plaza Suite.

"He's walking around with his head shaved," Sammy said, "and wherever he goes, he's got this entourage with him, I mean, twenty or thirty people, lots of girls, the Pied Piper. Of course, they're looking to get coke. It's totally unbelievable. He's got them all mesmerized. It's insane. Bizarre. I find out he's bringing people, painters, carpenters, to remodel the place. I put a stop to this. I said, 'Frank, you ain't doing nothing here until you own it. Till after the closing.'

"I can't make this up, what he's doing. He goes flying in his helicopter over some other neighborhood discos, discos that made guys own, part of my competition, with a bullhorn and he's yelling, 'Don't go there! Go to the Plaza Suite!'

"A captain in the Genovese family contacts me. 'Sammy, what are you doing with that helicopter?'

"I laughed. I told him, 'Bo, I ain't doing nothing. We're dealing with a nut who's looking to buy my joint. He did this. I had no knowledge of it. You think I would do something like that? Put a helicopter up while your customers are standing in line, yelling at them with a bullhorn? You know that isn't me. But come to think of it, maybe I should keep the joint and do that myself.'

"He laughs, too. We're good friends. 'Yeah, but the guy ain't with you, is he? 'Cause we'll open up his ass if we catch him.'

"'Nah,' I said. 'Do what you want. He definitely ain't with me. I'm taking no responsibility for him.'

"To keep tabs on him when I'm not around, I have Mike DeBatt play up to him. He tells Fiala that he wants to continue to work for him as a bouncer, how I always underpaid him. And now I know Fiala doesn't have a clue who I actually am. He's saying to Mike behind my back, 'Fuck this Sammy. Fuck this punk. When I take over, I'm doing this, that.'

"I hear this and I'm gritting my teeth. I tell myself business is business. Take it easy. Be quiet. Let me just get through this. Then, after that, so what? We're through with him and I got the million. I'll just swallow a little abuse. Be smart. It don't mean nothing. There'll be another time."

The closing was scheduled for Monday, June 28. On the previous Friday night, after Ingrassia had gotten the cash from the armored car company and Sammy had left for his New Jersey farm, Sammy learned that Fiala had already physically moved into his private downstairs office. Not only that, but Fiala had ordered work to begin breaking through an office wall for a staircase leading directly to the Plaza Suite, so he would not have to use the 86th Street building entrance and walk around the block to enter the disco. He had brought in Doberman guard dogs. He had armed men patrolling the premises. "I heard they were Czechoslovakian, whatever," Sammy remembers. "They didn't speak English. It started to look like a con-centration camp."

This ultimate affront enraged Sammy beyond redemption. He told Eddie Garafola, "I can't take it no more from this bum." Accompanied by Garafola, he arrived on the scene. He asked some of the girls on his staff if they were all right.

"Yes," they said.

"Where is he?"

"He's in your office. He's moved in. He's put in a lot of his stuff."

Sammy, followed by Garafola, stormed into his office. Fiala was standing behind Sammy's desk, smirking. He idly spun Sammy's chair around to sit in it. A brace of Dobermans growled menacingly.

Sammy ignored them. "Frank, what do you think you're doing?" he rasped. "This don't belong to you till the closing. Get the hell out of here."

Fiala reached into a desk drawer and pulled out an Uzi. He ordered Sammy and Garafola to sit down. They sat.

"Eddie turned white as a ghost, pure white," Sammy said. "That Uzi was pointed right at me. My body completely tensed up like it was a piece of steel. I figured the bullets are coming the next second.

"But this Fiala didn't pull the trigger. He said, 'You fucking grease-balls, you do things my way. You think you're so tough. The Colom-bians are really tough. The Colombians fucked with me and I took them out. You greaseballs are nothing.'

"I realized he's talking, not shooting. If somebody's going to kill you, he don't talk. He shoots. With that, I kind of caught my second wind. I said as calm as I could, 'Listen, Frank, take it easy. What are you getting excited about? This is a business deal. There's always little hur-dles you got to get over. On Monday, we'll go to the lawyers for the closing. You're right. The deal is already three-quarters done. You want to stay in the office? Fine. It's yours, Bo.'"

Sammy watched Fiala relax and lay down the Uzi on the desk. "So we're not going to get whacked. I tell Eddie to get up and we leave. I've never been so mad in my life. As soon as we're outside, I said, 'Eddie, this fucker is going tonight. He should have killed me right then and there. He would've had a better shot with the law than with me.'"

He instructed Garafola to round up Sammy's key men—Stymie, Milito, Paruta, Mike DeBatt, Huck, Nick (Nicky Cowboy) Mormando. They were to rendezvous at Stymie's bar, Doc's.

When Garafola started to advise caution, Sammy snapped, "Shut the fuck up. I'm not asking you for advice. I'm telling you what to do. Look at that guy sticking that Uzi in my face. Look what we created here. Again, it was our greed. That party wasn't enough. Even though you told me to go ahead and deal with him, I'm the biggest jerk-off because I'm the boss and I did it. Just don't open your mouth one more time. Thus guy is history and it's over with."

With the interior entry from Sammy's old office up to the Plaza Suite still unfinished, Fiala would have to exit the building on 86th Street, turn left, walk to the corner and proceed about sixty feet up a side street to the disco's front door. Some ten feet past the entrance was an alley.

Sammy stationed Nicky Cowboy in a car parked on the corner. He had a shotgun. If anyone in the group that normally accompanied Fiala drew a gun, he was to start shooting. Eddie Garafola would stand on the opposite corner of the side street. As Fiala neared the Plaza Suite, Garafola was to call out to him. Armed with pistols and wearing ski masks, Stymie and Milito would be hiding in the alley. Michael DeBatt would be at his usual post by the door. Huck was inside in case of trouble there. Sammy himself would be on the side street near the alley. At a prearranged signal from him, Stymie and Milito would leap out and gun down Fiala.

"Everybody is in place and we're waiting. Down at the corner, Eddie sees him coming and nods to me. I look at Mike DeBatt at the door and give him a nod. It's about to happen.

"Fiala rounds the corner. He has a small entourage with him, maybe eight or ten people. After he passes Eddie and is almost at the door, Eddie shouts, 'Hey, Frank!'

"Fiala starts to turn to see who's calling to him. In turning, he sees me. I am no more than six or seven feet away from him. He's looking at me, eye-to-eye. Maybe he picked up the fury in my face or eyes. You could see the puzzled expression he had. I said, 'Hey, Frank, how you doing?'

"As soon as Louie and Stymie heard me say 'Frank,' they run out of the alley. Louie gets him with a shot to the head. He flops to the sidewalk. Louie goes and stands over him. He leans down and puts his gun to one eye and blows it out. Then he puts the gun in the other eye and blows it away, too.

"There's pandemonium on the street. People are running every which way. They're screaming. Some people are trying to get into the disco. Others are trying to get out. Mike DeBatt by the door acts like he's panicking. He's yelling, 'Get down! Get down! Somebody's shooting.' He's holding the door, so nobody's getting in or out.

"I had another car, a getaway car, up the street. Stymie and Louie immediately head for it and take off. Down at the corner, Nicky Cowboy has his shotgun ready. But Fiala's people are in total shock. They ain't doing nothing.

"I walked right up to Fiala's body. I spit on him. Then I go to Nicky Cowboy's car. So does Eddie. We both had guns. We give them to Nicky and off he goes. The hit men are gone. The guns are gone.

"I'm ready to cross over to a parking lot with Eddie where our car is. But by now the cops are all over. They're telling everybody, even people on the sidewalk, not to move. We're stuck. Just then some kid starts running away, why I don't know, and a whole load of cops go after him.

"In the confusion, Eddie and me make it to the parking lot. A car is pulling into the lot with some neighborhood girls I know who are always in the Plaza Suite. I said to one of them, who I know the best, 'Listen, we came together.'

"She says, 'What happened?' and I said, 'Somebody got shot in front of my joint. I can't believe it. In case any cops ask, I was with you.'

"She says, 'Yes, absolutely,' and puts her arm around me. 'I'll be your alibi.'

"I said, 'I don't really need an alibi. But it's my place, and with something like this, I could wind up with a problem. I appreciate what you're saying.' And I kissed her on the forehead.

"So we're standing there like spectators. The cops come back dragging this kid and throw him in a squad car. An ambulance came for Fiala's body. One look and they knew he was gone. They just covered him up. The cops never came over to the lot. They never talked to me or questioned me.

"They questioned people who were still on the side street, but the best they got was that men in ski masks did it. They questioned people who were inside the Plaza Suite. They questioned Mike DeBatt, who said he was so busy at the door he didn't see anything. He said after he heard shots, he just wanted to stop people from coming out so they wouldn't get hurt and he was shouting at people outside to get down."

Sammy and Garafola left the lot without incident. The entire hit team assembled at Doc's. Sammy congratulated them on a "beautiful piece of work." The gun used to dispatch Fiala was thrown in the ocean. Louie Milito and Stymie were instructed to burn all the clothes they were wearing. Garafola was ordered to get in touch with his uncle, who was custodian of the building that housed the disco. He was to wash down the side street where the murder had taken place in case the police returned seeking forensic evidence.

According to the police, the murder occurred at approximately 2 a.m. on Sunday, June 27, 1982. A detective told reporters that "Fiala appeared to be a free-spending, eccentric, self-made millionaire, who was in the process of purchasing the discotheque." Another detective noted, "On the surface, he was a legit guy, but we're not sure. Obviously, he did something wrong to somebody." He added that federal and state law enforcement authorities would be contacted. It was reported that two Doberman guard dogs had been found in an office Fiala was using. The office was described as a "porn palace," filled with hard-core movies, books, magazines and "sex paraphernalia."

The Plaza Suite, it was learned, did not have a requisite operating license from the city's Department of Consumer Affairs. A spokesman for the State Liquor Authority acknowledged that actual ownership of the disco was murky at best. The original applicant for a liquor license, an insurance salesman, had apparently attempted to transfer ownership to an executive in a printing company. But because of a paperwork backlog, the transfer had yet to go through. Both men claimed they had never heard of Fiala. Employees at the Plaza Suite said that they had never seen either of the supposed owners.

Eyewitness accounts varied tremendously. There had been two masked gunmen. Or there had been four, possibly five, of them. The gunmen had burst out of a car double-parked in front of the disco. Another version had gunmen shadowing Fiala up the street, tapping him on the shoulder and shooting him when he turned around.

Admitting that they had no definitive leads, detectives were reduced to saying that Fiala's murder was carried out very professionally.

"Without question," Sammy said, "the entire neighborhood knew I did the hit. But nobody said a word."

from Donnie Brasco
by Joseph D. Pistone
with Richard Woodley

Joseph Pistone (born 1941) spent six years masquerading as a wiseguy with the Bonanno organized crime family. Some of Pistone's most artful and dangerous work occurred during his early efforts to meet and impress the right people. He teamed with writer Richard Woodley to tell his story.

W e had a list of places where wiseguy-type fences were known to hang out. This was going to be a seven-day-a-week job, going around to these bars and restaurants and clubs. The target places were not necessarily "mob" joints. Sometimes they were night spots and restaurants owned in whole or in part by the mob. More often they were just places where wiseguys and their associates liked to hang out.

I would cruise these places, mostly in midtown or lower Manhattan, have a drink or dinner, not talking much or making any moves, just showing my face so people would get used to seeing me. Places like the Rainbow Room in the RCA Building in Rockefeller Center, Separate Tables on Third Avenue, Vesuvio Restaurant on Forty-eighth Street in the heart of the theater district, Cecil's Discotheque on Fifty-fourth Street, the Applause Restaurant on Lexington Avenue.

We didn't concentrate on places in Little Italy because I would have been too obvious. You don't just start hanging out in places there without knowing anybody. You're either a tourist or some kind of trouble. I didn't try to introduce myself to anybody or get into any conversations for a while. Mob guys or fences I recognized were mixed in with ordinary customers, what wiseguys call "citizens," people not connected with the mob. After I had been to a place a few times, I might say hello to the bartender if he had begun to recognize me. The important thing was just to be seen and not to push anything; just get noticed, get established that I wasn't just a one-shot visitor.

I didn't flash around a lot of money because that tags you either as a cop or a mark. A mark is somebody that looks ripe for getting conned out of his money. And a cop typically might flash money when he was looking to make a buy of something illegal, like tempting somebody to offer swag—stolen goods—in order to make a bust. No street guy is going to throw money all over the place unless he's trying to attract attention. Then the question is: Why is he trying to attract attention? I didn't want to attract that kind of attention. So to do it right, you don't go in and start spending a lot of money or showing off stuff or trying to make conversation, because you don't know them and they don't know you.

You take a job like this in very small, careful steps, not just to avoid suspicion but also to leave behind you a clean, credible trail. You never know what part of what you do will become part of your history when people want to check on you. You want to establish right away, everywhere you go, that you don't have a big mouth, and that you don't have too big a nose about other people's business. You have to be patient, because you never know where anything will lead. Basically I wanted to keep my own personality, which was low-key. I felt that the time would come in conversation with somebody what my game was.

One of the first places I frequented was Carmello's, a pleasant restaurant at 1638 York Avenue, near Eighty-sixth Street and the East River. It wasn't far from my new apartment, and I wanted a place where I could stop in for a late dinner or drink near where I lived. This wasn't one of the primary places we had targeted, but we knew that some wiseguy types hung out there. Our information was that the restaurant was owned by Joey and Carmine Zito, who were members of the Genovese crime family, headed by Fat Tony Salerno.

For weeks I roamed around and hung out at these places. Time dragged. I rarely drink alcohol. I don't smoke. Before I came on the job as an FBI agent, I once had a job as a bartender, and it was one of my least favorite things, hanging out in a bar all night watching people drink and listening to drinkers talk. During these weeks, in the evening at a bar, I might start off with a Scotch, then I'd switch to club soda for the rest of the night.

Occasionally I saw somebody we had targeted. I recognized them from the pictures I had been shown in preparation. But I never got an opportunity to get into conversation with them. It isn't wise to say to the bartender, "Who is that over there? Isn't that so-and-so?" I wanted to get to be known as a guy who didn't ask too many questions, didn't appear to be too curious. With the guys we were after, it was tough to break in. A wrong move—even if you're just on the fringes of things—will turn them off. While I was having a couple of drinks or dinner, I was always interested in what was going on in the place. I was always observing, listening, remembering, while still trying to put across the impression that I was oblivious to who was in there.

All through October and November I hung out, watching, listening, not advancing beyond that. It was boring a lot of the time but not discouraging. I knew it would take time. It is a delicate matter, maneuvering your way in. You don't just step into an operation like this and start dealing. Associates of wiseguys don't deal with people they don't know or who somebody else doesn't vouch for. So for the first two or three months I had to lay the initial groundwork that would lead to being known and having somebody vouch for me.

All this time—in fact, for the entire six years of the overall operation—I never made notes of what I was doing. I didn't know if at any time I was going to be braced—somebody might check me out, cops or crooks, so I never had anything incriminating in my apartment or on my person. Every couple of days or so, depending on the significance, I would phone my contact agent to fill him on what was going on, who I had seen where, doing what.

One thing that went on at Carmello's was backgammon. Men played backgammon at the bar. I noticed that a lot of local neighborhood guys would hang out in there, come for dinner, then sit at the bar and play backgammon. And some of the wiseguys that were hanging around would get involved. They played for high stakes—as high as $1,000 a game. That looked like a good way for me to get in, get an introduction, get some conversation going with the regulars. But I didn't know how to play backgammon. I bought a book and studied up. Another agent whose undercover name was Chuck was a good backgammon player. Chuck had an operation going in the music business. He was a friend of mine. He would come over to my apartment, or I'd go over to his, and he'd teach me backgammon. We played and played, in order for me to get comfortable.

Finally, when I thought I was good enough, I decided to challenge for a game at the bar.

It was near Christmastime so there was a kind of festive mood in the place, and that seemed like a good time for a newcomer to edge in. On this night there were two boards going at the bar. I watched for a while to see which board had the weaker players. The way you got into the game was to challenge the winner, and that's the board I challenged the winner on.

The stakes for the first game were $100. That made me nervous because I didn't have a lot of money to spend. I won that first game, lost the next, and ended up the evening about breaking even.

But the important thing was that it broke the ice. I got introduced around as "Don" for the first time. And now I could sit down and talk to people. We could sit around and talk about the games going on.

After a couple weeks I retreated from the backgammon games. The money was getting a little steep. I played two games for $500 each, lost one then won one. My expense account then was maybe $200 to $300 a week for everything, and I couldn't go over that without going into an explanation for the accountants at the Bureau. It wasn't worth it, just to play backgammon with some half-ass wiseguys.

Anyway, by then I had accomplished what I had learned backgammon for. I had gotten to know some people, at least enough to be acknowledged when I came in: "Hey, Don, how's it going?"

So I wasn't a strange face any longer. I also got pretty friendly with the bartender, Marty. Marty wasn't a mob guy, but he was a pretty good knock-around guy who knew what was going on. I got to bullshitting with Marty pretty good near the end of December 1976, and early January of 1977. Conversation rolled around gradually, and he asked me if I lived around there, since I was in there so much. I told him, yeah, I lived up at Ninety-first and Third.

"You from around here?" he asked me.

"I spent some years in this area," I told him. "Lately I been spending a lot of time in Miami and out in California. I just came in from Miami a couple months ago."

"What do you do?" he asked me.

That kind of question you don't answer directly. "Oh, you know, not doing anything right now, you know, hanging out, looking around . . ." You bob and weave a little with the guy. I said, "Basically I do anything where I can make a fast buck."

He had a girlfriend that used to come in at closing, then they'd go out bouncing after work, around the city. A couple times he asked me if I wanted to go, and I backed off, said no thanks. I didn't want him to think I was anxious to make friends.

Still, I didn't want him or anybody else in there to think I didn't have anything going for me. So once in a while I'd bring a female in—somebody that I'd met in another bar across the street from my apartment or something—just for a couple drinks or dinner. And sometimes my agent friend, Chuck, would come in with me for a drink. You can't go in all the time by yourself, because they think you're either a fag or a cop. And it's good to vary your company so they don't see you with the same people all the time and wonder what's up. The idea is to blend in, not present yourself in any way at all that makes anybody around you uncomfortable.

Marty's girlfriend had a girlfriend named Patricia, a good-looking blonde who was going out with one of the wiseguys that hung out there, a bookie named Nicky. A couple times she came in when I was in there and Nicky wasn't, and she'd sit down for some small talk with me. At first it was just casual conversation. Then I figured she was coming on to me a little, and I had to be very careful, as an outsider, not to overstep my bounds. The worst thing I could do is appear to be coming on to a wiseguy's girlfriend, because there are real firm rules against that. If I made that kind of mistake I would have shot my whole couple months of work to get in there.

One night this Patricia asked me if I wanted to have dinner with her. "Nicky's not gonna be around," she said. "We could take off and find someplace nice."

"Thanks," I said, "but I don't think so. Not tonight."

Then I grabbed Marty the bartender off to the side. "Hey, Marty," I said, "I want you to know that I'm keeping my distance from Patricia because I know that she's Nicky's girlfriend. But I don't want to insult anybody, either."

Marty said, "I know, I've been watching how you handle yourself."

So I established another small building block in my character: The bartender knew that I knew what the rules were with wiseguys. Most guys who hadn't been around the streets or around wiseguys might have jumped at an invitation from a girl like that—figuring that, after all, if she makes the play, it must be all right. But with wiseguys there's a strict code that you don't mess. I mean, strict.

A week or so later Marty came over to me. "Hey, Don, I just want to tell you that Patricia and Nicky broke up, so if you want to ask her out for a drink or something, feel free."

I said, "Thanks, but I'm not really out hawking it, you know?"

He said, "After work tonight we're going to the Rainbow Room. Come on with us, and bring her."

The four of us went to the Rainbow Room and had a good time. I went out bouncing with him a few times more after that, and that got me in pretty solid in that place.

He started introducing me to the other guys that hung out in

Carmello's, including some of the half-ass wiseguys. I never did anything with them, didn't get involved with them, but at least they acknowledged me when I came in, and I began to have a "home base" where people knew me, in case anybody started checking.

It was also a place where I could leave messages and where messages would be taken for me. I would tell Marty, If a guy calls here looking for me, tell him I'll be in here at such-and-such a time. Sometimes I would call and ask for myself, and Marty would take the message and give it to me when I came in. So I established that I had some friends around, people I was involved with.

The important thing here in the beginning was not so much to get hooked up with anybody in particular and get action going right away. The important thing was to have a hangout, a good backup, for credibility. When I went other places, I could say, "I been hanging out at that place for four or five months." And they could check it out. The guys that had been hanging around in this place would say, "Yeah, Don Brasco has been coming in here for quite a while, and he seems all right, never tried to pull anything on us." That's the way you build up who you are, little by little, never moving too fast, never taking too big a bite at one time. There are occasions where you suddenly have to take a big step or a big chance. Those come later.

Finally it was time for me to make my move with Marty the bartender. Typically, what an undercover cop will do, in a buy-bust situation, is try to buy something from you. Cops always buy, never sell. I was going to sell. So I brought in some pieces of jewelry. A couple of diamond rings, a couple of loose stones, and a couple of men's and ladies' wristwatches.

When there was nobody else at the bar, I opened the pouch and showed the stuff to him.

"If you'd like to hold on to these for a couple days," I said, "you can try to get rid of them."

"What's the deal?" he asked.

"I need $2,500 total. Anything over that is yours."

He didn't ask if the stuff was stolen. He didn't need to, because it was understood. During the course of recent conversations I had given him the impression that I wasn't on the legit. So it was obvious. You say as little as possible in a situation like this. Actually, of course, the stuff was from the FBI, things that were confiscated during investigations and used strictly for this type of purpose.

He took the items and held on to them for three or four days. Then one night he said, "Don, some people want it, but I can't get you the price tag that you want."

Now, I don't know if he's testing me or what. You never take it for granted that somebody trusts you. I could have said, "Well, get me what you can for it, and I'll give you a piece." But that's not the way you work. Things have a certain street value, and a street guy knows what that is. I knew what the going rate for swag was from dealing with my informants before I went undercover. So I could talk sense about price for diamonds, gold, jewelry with anybody, whether I was going to buy or sell. So if I have swag worth $2,500, I stick with that. If you say, "Okay, just give me $800," then they might doubt that you know what you're doing.

So I said, "Okay, just give it back, no big deal. I'll be getting more stuff, so maybe we can do business another time."

He said, "Anything you come across, Don, let me see it. If I can get rid of it, I will. I can move a lot of stuff. I come across a lot of swag."

"The only thing I'm interested in," I said "are jewelry or good clothes for myself." But I never bought anything from him.

I did place some bets through him. He talked about Nicky, the bookie, told me about his business. And I placed some bets on the horses.

All of this served the purpose of solidifying my place.

My agent friend, Chuck, had an undercover operation going in the music business: records and concerts. Sometimes we'd hang out together, back each other up—as when he would come with me to Carmello's. Chuck was putting on a concert at the Beacon Theatre on Broadway, featuring the soul singer James Brown. He asked me if I'd give him a hand. That would help him and would also help me—it would show the mob guys downtown that I was doing something, that I was a mover.

He had sucked into his operation a couple of connected guys with the Colombo crime family. He introduced me to one of them, a guy named Albert. "Connected" means that you associate with Mafia members, do jobs with them, but do not share in all the rewards and responsibilities of an actual Mafia member. A true Mafia member is a "made guy" or "straightened out," or a "wiseguy." Albert's uncle was a made guy in the Colombo family.

Albert was a half-ass wiseguy—just a connected guy, not a made guy. He was a big guy, maybe 6′ 2″, about thirty years old. He was a con artist dealing in paper—a stocks-and-bonds type guy. I didn't think he ever did anything very heavy. He was a bullshit artist.

But he was not a bad guy to hang around. Chuck introduced me to Albert so that maybe I could get some introductions into the Colombo family. So I started running sometimes with Chuck and Albert, bopping around different night spots. Albert liked to hit all the in spots, discos, and restaurants.

When the James Brown concert was coming up, Albert and a couple of his buddies from Brooklyn came up with the great idea that they were going to stick up the box office. He came to Chuck and me and said, "Look, near the end of the concert, when the box office closes, let's stick it up."

He wanted to stick up our own box office. Chuck and I couldn't allow guys with guns to come in and do that, but we couldn't just veto it, either, without drawing suspicion. We really didn't know how the hell the thing was going to go.

We told Albert, "Look, if these guys come in and knock off the box office, that's less split for us, because we're gonna cop this box office, anyway. We can split it three ways. If you bring in your two friends to stick it up, that's a five-way split."

He went back to his guys with that explanation, but they wanted to do it, anyway. They wanted it all.

It was the day before the concert. We didn't know what to do. We couldn't tip off the cops, because the tip would have been traced right to Chuck or me.

"What should we do?" Chuck says to me.

"I don't know," I say, "this is your operation. I'll go along with anything you want to do as long as we don't jeopardize *my* operation."

Chuck had an idea. "I think I'll hire a couple of off-duty cops, just have them hang around the front of the lobby, like for crowd control, and maybe it'll deter these guys."

He hired the off-duty cops. They arrived in uniform and stood around. Albert and his friends showed up.

"What the fuck's with these cops?" Albert said.

I said, "I don't know. Probably they're on the job and figured they'd stick around and hear James Brown. I don't know."

"What the fuck," Albert said to his friends. "How can we stick up the place with cops around?" They discussed it for a few minutes, standing outside, watching the cops in the lobby. They decided it was a no-go.

So we slipped that one. And it helped me out, because now I could tell guys that I had a piece of this guy, Chuck, who's got this Ace Record Company in his pocket.

I was trying to get home to my wife and daughters at every opportunity, even if it was just for breakfast. I would often just end up the night and head across the George Washington Bridge to New Jersey to spend a few hours at home. My wife and I socialized very little when I was home, and our few social friends were Bureau people. And while of course they knew I, too, was with the Bureau, they didn't know what operation I was on.

I was very friendly with an agent named Al Genkinger in the New York office. All during the time I was undercover, Al and his wife stayed close to my wife, took care of anything that came up. Anything my wife needed, she would get in touch with them. That was a comfort.

We told neighbors and others that I was a salesman, on the road a lot.

My daughters were already developing the habit of evading conversations with others about what I did, or even of not asking me questions about my work. They would say, "What do you do when you go to work?" And I would say, "I just do my work like anybody else." After a while they stopped asking.

They were becoming cheerleaders at school. My oldest daughter had boyfriends. My wife and I became friendly with a lot of boys on the athletic teams. We went to high school wrestling matches on Wednesdays when I could make it home. She went without me if I couldn't make it.

I set up a weight lifting program for some of the guys in our basement. I had been a weight lifter for a long time. They ate it up. They didn't ask personal questions. They would come over regularly and follow the program I set up. My wife made pizzas.

It seemed I was home very little. My wife and daughters were not happy with the extended absences, especially when I didn't give much explanation. We didn't know it then, but that period gave me the best home time that I would have over the next five years.

I bopped around with Albert and got to know him pretty well. I took him up to Carmello's a few times, so he could see that guys there knew me. It's the kind of thing that feeds on itself: He sees that people know me and acknowledge me, so he feels he can introduce me to other people who know him. It enhances my credibility to be hanging out with a connected guy whose uncle is a wiseguy in the Colombo family. For his part, Albert sees that I'm accepted where I go, so it's good for him to be seen with me.

Getting established is a subtle business, a matter of small impressions, little tests, quiet understandings.

Albert lived in Brooklyn. But he loved Manhattan. One night there was a big snowstorm and he didn't want to drive home to Brooklyn. So I let him stay over in my apartment. From then on he was always trying to weasel in, to stay over at my apartment so that he didn't have to drive home to Brooklyn. I wanted to keep cultivating him, but I didn't want him parking in my apartment.

Between trying to get myself set up, establish credibility, and hanging around with Albert and others, I hardly got home at all during the month of December—maybe two or three evenings up to Christmas. So I was especially intent on getting home at a reasonable hour Christmas Eve, to spend that and part of Christmas Day with my family. I planned to knock off early Christmas Eve and get home by maybe eight o'clock. I had bought presents for everybody and stashed them in the trunk of my car.

In order to get home to my family, I started celebrating Christmas early in my Don Brasco world. On the afternoon of Christmas Eve, we started bouncing around to the various spots, having drinks and wishing people we knew Merry Christmas. Chuck, who was a bachelor, and Albert, who didn't ever like going home, brought along a couple of girls they had been going out with.

One place led to another. I had to act like I wasn't in a hurry to get anyplace. It was after ten o'clock. We were going down Eighty-sixth Street, heading for Carmello's. The street was pretty empty. On the corner there was a guy still selling Christmas trees. I happened to mention, "It's Christmas, and I don't even have a Christmas tree in my apartment."

Albert yells, "Pull over! Pull over to that guy there—he's got trees! I'm gonna buy a tree!"

I pull over at the corner. Albert jumps out and goes over to where the guy has Christmas trees. The guy has only three or four trees left. They are barely trees, more like sticks tied together. Albert picks one out and brings it over to the car. I never saw anything so scraggly. There was a trail of needles from it on the sidewalk. The top was bent over.

"What are you gonna do with that?" I ask.

"Let's put it up and decorate it in your apartment!"

"Come on, I got no decorations. All the stores are closed."

"We'll find something to decorate it with," he says, "won't we, girls?"

"Yeah, yeah!" they say.

"We can't let you be alone on Christmas Eve," Albert says.

So we go up to my apartment with this scrawny tree. When we stood it up, you could see that it was even missing some branches. "I got no stand to put it up in," I say.

"We'll use this!" he says. I had one of those big water-cooler bottles that I threw pennies in.

They put the tree in that. Then the two women rummaged around in the kitchen and came back with some tinfoil. They started making Christmas balls and decorations out of tinfoil. They hung these things on what few branches there were. Every time they hung a tinfoil bird up, a million needles fell on the floor.

"We couldn't let you go without a Christmas tree," Albert says. "Bad enough you don't have a date on Christmas Eve."

They all proceeded to make sure I enjoyed Christmas Eve and wasn't lonely. They sang Christmas carols until after midnight, sitting around this ugly tree, Albert and the girls all boozed up.

I was thinking about my kids, and all the presents in the trunk of my car, and I was angry for letting myself get into this situation.

I said, "Come on, everybody, that's enough, I've had it with Christmas."

They wanted to keep partying. I took Chuck aside and said, "You gotta get 'em out of here. I want to go home."

So he herded them up and left. I waited about a half hour, then I went down to the garage, got my car, and headed home.

I managed to have Christmas morning with my family. I was back on the job in the afternoon. Five more Christmases would pass by before I would have a normal one with my family.

Things began to happen, some movement. Shortly after the first of the year, 1977, Albert introduced me to some active Colombo guys. We were out bouncing, and we went to Hippopotamus, the popular disco at Sixty-first Street and York Avenue. A lot of mob guys hung out there.

Albert said he'd like to introduce me to a Colombo guy that did a lot of business with swag.

He brought me over to a table and introduced me to a guy. "Jilly, this is Don, a friend of mine."

Jilly was maybe five years older than me, average build, 5'9", 160, with dark hair, prominent nose.

We sat down and talked for a while, and Albert told Jilly and the guys with him that we had been hanging out for a few months. Jilly headed up a crew that hung out mainly in Brooklyn. He said I should stop by his store over on 15th Avenue and 76th Street in the Benson-hurst section.

"Yeah, maybe I'll do that," I said.

For a couple of months now I had been playing this game of trying to be noticed without being noticed, slide into the badguy world and become accepted without drawing attention. You push a little here and there, but very gently. Brief introductions, short conversations, appearances one place and another, hints about what you're up to, casual mannerisms, demeanor, and lingo that show you know your way around—all these become a trail of credibility you leave behind you. Above all, you cannot hurry. You cannot seem eager to meet certain people, make certain contacts, learn about certain scores. The quickest way to get tagged as a cop is to try to move too fast. You have to show that you have the time to play it by the rules of the street, and that includes letting people check you out and come to you.

You have to have confidence in how you're handling yourself, because while you're playing this game, much of the time you don't know where you stand. Nobody tells you you're getting in solid or getting to know the right people or heading in the right direction. Nobody tells you if you're safe. You have to sense it. Badguys on the street are sensing you. You can be wrong. Obviously, so can they. But the street is no place to doubt yourself.

These initial months were not a time of high excitement in terms of events. But I felt excitement. I had a foothold. Nobody in the outside world knew where I was or what I was doing, hour by hour, day by day. On the street, people didn't know who I was or what I was really doing. I was on the job and on my own. There was excitement in that.

One night I came out of Carmello's and started to drive downtown to make the rounds of the regular spots. I thought a car was following me. To check it out, I didn't try to shake them right away. I just led them on a wild-goose chase for a while. I went across the George Washington Bridge to Fort Lee, New Jersey, turned around, and came back. The other car stayed with me but made no move.

It had to be some sort of law-enforcement unit. Nobody else would have reason to follow me. My assumption was that there was an informant in Carmello's, or one of the other places, who had passed on the information that there was a new guy hanging around, making friends with badguys, a guy who obviously doesn't work and yet has money to spend. Or else they could have been spot-checking the place, surveilling it, and they saw my car there a few times, with out-of-state tags, saw me come and go, and got into it that way.

Law-enforcement units—New York Police, FBI, Drug Enforcement Administration, all the others—have organized crime figures under surveillance all the time. It is standard practice. None of these outfits—including the FBI, for the most part—knew who I was. So if I started coming into their picture, buddying up with badguys, naturally I would become a suspect just like the rest of them.

If it wasn't cops, it could be wiseguys checking me out. I didn't want anybody on either side tailing me. If I was going to meet my contact agent, or going home to see my family, a tail could have blown the whole operation. So every time I left a place, I was tail-conscious. I always "cleaned" myself. I never went directly to my destination. I would ride around, keep checking my rearview mirror to see if I was being followed, lose any suspicious cars with a series of turns and double-backs. When I parked someplace, I would notice whoever parked near me, and anybody who came in a place with me.

The first time I was rousted, I was near Carmello's. I hadn't had time to get rid of the car tailing me. They pulled me over. A couple guys in plainclothes with drawn guns ordered me out, told me to put my hands on my head. They patted me down, checked inside the car. They didn't find anything on me or in the car. When they were finished, they said it was a routine license check because I had Florida plates on the car.

The only thing it was routine for was wiseguys, because they get rousted all the time. That's why you don't usually carry a gun. These guys here who rousted me didn't even identify themselves. I don't know who they were.

I was tailed a few times, stopped and searched a couple of times. It was an inconvenience, but it also made me feel that I was doing the job right.

I drove over to Brooklyn, to Jilly's store at 7612 15th Avenue. The neighborhood was very clean, quiet, working-class, two- and three-story residential buildings with a lot of storefronts on the ground floors. Jilly's store was in the middle of a block of glass fronts. There was a small grocery store, and the Park Ridge Pharmacy on the corner.

A big sign over the door of Jilly's store read ACERG. Jilly's last name was Greca, his store was the name spelled backward. The store part was the front room. Plain metal racks of expensive clothes, mostly women's stuff: leather jackets, pants, blouses. Everything was marked cheaper than it would be at a regular store. The store was open to the public, but nobody would be coming there from Manhattan. It was a neighborhood store in the kind of neighborhood where outsiders are spotted in a minute.

Everything was cheap because it was all swag. Jilly's crew were hijackers, burglars, all-around thieves. The store sold their loot.

The Acerg store was in the front, and anybody in the crew could act as salesman. There was a back room with a desk and a couple of card tables. That's where the crew hung out during the day. That's where I was introduced to a few guys, ranging in age from maybe late twenties to early forties, who were sitting around playing and bullshitting. First names and nicknames only: Guido, Vito, Tommy the Chief, Vinnie, and so on.

I started hanging out there with Jilly's crew. Because I was "known" by other people that this crew knew, and because I was introduced to them by somebody they knew, they were pretty open around me.

Although these were lower-echelon guys in the mob, they always had something going. They always had money. They were always turning things over. They always had swag around. Swag was always going in and out. Everybody dressed well. Ninety percent of what they wore was swag. Latest styles. Sports shirts, slacks, sweaters, and leather jackets. If they had jeans on, they were always designer jeans.

You name it, they stole it. Jilly's crew would hit warehouses, docks, trucks, houses. There was nothing they wouldn't consider stealing. They considered all the time. There wasn't one hour of one day that went by when they weren't thinking and talking about what they were going to steal, who or what or where they were going to rob. There was always a load to go after, or somebody else's load you might get a piece of, always something to hustle.

When they got up in the morning, they didn't think about going to work and punching a time clock. They didn't think about spending time with their wives or girlfriends. The mob was their job. You got up, went to the club or wherever you hung out, and spent your day with those guys.

You've got to be up all day figuring out what you're going to do that night, what scores you're going to go out on. The day basically was: You got to the club at ten-thirty or eleven o'clock in the morning, then sat around all day and discussed scams and scores and hustles, past and future. Somebody would have an idea about a burglary or hijack, and they'd kick it around to see if it was worthwhile. Or somebody else had pulled a score and was looking to get rid of jewelry, furs, or whatever. And they'd discuss the possibility of "middling" it—selling it.

All day long, while they schemed, they'd sit in the back room at the Acerg store and play gin and smoke cigarettes and cigars. I don't smoke. They never opened a window. Even with air-conditioning, it got to be pretty dense. There might be two games going, depending on how many guys were in there. I don't even like to play cards. You play gin— never any other game—for maybe ten cents a point. Even while you're sitting around playing gin you're still talking about making a dollar, what the hustle of the day is. Maybe you go over to somebody else's club, play gin there, or talk up some scheme. Maybe you talk to somebody about a score you're trying to set up or trying to get a piece of. If they had a potential job to case, a couple guys would go out during the daytime and look it over.

If they weren't scheming and dreaming, they were telling war stories, reminiscences about their time in various jails and prisons. Everybody did time in the can. It was part of the price of doing business. They knew all about different jails, cell blocks, guards. I had enough phony background set up to establish my credentials as a serious criminal, to show that I was tough enough to do time if I had to without turning rat. But I never claimed to have done any prison time because I didn't know those places, and that could have just tripped me up. If you do three to five years you get to know the guards—what guard's on what tier. You get to know the inmates, guys who are doing fifteen to twenty, guys who are still there. They knew the lingo and the slang. Everybody remembers those relationships and that time.

My thinking is, if it's not necessary to have done something, don't claim to have done it. When these guys talked about prison time, I just listened like an ordinary citizen.

For lunch somebody would go out to bring in Chinese food or hero sandwiches. Maybe around four-thirty or five o'clock, the guys would split, go home to their wives or whatever, have supper, then go back out on the street, pulling off their scores or bouncing around the night spots or doing whatever they did.

On Tuesdays we went to Sally's club for lunch. Sally was an old-time wiseguy, a capo in the Colombo family. He had a social club on 17th Avenue, not far from Jilly's. Sometimes we'd hang out over at Sally's, divide the time between there and Jilly's. But every Tuesday afternoon Sally cooked a big lunch for our whole crew of about eight, and his own, altogether maybe eighteen or twenty guys. He had a regular kitchen, and he would cook meatballs, macaroni, sausages, peppers, everything. For this lunch we would set up a long folding table. We would sit at the table all afternoon eating lunch, drinking jugs of homemade red wine that Sally produced, and bullshitting.

My day would pretty much follow the same routine as theirs. I'd get to the club between ten and eleven and hang out all day with these guys. By late afternoon or early evening, I'd go back to my apartment, maybe take a nap for an hour, get up and shower, and about nine o'clock or so go back out on the street to wherever it was we were going to meet. Sometimes I would go back to Brooklyn, sometimes bounce around in Manhattan; sometimes with them, sometimes by myself in places where people had gotten to know me through these guys.

But even when we'd cruise around to the different night spots, the talk was always on whatever scams or hustles were going on or coming up. What they did for a living was on their minds more than it was with ordinary people. They never put that aside. Nobody ever had enough money, no matter how much they had, and it was always feast or famine. Half the time their schemes came to nothing. Or worse, they went bad in the execution and cost them either money or jail time. But that didn't cool their dedication. They did not have a sense of humor about their failures, or those schemes they came up with that were harebrained. They stuck to their routine.

A small-time fence named Vinnie, who hung around Jilly's, was over-weight and had a bad heart, for which he took some pills—maybe nitroglycerin. One afternoon we were all in a card game. It was a hard game, for quite a few bucks. And at the same time they were kicking around the prospects for a house burglary over in Bayonne, New Jersey.

All of a sudden Vinnie falls down on the floor, gasping for breath and grabbing at his chest.

"Hey, you guys," I say, "Vinnie's got a problem."

Nobody moves. They keep playing cards. Vinnie is gasping and grabbing, and still nobody moves.

"He's having a heart attack!" I scramble over to him. "We gotta get him to the hospital! Come on, somebody help me with him!"

"Aw, he does that all the time," one of the guys says. "He's just having one of his regular attacks. Let him pop a few pills, he'll get over it."

This was one of the situations that often came up where I wanted to fit in with the badguys, but I still had my own sense of morality.

I can't just let the guy croak. I manage to get him up and out to my car. I drive him to the emergency room. A couple of hours later he comes out. "I ran out of my medication," he says.

We drive back to Jilly's. They are still playing cards. "See?" somebody says. "We told you he'd be all right."

It was easy to get lulled by this daily routine with these guys. Most of the time it was boring. They were not Phi Beta Kappas, but they were very streetwise. Just under the surface of their routine there was always something lurking that could trip me up. While I was constantly taking mental notes in order to report relevant information to my contact agent, I had to be alert for traps. Most of these guys were, after all, killers.

The FBI wouldn't let me actually go out on hijackings and burglaries, because the crew went armed. There was too good a chance somebody would get shot. In these pioneering days, thinking upstairs in the bureaucracy was very conservative. Somebody suggested that if I went along on crimes where guys were packing guns, I might be liable for prosecution myself.

The guys would ask me to go out on jobs with them. I would find ways to back off. I would tell them, "Hey, packing a gun and all that stuff, that's too cowboy for me. I'll help you out later on with the unloading." And they had enough guys so that adding me didn't mean anything. It wasn't like I was crucial. Plus the fact that for every man that doesn't go along on a job, that's less split they had to do on the proceeds.

They bought it. But if I had tried to push for myself to go along, get all the information I could about the score, and then back out of it— that would have made them very suspicious. I was always up-front with them.

I stayed low-key, and it was no big deal that I was around.

But once they got a little used to me, they let me sit in on their planning sessions. I'd go out with them when they cased a score. And gradually I started imposing myself. They would come and ask my advice on certain scores. I would sit down with them and go over the plans of the job, pick out flaws in it. That showed them that I knew something about what I was doing. In some cases when I could show them what was wrong with pulling a job, it deterred them from pulling them—part of my job, after all.

It was a delicate situation. I couldn't initiate or encourage crimes. Yet to be permitted to hang around I had to participate in some fashion. The Bureau didn't have any fine guidelines for everything I could and couldn't do. I was pretty much on my own. It required some tap dancing.

I helped unload stuff at the store. They would hijack any kind of truck, from eighteen-wheelers down to little straight jobs. They would seize the truck, unload the stuff into smaller trucks or vans, and take it to the "drop," which might be a vacant warehouse or factory, and bring samples to Acerg to show prospective buyers. The load would be parceled out to fences who could get rid of it.

When they hijacked a truck, they would usually just tie the driver up. But most of the hijacked loads were giveaways—setups. The drivers of the heisted trucks would be in on the heist for a percentage. The crew would go wherever they got the information that a guy had a good load on. Most of the heists were in the city. They'd pull them right on the streets in Brooklyn. Some were in Jersey.

Their burglaries were all over—in the city, out on Long Island over in New Jersey, in Connecticut, in Florida. Stuff came from the airports all the time. Jilly had a steady supply from JFK International Airport, utilizing somebody inside the cargo operations.

I'd unload cases of coffee, sugar, frozen food, whiskey, bags of cocoa, truckloads of sweaters, blouses, jackets and jeans. They would take anything. The best loads were food loads—shrimp, coffee, tuna—because you can get rid of that stuff anywhere, like restaurants and supermarkets. Frozen shrimp and lobster were favorites. Pharmaceuticals—over-the-counter stuff like razor blades, aspirin, toothpaste—were prime targets because so many stores wanted them and the markup was great, even on the straight market. Clothes were good, especially leather, and women's clothes. Liquor was always a big item, especially around Christmastime. There were women's leather gloves, ski gloves, even a load of hockey gloves.

The commodity didn't make any difference, as long as they could sell it. Now, something like men's hockey gloves—where would you move them? They might have gotten stuck with them. But it was a load they could take, so they took it. It doesn't cost anything to steal hockey gloves.

Managers at places like restaurants and supermarkets had to know the stuff was hot, because the price was below anything on the wholesale market. But they bought it, anyway. Some of the best places. When you see how that works, it changes your view of some of the bargains and discount stores. It makes you more cynical. Sometimes the circle was very neat. They would burglarize an A&P warehouse one night, sell the cases of coffee and tuna to other stores a couple of days later.

TVs and VCRs were big. Robbing boxcarloads of them from the railroad freight yards was nothing unusual. They had a railroad employee who would give them a bill of lading and point out the right boxcar. Just back up a truck and load it.

When they hit houses, they were usually looking for jewelry, stocks and bonds, cash, or guns.

Anything that wasn't tied down, they would steal. Those were the days when Mopeds—motorized bikes or motor scooters—were popular. They would steal Mopeds off the street and rent them by the day out of the store.

I maintained a low profile, the way I'm comfortable. I didn't volunteer more about myself than was necessary; I didn't ask questions that didn't need to be asked—even though information I wanted was often just out of reach. But I knew that certain things I did would catch the eye of people or have people talking. I had to be patient, just let things develop.

• • •

Guido was Jilly's right-hand man, and he was a tough guy. He was tougher than the other guys in this crew. He looked different too. An Italian with blond hair and blue eyes. He had a mustache. Because he wasn't a made guy, he, like me, could have a mustache. He was about 6'1", 200 pounds. Late thirties. His arms were tattooed with snakes. He wore tinted glasses. He told me he had been in and out of jail most of his life, for various offenses. He was a shooter, but he had never been convicted of murder. Guido's crew under Jilly was sophisticated enough to operate with walkie-talkies. Jilly told me he thought Guido was too much of a cowboy, took too many risks, but that he had done a lot of "work" for the Colombos, meaning he had participated in hits.

If Guido was your friend, he would be with you till the end. If he was your enemy, forget about it—he would get you. Everybody showed respect for Guido.

One day soon after I started hanging out with the Jilly crew, Guido and I were riding around in my car.

He said, "Hey, Don, what's that squeak?"

"I don't know," I said. "Doesn't bother me."

"Yeah, it's a squeak," he said, leaning forward and cocking his head, "in the dashboard."

We got back to Jilly's, and I pulled up at the curb across the street.

He said, "I'll take that dashboard off and find that squeak and fix it."

"Hey, Guido, don't waste your time. It doesn't bother me."

"It bothers me. It won't take long."

Guido always carried a set of burglar tools in a toolbox in his car. He went and got them and crawled in under the dashboard and started taking it apart.

I said, "Why go through all this trouble just to find a squeak? It's no big deal."

In five minutes he had the whole dashboard off. He looked all over behind it. "It's okay," he said. He started putting it back in place.

"Well, what the hell did you take it apart for?" I said.

"To tell you the truth, you're new around here. I just wanted to see if your car was wired up or anything. It's clean."

"Well, fuck you," I said. "You think I'm a fucking cop with a fucking recorder in my car? Why don't you just ask me, face-to-face?"

"Take it easy, Don. We gotta be careful, that's all. There's lots of operations they got going on around here. You're just new to us, that's all. Forget about it."

Actually I wasn't all that surprised to have somebody snooping around to check me out. If they did it once, they could do it again. So for all the years I was on this undercover job, while I would eventually have reason to wear hidden transmitters and tape recorders and would ride around in other agents' cars which were equipped with recorders, I would never have my own car wired.

I couldn't play it entirely safe. Any chance I would get, I myself would snoop around. If the guys were out front in the store or outside, and I was alone for a couple of minutes in the back room, I would always be looking in the desk drawers. There would usually be guns, both automatics and revolvers. There would also be other burglary paraphernalia stashed in there, like wigs and ski masks. If anybody had come in, my snooping would have been fatal. But my job was to find out what was going on, after all. I wasn't just curious.

If I was who I said I was, I couldn't just be sitting around listening to their schemes. I had to have some things of my own going.

Early in 1977, I made a few small deals with Vinnie the fence. Vinnie wasn't a heavy-duty guy. He was a family-type guy, from Staten Island, who used to hang around Jilly's during the day and then go home to his family at night. He didn't go out on actual jobs; he wasn't a tough guy. He just got rid of swag for people.

I wanted to make it look like I was moving stuff here and there to make a few bucks and trying to work my way up the line to bigger fences. Vinnie started me out with perfume.

We arranged a meeting for downstairs from my apartment, outdoors at the corner of Ninety-first Street and Third Avenue. Around noon he arrived driving a rented white Ford Econoline van. It was filled with cartons of perfume—by Lanvin. "I pick this up every week right at the factory where they make it," he said "I pay a couple of guys who work there."

Perfume wasn't really my line, but it's not too far removed from jewelry. And mob thieves don't turn up their noses at anything where they can make a profit. You want to be a good customer, but not so good that you become a mark. I bought one carton of the perfume—Eau My Sin and Yves St. Laurent Rive Gauche—for $220.

The perfume, like everything else I bought in my role, I turned over to the FBI.

A few days later I met him at the Woodbridge Auction on Route 9 in Woodbridge, New Jersey. The auction was like a flea market and drew big crowds. Vinnie had a booth there where he sold swag that he hadn't sold to other fences. There, with the public and families all milling around, Vinnie would be in his booth selling stuff from hijacks or burglaries. I used to swing over there to see what new stuff he had, or if I had something that he might want to sell out of the auction. He got rid of a lot of swag from that booth.

I even took my wife there once. I got to spend so little time with her in those days that I figured the risk was tolerable. She got a kick out of it. The only problem was that once, right in front of Vinnie, who called me "Don," she called me "Joe." But he didn't seem to pick up on it. And, anyway, supposedly she was just some broad I knew—I could have been using any name with her.

He had some Enigma perfume for me, $250 a case, which contained fifteen boxes. "This stuff retails for forty dollars a box," he said. I bought a case.

I told him I had made a score, and had fifty to sixty watches and a good haul of fine turquoise jewelry. I showed Vinnie two sample wristwatches—gold Pateau Mitsu Boshi Boeki digitals, which were fairly new at the time, with red faces, worth maybe $80 apiece—and he bought them for $20 each. "I'll show these to Jilly in Brooklyn," he said, "and see how many more he wants."

Most of the "swag" I sold was stuff confiscated by the Bureau, loot recovered from previous thefts but which could not be traced back to the owners. These watches and jewelry were not from the Bureau. I had wanted the stuff in a hurry to make this deal, so I had bought them at a wholesale place on Canal Street. I worked it this way a few times. It meant there was no paperwork, nobody would know where the stuff was going. Like some other things I did, it might have left me open to internal criticism, but I had to make the decisions about my own security and pace. And nothing I did was a shortcut that would damage a case.

Vinnie said that he and his partner were about to make a score on a load of Faded Glory jeans, for which a buyer had already agreed to pay $125,000. "The load is a hundred and twenty-five thousand pairs," he said, "so it comes out to a buck a pair."

Three weeks later he called and said he wanted fifteen more watches, which I sold him for $300, and some of the turquoise jewelry. I sold him necklaces and bracelets for $150.

I said, "Did you get that load of jeans?"

"Part of it. The guy who took it, he made a couple other deals. So we only got part. You know how it is."

These small deals helped me get accepted by the crew at Jilly's store and the people they associated with. One of the first things Jilly himself offered me was a white sable coat, part of the haul they had taken in a burglary the night before. "It's worth eleven grand," Jilly told me. "You can have it for twenty-five hundred bucks if you want it."

I passed on that, told Jilly I didn't think I could move it.

There wasn't any sense in buying anything expensive that I couldn't identify, couldn't eventually trace back to the owner. If you can't trace an item back to the owner, you can't prove anything in court. Jilly didn't tell me where he got the coat, and you don't ask somebody where they got something like that. Unless he had, say, seven or eight of them—a really big score. Then you might say, "Hey, where'd you make a score like that?"

At that point the only reason I had for buying the stuff was to establish credibility, as I'd done with the perfume. But I didn't need to spend $2,500 for credibility.

The crew was either talking about, or bringing in, loads every day. Price isn't always negotiable. Even if a potential buyer feels that the price is too high, that doesn't mean the sellers will drop the price. The high price probably means that they have to give somebody else an end of it: Whoever they got it from wants x amount of money, so for these sellers to make anything they have to put a few bucks on top of that, and they can't really drop the price. No deal is ever really dead, it just keeps being shopped around.

Tommy the Chief was a fat hood, probably in his fifties. He brought in a case of crushed salted almonds, the kind used in making ice cream. He told Jilly he had fifty-eight more cases in his cellar, stolen from Breyer's Ice Cream in Long Island City. He had a list of other stuff he said he could get—cocoa, dried milk, and so on, from Breyers. "We got it set up with one of their guys that works as a roaster inside," Tommy said. "And we also got the security guard who will be on duty when we go in next week. The haul will be worth a hundred G's."

Jilly decided to go for it, to rent three twenty-two-foot trucks to haul the stuff away, and a garage to store the swag in over the weekend, until it was moved to the buyer. They brought one truckload of cocoa to the club. They just parked the truck right on the street, and I helped unload it. In that neighborhood, who's going to say anything about what goes on at the Acerg store? Two days later the load was sold to some guy in Yonkers.

One night Guido took a crew to burglarize a warehouse. They were going to heist four thousand three-piece men's suits. They had some kid with them to be the outside man, the lookout. While they were inside, somebody tripped a silent alarm. The owner arrived at the warehouse. The outside man panicked and took off without notifying anybody inside. The crew heard the owner coming in and managed to sneak out the back.

When Guido was telling Jilly this the following day, I wondered what the punishment might be on the kid. The crew boss had a wide range of options. Punishment depended on who the boss was and what kind of mood he was in. If Jilly was really ticked off, they might do a bad-number on the guy.

Jilly decided they would go back in the next night. As for the lookout, all he said was, "I don't want that cocksucker with you when you go back in. He can't come around no more."

They went back into the warehouse. They didn't get all four thousand suits. They got about half of them.

I was always on the lookout for an opening to get to the bigger fences, the guys Jilly's crew was selling to. But whenever I'd suggest that I might be able to use a couple of contacts, they'd say something like, "Give it to us, we'll bring it to the guy. Don't worry about it." And if I said I might have some big score coming, their reaction would be, "Hey, you got a big load, we can get rid of it for you." They weren't about to give up their fences.

There was no acceptable reason for me to push to meet the bigger fences, except by coming up with bigger swag to sell.

I wasn't spending all my time in Brooklyn. I kept poking around in other directions. While bouncing around the Manhattan night spots with the Colombo guys, I met Anthony Mirra. I was introduced to him in a disco then named Igor's, which later became Cecil's, on Fifty-fourth Street.

I knew who Tony Mirra was. He was a member of the Bonanno crime family. He had done about eighteen years in the can for narcotics and other convictions, and he had only gotten out a year or so earlier. I knew that he was involved in anything and everything illegal to make money—gambling, drugs, extortion, and muscle of the type that leads to "business partnerships." I knew that he was a contract man, with maybe twenty-five hits under his belt. He was mean, feared, and well connected, a good guy for me to know.

I started hanging out with Mirra while I was still running with the Brooklyn guys. Through Mirra I met a good thief. I needed some more potent swag to bring to Jilly's crew. This thief had a haul of industrial diamonds. I decided to take a shot with these diamonds. I asked the thief if I could take a few samples on consignment to see if I could "middle" them—be the middle man for selling them off. He agreed and gave me ten diamonds.

Selling stolen property like this would not have been sanctioned by the Bureau. I didn't want to argue with anybody about it. I decided it was worth the chance.

The diamonds I had were worth about $75,000 on the street. I didn't really want to sell them to Jilly's crew, I just wanted to show them what I could do. I decided on a price that would be higher than a good street price—to discourage the sale—but not so high that it would look like something was wrong or I didn't know what I was doing.

I brought the pouch of diamonds into the store and showed them to Jilly and the guys.

"I hit a cargo cage out at the airport," I said. "I got a guy inside. I give him a cut. I got a buyer already, down on Canal Street. But if you could sell them, I'll give you the shot. All I want is a hundred grand out of the deal—seventy-five thousand for me and twenty-five thousand for my inside man."

"That's kind of high," Jilly said, "a hundred grand."

That price would force them to ask for $150,000 to $200,000 in reselling them.

"Hey, what can I tell you?" I said. "My inside guy that set it up wants twenty-five grand. The guy on Canal Street is willing to give me a hundred grand. I'm giving you a shot because I'm with you guys. I need seventy-five grand. So if you could sell them for more than a hundred, anything over that is yours."

Jilly said to give him a couple days to check with a guy who was out of town. I did. He checked with the guy and said to me, "He's willing to go for seventy-five."

"I can't do it, Jill. I would only get fifty thousand out of the deal, and it's not worth it. I'll just off 'em to the guy down on Canal Street."

"Yeah," he said.

Jilly understood, which was just what I wanted. I had made some moves, got some stones—no cop is going to come up with $200,000 of diamonds to sell—showed them that I knew what I was talking about. If Jilly had come back with an offer of, say, $125,000, I couldn't have backed out of the deal. I would have had to keep my word and sell them to him. That was the chance I took.

It gave me a jump up in credibility, up from the ground floor.

from Mafia Business
by Pino Arlacchi

American mafioso apply their own meanings to terms like "honor" and "respect." What's honorable or respectable about shooting an associate in the back of the head or poisoning an innocent witness to a crime? Pino Arlacchi (born 1951), United Nations Under-Secretary-General and a long-time opponent of Italy's powerful mafia, can explain.

S ocial research into the question of the mafia has probably now reached the point where we can say that the mafia, as the term is *commonly* understood, does not exist:

. . . Most people, and especially most people outside Italy, have a fairly clear image of the mafia as a centralized criminal association, with a strict code of honour and its own constitution and initiation rites. Information has been freely available to the public in the specialist literature, as well as in the daily press, in detective stories and horror comics, and in sensational TV series. But to try and find out more, to go back to the sources, is to get an altogether different picture . . . and conclude that Mini [the accused in a mafia court case] was speaking nothing but the truth when, asked whether he belonged to the mafia, he replied, 'I don't know what that means'. In fact, he knew that an individual was what we call a *mafioso*, not because that individual belonged to a secret society, but because he behaved in a certain way—behaved, that is, like a *mafioso*.[*]

What did it mean to *behave like a mafioso?*

It meant to *make oneself respected*. It meant to be a 'man of honour', *un'uomo d'onore*, strong enough to avenge himself for any insult to his person, or any extension of it, and to offer any such insult to his enemies. Such behaviour, whether defensive or aggressive in kind, may run counter to the state's prohibition of violence; but in the culture which the *mafioso* inhabited, it was not just accepted, but encouraged and idealized. Indeed, the fact that the comportment of the *mafioso* openly violated the rules and judicial institutions of officialdom was one important factor in the prestige that it conferred.

The mafia was a form of behaviour and a kind of power, not a formal organization. To behave as a *mafioso* was to behave honourably *(onorevole)*. It was to conform, in other words, to certain rules of cunning, courage and ferocity, of robbery and fraud, that even as late as the 'forties of the present century continued to play a crucial role in the culture of many areas of western Sicily and southern Calabria. 'He was really a tough customer, nobody could stand up to him'; 'he wasn't violent as a rule, but when he had to be, then he amazed everyone, he stunned his enemies. This happened six or seven times, and people still talk about it like something from a legend'—this is how a village *mafioso* is described in a book that might be taken as a kind of popular manual on the traditional mafia. To members of the society depicted in *The True Story of the Outlaw Marlino Zappa*,[**] the word *'onorevole'* ('honourable') denotes, simply, the possession of superior strength and force. To be 'honourable' is to be 'exceptional', 'worth your salt'; it is to be 'overbearing'. An honourable act is, in the last analysis, not much more than a successful act of aggression (whether in response to some previous insult or on the aggressor's own initiative).

[*] H. Hess, *Mafia*, Bari 1973, p. xi.
[**] P. Familiari, *La vera Storia del brigante Marlino Zappa*, Vibo Valentia 1971.

Until a few decades ago, most of the population of Reggio Calabria
province used the Greek word 'ndrangheta to indicate a high degree of
heroism and virtue. This was embodied in a superior élite, the
'ndranghetisti. 'Ndranghetista means 'member of the honoured society', but
more generally it referred—as in classical Greece—to any brave man who
was proud of his valour, scorned danger, knew no scruples and was ready
for anything.[*] The key to the 'ndranghetista's system of ideas was omertà,
which means *the ability to be a man ('uomo)*. To keep to the rules of omertà
was to follow a *double moral system*, with one set of norms applying among
the members of a given group, and another, opposing set governing relations with those outside.[**] In relations with fellow-'ndranghetisti, 'tact
and fine manners' were required, together with 'education, courtesy, kindness, and persuasion by argument and without compulsion'. But dealings
with the common people and with one's enemies obeyed the opposite
principle of *false omertà*, 'feigned omertà: 'false kindness, false condescen-
sion, false courtesy, which are snares concealing death to unsuspecting
trouble-makers . . . and to the wicked and contemptible.'[***]

Despite the formal hostility of the official authorities, the
'ndranghetisti enjoyed popular admiration and esteem. Traces of this
attitude occasionally filter through into important judicial documents.
In 1939, a local mafia chief, Paolo D'Agostino, was found killed near a
shrine in the commune of Ardore, in Calabria. Sentence was passed on
his murderers by a court at Locri, 12 of the 142 accused receiving life
sentences and the remainder being acquitted. The judgment described
the murdered man as 'a dangerous character, whose personal courage
was matched by his daring spirit, his rare determination to have the
upper hand, and his readiness to take advantage of others at the first
opportunity. He had the courage needed to make these qualities count,
and was able not just to defend himself against two or three antagonists,
but to take the offensive and put his enemies to the slaughter.'[****]

---

[*] P. Martino, 'Storia della parole,' 't'ndrangheta,' in *Quaderni Calabresi*, 44 (1978).
[**] M. Sahlins, 'La sociologia dello scambio primitivo', in *L'antropologia economica*, Turin
1972, pp. 113-116.
[***] L. Asprea, *Il previtocciolo*, Milan 1971, p. 174.
[****] S. Gambino, *Mafia, La lunga notte di Calabria*, Reggio Calabria 1976, p. 74.

Mafia and *'ndrangheta* are synonyms, as are *mafioso* and *'ndranghetista*. They are terms denoting the idea of honour and the man of honour in the eyes of the local population. In the traditional mafia areas of Sicily and Calabria, honour was the unit that measured the value of a person, a family or a thing. It was expressed in the respect and esteem in which certain people were held, and was strictly linked to the possession of particular qualities and the accomplishment of particular *gesta*—feats, deeds and actions.'[*] The behaviour of the *mafioso* was part of a cultural system whose central theme was honour attained through individual violence. These values are to some extent expressed in the well-known definition of the mafia, and of the *meaning* of the *mafioso*'s acts, which Pitré gave at the end of the nineteenth century:

> The mafia is neither a sect nor an association, and has neither rules nor statutes. The *mafioso* is not a robber or a brigand . . . The *mafioso* is simply a brave man, someone who will put up with no provocation; and in that sense, every man needs to be, indeed has to be, a *mafioso*. The mafia is a certain consciousness of one's own being, an exaggerated notion of individual force and strength as 'the one and only means of settling any conflict, any clash of interests or ideas'; which means that it is impossible to tolerate the superiority or (worse still) the dominance of others.[**]

Honour

The concept of honour referred, intrinsically, to two fundamental ideal attributes: virility in the case of men, virginity and sexual shame in the case of women. Apart from the very lowest class, every member of the

[*] J. K. Campbell, *Honour, Family and Patronage*, Oxford 1964, pp. 268–297. G. Pitré, *Usi, costumi e pregiudizi del popolo siciliano*, vol. II, Bologna 1969, p. 292.
[**] G. Pitrè, *Usi, Costumi e pregiudizi del popolo Siciliano*, Vol. II, Bologna 1969, p. 292.

local community was held to be *naturally* endowed with a certain degree of honour. But in the conditions of insecurity and competition typical of the society where the mafia flourished, it was easy to forfeit either virility (or—the term was synonymous—*diritezza*, 'uprightness': the capacity to 'stand up for oneself,' acknowledging no superior) or virginity. 'To be a man—that's the hardest thing, in this lousy life we lead', exclaims one of the characters in the novel *Il selvaggio di Santa Venere.* *

In a mafia area, 'to be a man' meant to display one's pride and self-assurance, and to show oneself ready and able to respond quickly to the threats that life constantly posed to one's own honour and that of one's family. 'To live in these parts,' writes L. Asprea in his autobiography, 'you needed to be not so much a peasant or a worker as a wild beast. You had to be cautious, you had to show respect; but if anyone provoked a fight, you had to be ready to bite them.' **

Virility and sexual shame were linked to a clear opposition between the sexes that governed a large part of the *mafioso*'s cultural world. Except among relatives, the two sexes represented qualities in constant antagonism: the *uomo di rispetto* ('man worthy of respect') had the task of demonstrating his virility at every opportunity, even if this meant committing violence against women or seizing them by force.

In terms of the honour of any given family, however, virility and virginity-shame complemented one another. The virility of the men in the family protected the women's honour against threats and insults from outside. The women, for their part, had to preserve their virginity and their modesty if their menfolks' virility was not to be dishonoured.

Among the limited category of possessions crucial in determining the degree of honour of an individual or group, women represented something especially precious. Indeed, they were themselves the most precious of possessions, to be guarded with unflagging watchfulness. *** Women who, through some particularly unfortunate chain of events, found themselves without menfolk to defend them were hard

* S. Strai, *Il selvaggio di Santa Venere*, Milan 1977, p. 127.
** L. Asprea, op. cit., p. 23.
*** Gambino, op. cit., pp. 57–58.

put to retain the respect or consideration of society. In most cases they
fell to the lowest social stratum, and passed their own dishonour on to
their descendants.

In mafia areas, feminine honour typically symbolized unbroken
family honour. If an outside enemy destroyed it, he gained superiority
over his victims, proving himself the more powerful by exploiting a
potential weakness of his adversary. He showed that he could oblige a
member of another group to violate the sacred bonds of loyalty in
order to satisfy his own desire. Under such circumstances, blood-
vendetta was the obligatory recourse: the father or brother must first
kill his own daughter or sister, and then her violator or lover. A husband, in the same way, must kill first his unfaithful wife and then her
lover. Not to pursue the vendetta was to forfeit beyond recovery any
claim to social standing: individuals and groups who lost their honour
in this way were very often excluded from the local community. In his
autobiography, L. Asprea describes a Calabrian village of the 1930s
where those in the category of the irretrievably dishonoured were seg-
regated from the rest of the community even in the literal, territorial
sense:

> To the south of *il Calvario* was *il Piliere* . . . There, alongside
> the main sewer of the town, was a string of huts, battered by
> the east wind . . . They were unbelievably smoke-blackened.
> This was the refuge of the most wretched and feeble-hearted
> men: their women, wives and daughters, were at the mercy
> of any more powerful man.[*]

Social life had no place for individuals and groups who had lost their
honour. For this reason, emigration was often the only alternative to
civil death:

> In one quarter of Taurianova, during the war, a peasant-
> woman whose husband was in the army became the love of

---

[*] Asprea, op. cit., pp. 14–15.

an *'ndranghetista* who had managed—*per diritezza,* he said: because he knew how to stand up for himself—to avoid going to the front. When the husband got back, he realised at once, from the coldness of people's greetings, that something serious had befallen his own and his family's honour. When he had found out from his old father what had happened, he didn't have the courage to kill either his wife or the *'ndranghetista.* A few months later, he had to leave for America. Nobody held him in the slightest regard any longer. Even the children in the street had started to make fun of him. [*]

Heightened sensitivity in matters of feminine honour was one of the most frequent sources of conflict between *uomini di rispetto* in traditional Calabria. Of all the mafia-type murders committed between 1940 and 1950 in the Plain of Gioia Tauro, over 60 per cent stemmed from conflicts caused by acts of sexual violence, abductions of women, or broken engagements. In this last case, conflict arose, not from any direct physical attack on the woman's honour, but from the implicit suggestion that for some reason or another she was not worthy of becoming a wife. In these communities—in ordinary families, as well as among the mafia—marriage was entered into only after long discussions and searching enquiries. No-one, therefore, could say their decision was mistaken, and any attempt to go back on what had been settled was seen as a challenge to the family honour.

Challenges, Combats, Competitions

In cultural systems of the mafia type, the individual's personal strength and force had a more immediate and obvious role than elsewhere in determining the degree of honour accorded to competing individuals and family groups. Neither birth nor institutional factors were decisive in determining the distribution of honour. Men of honour were made,

[*] Interview no. 6

not born, and the pursuit of honour was a free competition, open to all. The élite of men of honour was formed by a demanding process of selection, based on competitive confrontation between individuals. The culture of the mafia differed from other cultures in that such antagonistic confrontation was a matter of course within it, and found expression in a whole range of events. Balls, festivals and pilgrimages were among the classic opportunities for status and prestige to be assessed. Hundreds and even thousands of people, drawn from a wide area, came together for these annual festivities and collective celebrations, making them an ideal arena for trials of honour and for the spreading of mafia values.

One of the most important of these recurrent festivals was the pilgrimage made each year to the shrine of the Madonna di Polsi, in the heart of the Aspromonte region. Here, 'the young men have to make an impression, they have to show the whole family what they are made of (literally, that they are *mascoli di fegato* : "men of liver")'.[*] It was during a festival that don Nino, the mafia chief described by Strati, demonstrated before a crowd of two thousand people that he was precociously endowed with the qualities of a man of honour:

> During a summer festival which was taking place outside a church in the open country, one silly fool tried to make himself look big by taking Nino's place at the head of the dance, which he had been leading. With a single backhanded slap, Nino sent his head spinning. The women cried out in fright, and everyone grew excited and uneasy. The two *carabinieri* on duty came running to restore order, but Nino was in such a rage that he lifted one of them bodily in the air and threw him against a wall. The whole crowd gathered round, to see what was going on and say what they thought of it.[**]

● ● ●

[*] Strati, op. cit., p. 97.
[**] Ibid., pp. 56–57.

In mafia areas, competitions, challenges and fights were also the fundamental means by which people were socialized. The distribution of
power and prestige within the family was not preordained, as in families of the patriarchal type; rather, it was established through a series of
very intense conflicts. The entire domestic world was dominated by *ver-
tical* relations (parents-children; husband-wife; elder brother-younger
brother, and so on). Family solidarity prevailed only in the case of conflict with another family group. Relations within the family obeyed the
rule, not of *intimacy* or *solidarity*, but of *subordination*, which involved a
mass of obligations and values emphasizing the prerogatives attached
to each position within the reigning domestic hierarchy.

The father-son relationship, for instance, was not based on an established, stable hierarchy derived from the parent's greater age and experience, but on the latter's ability to emerge victorious—through
physical strength and through cunning—in any competition for
supremacy. What mattered was the establishment of a hierarchy based
on the predominance of the strongest. The strongest member of the
domestic group might also be the oldest, or he might simply be the
most aggressive or the wiliest. Family roles were thus fluid and temporary, and subject to considerable tensions and reversals. In time, one of
the sons might grow sufficiently bold to 'challenge' the father's superiority, struggle against it, and dethrone it.[*]

Success in competition was an end in itself, independent of the
material advantages that victory brought within reach.

Mafia culture therefore offered numerous symbolic representations
and simulated forms of competition for honour. These found their
fullest expression in the game of *passatella*. A number of players, whose
roles and hierarchical relations were fixed as required by the drawing of
lots or by suitable sub-competitions, competed for the control and distribution of a resource, represented by wine, beer, fruit, or even water.
The way in which this was to be distributed was decided in negotiations
that could last for hours, and whose course depended on the changing

[*] Ibid., pp. 8–10.

relationships of alliance and antagonism between the players. As the game proceeded, its ruthless and dramatic character often transformed it into a *real* struggle for supremacy, with fights, wounding, and murder. A case in point is recounted in the biography of Gerolamo Piromalli, the most important Calabrian *mafioso* of the post-war period:

> Towards midnight on 27 August 1950, a seriously injured man was admitted to the General Hospital at Reggio Calabria. This was Francesco Ippolito—the late Francesco di Pellegrina di Bagnara. He was immediately operated on, and died without informing the authorities of the name of his attacker . . . The local *carabinieri* proceeded to investigate . . . The events leading up to Francesco Ippolito's death can be reconstructed as follows: on the afternoon of 27 August, Francesco Ippolito, his brother Carmelo, Girolamo Piromalli and Carmelo Marafioti met up near the Pellegrina Railmen's Club . . . They passed the time with a game of *padrone e sotto* (that is, *passatella*), adding interest to the game by using bottles of beer as stakes.
>
> It fell out that chance more than once favoured Francesco Ippolito, making him the *padrone* of the beer; and he, while offering drink to his other friends, each time left Piromalli *all'olmo* (without a drink). Piromalli took good note of this, and eventually—perhaps because Ippolito was giving himself airs on account of his good luck—he declared that Ippolito was nothing but a kid, and that he for his part had come along to have some fun and not to quarrel.
>
> Ippolito answered by saying that he was afraid of no-one, and that even if the other was Mommo Piromelli, he was not going to eat dirt. This exchange of insults inevitably created a tense atmosphere among the players. However, the game continued; and when chance made Piromalli *padrone* of the beer, he repaid Ippolito in kind, leaving him *all'olmo* in his turn.

With the game going on in this way, the tension showed no sign of breaking. Indeed, it must have been clearly apparent, for when Vincenzo Oliviero arrived he realised that 'something must have happened between Piromalli and Ippolito'. In fact, understanding the situation and what it might lead to, Oliviero suggested to the onlookers that the game should be brought to an end.

. . . The game ended and, once they had paid for the beer they had drunk, everyone went out, stopping for a few moments outside the bar. Here . . . Ippolito went up to Piromalli, and the two of them moved a few paces away from the others. They exchanged a few words . . . Everyone felt certain that they had challenged one another, and had made an appointment to meet again. . . . "[*]

In communities where the mafia was present, this general tendency towards combativeness in its most extreme forms, regardless of the rules laid down as the basis for competition, sometimes made itself felt even in the most innocuous encounters, such as football matches or children's games.[**] The competition for honour was not precisely delimited and institutionalized, as it is in modern forms of sporting, scholastic and commercial competition, and in the struggle between classes and groups. As in war, rules were reduced to a minimum, and any means were justified. Struggle between people thus resembled the most primitive forms of social conflict: robbery, wanton destruction, the taking of prisoners, slaughter. Aggression was a socially sanctioned form of action.

Intermediate kinds of institutional regulation, such as the duel, never became established. Thus even where conflicts between *mafiosi* began by acknowledging the rules of chivalry, their outcome was determined by the unbounded use of fraud and deceit.

This is well illustrated by Familiari's account of the clash between

---

[*] Reggio Calabria Court, *Procedimento contro Piromalli Gerolamo, Protocollo*, no. 298/50, 1950.
[**] Asprea, op. cit., p. 13.

the mafia chief, Criazzo, and his young challenger Gemina. Gemina, a goat-herd, accused Criazzo of having colluded with the judicial authorities and with the wealthy people of the district in order to 'get something out of it for himself.' The duel between the two ended in victory for the younger *mafioso*, and the mafia chief, seriously wounded, was taken to hospital. 'After two months and five days in bed, Criazzo returned home. The following night, he went round to see Vincenzo Gemina, who was sleeping in a hut. He called him outside and killed him in the doorway with two rifle-shots . . . The funeral was an impressive one. The whole town followed the brave goat-herd's coffin, and his murderer was in the first row.'[*]

In mafia areas, acts, people and events were habitually judged in terms of the honour acquired through victory in struggles and competitions. It follows that aggressiveness and violence were positively endorsed. In consequence, those who for biological and cultural reasons were least disposed to take part in conflict (such as women, children, and the elderly) found that their participation in the life of the community was severely limited—unless they adopted the manly and pugnacious bearing of those in the superior categories. Asprea, describing his mother, emphasizes her strength, her courage, and her rather bloodthirsty temperament.[**] In the eyes of the inhabitants of Reggio Calabria province (and of the author of the novel *Emigranti*), the women of Bagnara owe their fascination to the fact that 'people said they wore razors in their hair, and used their knives with more daring than the men.'[***]

The society into which the *mafioso* was born was a tragic and brutal world, sparing neither the weak nor the defenceless. Although women and children, being excluded from the competition for honour, were rarely involved in woundings and killings, members of the marginal categories of the local community sometimes became the object of the most sadistic crimes. The mafia chief Michele Navarra, a doctor from

[*] P. Familiari, *La vera storia del brigante Marlino Zappa*.
[**] Asprea, op. cit., p. 18.
[***] F. Ferri, *Emigiranti*, Rome 1976, p. 198.

Corleone, had no hesitation in killing a boy, the son of poor shepherds, with a cyanide injection simply because the child might *perhaps* have been present at the scene of a murder which Navarra had committed.[*] And at Oppido Mamertina, Peppinello, the son of a prostitute, was killed by a group of young men on Easter Monday afternoon. The youths had made the child their target in a shooting-competition.[**]

Honour and Justice

One important consequence of the war of each against all that prevailed in mafia areas was the fact that nothing, at bottom, could be really unjust. Honour was connected less with justice than with domination and physical strength. The local community remained largely indifferent to questions of 'right' and 'wrong', or 'justice' and 'injustice', when there was a conflict between two families, groups of relatives, or individuals. The preference tended to be given to whichever party proved victorious in the end, irrespective of the original causes of the conflict:

> The assassination of Andrea in Genuardo in 1919 and that of Cesare in the following year were carried out by Alessandro Cassini to get his territorial claims recognized. In the village of Genuardo, these claims were not disputed: Andrea's father accepted defeat, and even complied with the action of the Cassinis by charging innocent persons.[***]

In the carrying out of his day-to-day 'duties', the *mafioso* did not follow any abstract ideal of morality and justice. He sought honour and power, and in pursuit of his goals he was quite ready to flout *any* established rule of conduct. There does not exist, and there never has existed, any

[*] D. De Masi, 'Sopraluogo nella Sicilia della mafia', in *Nord e Sud*, 46 (1963), p. 23.
[**] Asprea, op. cit., pp. 58–59.
[***] A. Blok, *The Mafia of a Sicilian Village, 1860–1960: A Study of Violent Peasant Entrepreneurs*, New York and Oxford 1974, p. 174.

coherent system of 'just, unwritten laws', enforced by the power of the mafia as against the 'unjust written laws' imposed by the State.

As we shall see below, traditional *mafiosi* assumed public functions, safeguarding the socio-economic *status quo* against the threat posed by subversive forces. Such functions, however, were the product—recognized as such both by the local society, and by the State—of the mafia's possession of a territorial monopoly of physical violence, and not of its general 'allegiance' to any traditional order. If anything, this 'allegiance' is a later rationalization, temporally and logically consequent upon the gaining of the monopoly of violence.

The conviction that the law is an instrument of physical force has deep roots in mafia culture. When an enemy threatens him with recourse to the State's laws, the *mafioso* of *La famiglia Montalbano* replies that 'law is force, and can never be separated from force'.[*] Force and supremacy, here, create the law much more than they represent the efficacy of any law valid in itself. Of all historical and social worlds, none demonstrates more clearly than the world of the *mafioso* the extent to which physical force can be independent of any pre-established distributive justice. Individual *mafiosi* were perfectly aware of the ultimate foundation of their power, and on some occasions took care to emphasize how the concrete 'justice of force' prevailed over the ideal force of justice.[**]

When power was at stake, *mafiosi* had no hesitation in violating the most deep-rooted cultural and ethical norms. '*Mafiosi* used to stress relations of friendship in order to accomplish a killing effectively without raising the suspicion of either the victim, public opinion, or the law,' wrote Blok. Blok also recounts a struggle that took place in 1922 between two western Sicilian mafia groups. A serious disagreement had broken out between Bernardo Cassini, a member of the leading mafia cell *(cosca)* in Genuardo, and the *cosche* of Adernò, Corleone and Bisacquino. When his brother was killed and his animals were stolen, Bernardo realised that his own life was in danger, and that

[*] S. Montalto, *La famiglia di Montalbano*, Chiavalle Centrale 1973, p. 84.
[**] Familiari, op. cit., pp. 20–21; Strati, op. cit., pp. 17–18.

he would have to give in to his opponents, whose leader was the famous Vito Cascio Ferro.* Bernardo asked for a meeting to be organized, at which the whole affair could be discussed. It was decided that Bernardo must pay a money indemnity to each of his adversaries. He went to Corleone and paid up. He then took money to Bisacquino, to Cascio Ferro's house:

> Cascio Ferro himself and the other mafiosi involved reassured Bernardo and told him that he could leave the house without incurring any danger. Thus appeased, Bernardo did not suspect that his 'friends' were preparing his elimination. Bernardo was shot twice by Don Pipineddu, one of Cascio Ferro's right-hand men.**

What determined the power of the *mafioso* was victory in the struggle for supremacy—victory by whatever means. Respect for traditional legal and cultural obligations was a subsequent, derivative phase in the dynamic of mafia power (which we shall, however, discuss later in this account). The fact that all hierarchical relations operating in mafia areas were governed by this strict link between right and might, law and physical force, gave them a distinctive formal character, which could recoil at any moment upon the heads of those currently in power. When the leader of a cell was physically eliminated or defeated in a fight, his followers accepted the new state of affairs quite calmly, and the victor was quickly installed in his place: 'Guiseppe Damati . . . was only twenty-six years old when he killed and replaced the much older and established Bernardo Cassini in November 1922.'***

It was just this formal quality of mafia power, linked to its honorific-

---

Vito Cascio Ferro : Together with Calogero Vizzini and Genco Russo, Cascio Ferro was one of the most important traditional Sicilian *mafiosi*. Born in Bisacquino, in the province of Palermo, he emigrated to the USA for a time at the beginning of the century. He was arrested under the fascist regime and condemned to life imprisonment, dying in jail in 1943.

** Blok, op. cit., p. 173.

***Ibid., p. 173.

competitive origins, that explained the apparently curious phenom-
enon of the 'transfer' of authority from one man to his opponents.

His understanding of these 'Hobbesian' roots of mafia power
brought the *prefetto* (Prefect) Cesare Mori much early success in the
anti-mafia campaign that he began in Sicily in 1924. 'If Sicilians are
scared of the mafia,' Mori told his colleagues, 'I shall convince them
that I am the most powerful *mafioso* of the lot.'[*] The linchpin of his
whole strategy was the setting up of a competition for honour with the
mafiosi of Sicily, a competition that would take place partly on their
own terrain but which also relied upon the State's military and organi-
zational superiority.

His language and his methods were thus steeped in the spirit of the
mafia. When the elite of Palermo gathered in the Teatro Massimo to
celebrate his victory over the mafia brigands of le Madonie, Mori
declared that it was 'no good trusting in the inadequacy or incom-
pleteness of the law. The law will be rewritten, completed, and put
right. And in any case, wherever it is lacking, we shall step in, with argu-
ments of unquestionable force.'[**] His struggle against the *mafiosi* of le
Madonie clearly shows how he tried to bring about a transfer of collective authority from outlaws to State officials by demonstrating his
superiority in political, military and—above all—honorific terms.

After surrounding the town of Gangi, where the *mafiosi-banditi* had
taken refuge, and occupying it with a military force for some ten days,
Mori gave the bandits twelve hours to leave their hiding places and surrender:

> It was my firm intention to deny them the honour of armed
> combat. I did not want the prestige of crime to benefit once
> again from the glory . . . of a battle with the forces of law
> and order. I proposed not just to win—that is, to bring the
> bandits to justice—but to give the people concrete proof of
> the cowardice of crime.[***]

[*] A. Petacco, *Il prefetto di ferro*, Milan 1975, p. 105.
[**] Ibid., p. 105.
[***] C. Mori, *Con la mafia ai ferri corti*, Verona 1932, p. 296.

• • •

However, the police campaign achieved no notable success until Mori put into practice his plan of showing himself to be 'the biggest *mafioso* of all':

> His first trick was to have rumours spread that the Gangi hostages were suffering all kinds of maltreatment in prison, and in particular that 'the cops are screwing the bandits' women'. The ruse was only partially successful . . . Many of the bandits came into the open and gave themselves up to the authorities . . . But from the chiefs, there was not the slightest movement . . .
>
> . . . 'If these characters care nothing for the virtue of their womenfolk,' Mori commented ironically, 'let's see how they react when their interests are attacked.'
>
> There and then, he published a decree confiscating all the bandits' goods. The confiscation was carried out in broad daylight, and so publicized that no-one could avoid noticing it . . . Mori then had the fattest calves from the confiscated herds slaughtered in the *piazza*, ordering the meat to be distributed free to the public. The people, hungry after the long siege, all came rushing to collect the unexpected gift. The giving out of the meat became in some ways like a town festival. The policemen-butchers made the most of the public mood, pouring scorn on the timidity of the bandits.
>
> . . . Cesare Mori continued with his psychological warfare, authorizing his immediate colleagues to issue personal challenges to the most celebrated brigands. He himself challenged Gaetano Ferrarello: 'Let it be known to the so-called King of le Madonie,' he proclaimed, 'that I am ready to meet him single-handed and carrying my musket. I shall be waiting for him this evening at six, in the *fondo Sant'Andrea*. If he is a man, he will be there.'

Similar challenges were then issued by Francesco Spanò to Carmelo Andaloro and by the police-chief, Crimi, to Salvatore Ferrarello. These pieces of bragadoccio may at first sight seem transparent, and it is clear enough that the bandits never had the slightest intention of accepting the challenges. But Mori's aim was in fact to make an impression on the imagination of the people, who were accustomed to respect only those who behaved like *mafiosi*.

It was at this point that Mori decided to issue his ultimatum to the bandits in hiding . . . But it proved unnecessary to wait for the full period to elapse . . . Gaetano Ferrarello emerged from his hiding-place, which was actually in the attic of the building that housed the police-station.

'My heart is pounding,' he said in an agitated voice. 'For the first time in my life, I am face to face with justice.'[*]

Honour and Murder

In a system whose basis was the struggle for supremacy, the most unequivocal way of asserting one's own pre-eminence was to take another man's life. When Bernardo Cassini was murdered, as Anton Blok describes, his killer gained not just land and power, but the honorific title *don*. In the mafia scale of values, where conflicts of honour played such a central role, it was in the highest degree honourable to take life and to kill a fearsome adversary. 'So-and-so is an exceptional man; he has "got" five murders'. 'He is *un'uomo di rispetto* : people say that he's "rubbed out" four people'—phrases of this kind recur in mafia conversation. The more fearsome and powerful the victim, the greater the 'worth and merit' of the killer. Vito Cascio Ferro boasted of how he had killed with his own hands his long-standing adversary Joe Petrosino, the New York police lieutenant, enemy number one of

[*] Petacco, op. cit., pp. 91-93.

the American mafia, who had visited Palermo secretly in 1909: 'In my whole life I have only killed one person, and I did that *disinterestedly* . . . Petrosino was a brave adversary, and deserved better than a shameful death at the hands of some hired cut-throat.'[*]

Any man of honour had to commit at least one act of murderous violence. Without killing someone, nobody could hope to inspire fear or to gain the recognition and respect due to a *mafioso*.

> It often happens that the *campiere* (estate guard—often an agent and representative of the mafia) gets the name of having pegged out one or two scalps to dry—that is, of having committed one or two murders. And then, because of the aura this gives him, he is made. Everyone's afraid of him. He becomes someone who causes an impression, makes an impression. People can't do without him and for that reason his services are better paid.[**]

Murder was the root of the *mafioso*'s prestige, transforming an anonymous shepherd or farm labourer into a man who must be reckoned with. Among the mafia of Sicily and Calabria, the act of murder—especially if committed in the course of a struggle for supremacy, of whatever kind—was a mark of courage and manly force, and automatically enhanced the killer's credit. This was an important form of *conversion* between illegal action and mafia action: to break the law of the State was honourable, because it showed contempt and defiance of powerful persons and institutions. Many *mafiosi* began their careers (and still do so) in the ranks of common criminals:

> It is by a series of well-defined steps that the *mafioso* enters the world of crime. These steps are always the same. They are monotonously familiar in judicial life-histories. At a very early age—as young as fifteen or sixteen—there will be a

[*] A. Petacco, *Joe Petrosino*, Milan 1978, p. 182.
[**] A. Cutrera, *La mafia e i mafiosi*, Palermo 1960, p. 95.

charge of illegal carriage of firearms. Next comes a charge or conviction for causing actual bodily harm. This accusation of wounding is a sign that the young man of honour has distinguished himself by his arrogance and boastfulness at some brawl or in some vendetta, though as yet the affair is only a minor one. At this stage, he is not yet certain to become involved with the mafia . . . Then the young man's desire for dominance, his wish to be a cut above the rest, and his friendship with undesirable characters push him a step further. He finds himself convicted of robbery or extortion. The more serious the offence, the better for his reputation in the underworld. And so he attempts a murder, and then commits a murder, or carries out a massacre—by which he gains, so to speak, his battle honours, and is entitled to 'claim his place' alongside other men of honour.[*]

Anyone who studies the careers of the most important *mafiosi* will indeed be struck, not only by the number and gravity of the conflicts from which they have emerged victorious (especially during the early part of their apprenticeship), but by the fact that there does exist a progression of illegal acts tending always to pass through the same stages. Thus the *curricula* drawn up by the judicial authorities for the lives of Gerolamo Piromalli (the mafia chief of the Tyrrhenian part of the Reggio district) and of Antonio Macrí (the Ionian mafia leader) are almost identical in their earlier phases (see Table I on page 70).

This honorofic dimension of murder, with homicide seen as an expression of the killer's predominance and of his ability to avenge himself, casts a haze of glory over every murderous act and over its agents and accessories. To get an idea of the impact which a murder makes on the population of a mafia area even today, one need only flick through the best-selling Reggio Calabria newspaper the day after the murder happens: page after page is crowded with photographs,

[*] Interview no. 4.

including close-ups, together with the most minute particulars of the victim, all giving the event a touch of symbolic grandeur. The reports usually emphasize the execution's cruellest and most violent phases; they tell how the blood spilled out, how the dead body was mutilated, how the victim spent his last hours, and how his disconsolate relatives are coping with their grief.

Table 1

Judicial curricula for the lives of Antonio Macrí and Gerolamo Piromalli

	Antonio Macrí	*Gerolamo Piromalli*	
Year	*Charges and Convictions*	*Charges and Convictions*	*Year*
1929	illegal carriage of firearms	illegal carriage of firearms	1939
1932	grievous bodily harm	grievous bodily harm	1940
1945	robbery with violence	robbery with violence	1944
1947	attempted murder		
1958	murder (with aggravating circumstances)	murder	1950

To carry and use firearms was a mark of honour in mafia areas. In Reggio Calabria province in 1950, several thousand licences to carry arms were issued; there was a still larger number of statutory declarations in respect of the domestic keeping of rifles, pistols, knives and bullets; and a yet larger number of cases of unlawful carriage and possession of arms.

The G-Man and the Hit Man
by Fredric Dannen

Law enforcement officials rely upon criminal informants to help them monitor and disrupt organized crime operations. That dependence often leads to conflicts of interest—legal, ethical and emotional. Fredric Dannen (born 1955) offers this account of one senior F.B.I. agent's controversial relationship with a particularly brutal mobster.

I n 1991, the Colombo crime family in Brooklyn went to war with itself: a rebel faction tried to seize control of the family from its boss, Carmine Persico, who was serving life in jail. Gregory Scarpa, Sr., a sixty-three-year-old mobster, immediately took command of the armed faction loyal to Persico. Scarpa was seriously ill: as the result of a blood transfusion, he was H.I.V.-positive. His body had shrivelled from a muscular two hundred and twenty-five pounds to a gaunt one-fifty, his stomach had been removed during surgery, and he digested his food with pancreatic-enzyme pills. Yet Scarpa, a multiple murderer, hadn't slowed down. During the seven months that the shooting war lasted, he could be seen driving with his troops along Avenue U, in Brooklyn, scouting out the social clubs and bars where members of the enemy faction were likely to be found. Sometimes he drove past the rebels' houses, and one night he surprised a rebel who stood on a ladder, with his back turned, hanging Christmas lights on his house. Scarpa rolled down his car window, stuck out his rifle, and picked the man off with three shots. Then he paged his consigliere with the satanic code 666, to signify a fresh kill.

By the time the war ended, in June, 1992, ten people had died, including an innocent man of eighteen who was shot accidentally at a Brooklyn bagel shop. Ten more people had been wounded, among them a fifteen-year-old bystander, who was shot in the head. By far the most violent participant in the war was Scarpa: he murdered four people and wounded two.

At the Manhattan office of the F.B.I., squads had been in place since the eighties to investigate all five New York Mafia families. The supervisor of the squad for the Colombo and Bonanno families was R. Lindley DeVecchio, a dapper, curly haired man of average height, with a mustache, whom friends and colleagues called Lin. He was a well-liked veteran who had been with the Bureau since the J. Edgar Hoover era, and he had come up through the New York office as an older colleague of F.B.I. director Louis Freeh. The Colombo war presented a unique challenge to DeVecchio. The F.B.I. had a duty to try to prevent violence of every type, even among criminals. If it could learn, perhaps from an informant, when and where a hit team was to be mobilized, the shooters could be intercepted in the act. DeVecchio did, in fact, have an informant inside the Persico faction of the Colombo family. That informant, however, was hardly likely to divulge the activities of the faction's hit team, for the simple reason that he was its leader— Gregory Scarpa himself.

Scarpa had had a secret relationship with the F.B.I. since the early nineteen-sixties, though for two extended periods he had been "closed," which is to say that he and the Bureau had had a falling out, and no agent was authorized to make contact with him. In 1980, DeVecchio had taken the initiative to seek out Scarpa, win back his good graces, and reopen him for the first time in five years. It had been a spectacular career move. Scarpa was no ordinary informant; he was classified as a T.E., for "top echelon," source. DeVecchio was promoted to squad supervisor in 1983. Largely because of his work with Scarpa—and with a second, unidentified mobster, it was said—DeVecchio became one of the Bureau's most admired experts on dealing with informants, and was accorded the honor of being asked to teach informant development to recruits at the F.B.I.'s training academy, in Quantico, Virginia.

DeVecchio told his students that when it came to building a rapport with an informant, training alone was no substitute for having the right personality. He was a natural himself, even if his upbringing—he is a native of Fresno, California, and the son of a decorated Army colonel buried at Arlington National Cemetery—could not account for it. DeVecchio had become a flashy dresser: at work, he wore a gold bracelet, silk pocket squares, and shirts with monograms. He was also an avid gun collector. He had learned the moves and the jargon of mafiosi on the streets of New York, and he was proud of it. "I've spent virtually twenty-nine years of my life talking to wise guys," he said recently. "You either know how to talk to them or you don't. Many a competent agent doesn't have the street sense." DeVecchio, who has a coarse sense of humor, recalled that his standard opening remark to the students was "I have two college degrees, and my vocabulary has degenerated to four-letter words, and if that bothers you—*fuck you!*"

Even agents with the keenest street sense might have found it intimidating to deal with Scarpa, an imposing man with a deep voice, who once said of himself, "The sign of my birth is Taurus, which is a bull," and who, in a wiretapped conversation during the eighties, convincingly made pronouncements such as "I don't have my money by Thursday, I'll put him right in the fucking hospital." Whatever chemistry existed between him and Lin DeVecchio, it was strong. Informants are supposed to be handled by two agents at a time, and the Bureau discouraged anyone of supervisory rank from operating an informant. Those guidelines were waived for DeVecchio because, he insisted, that was how Scarpa wanted it—there was no other agent he trusted. For more than a decade, DeVecchio was almost always unaccompanied when he met with Scarpa—at an apartment rented by the F.B.I. or in a hotel room, or at some other prearranged location. Sometimes DeVecchio delivered cash to Scarpa. The two men left each other phone messages as "Mr. Dello," their shared code name, and spoke frequently via a special telephone at the F.B.I. building called the hello line, which could not be traced. F.B.I. reports show that during the seven months of the Colombo war they met or spoke, on the average, at least every ten days.

During the war, DeVecchio maintained that Scarpa was not an active participant, but some younger agents were hearing repeated reports to the contrary. They were alarmed. In 1980, the Department of Justice had issued detailed guidelines: if an informant was suspected of involvement in any "serious act of violence," the supervisor in charge was required to consider closing him and targeting him for arrest. While it was understandable that DeVecchio might be reluctant to close a top-echelon informant—particularly someone who had helped make his career—that seeming reluctance put him at odds with some of his own agents. Eventually, four of them reported to the Bureau that, in an apparent effort to protect Scarpa not merely from arrest but from his enemies in the Mob, DeVecchio had leaked sensitive, confidential information to him. One agent has alleged that DeVecchio became compromised to the point of helping Scarpa locate people that Scarpa wanted to kill.

In early 1994, DeVecchio was placed under investigation, but in the meantime he was neither discharged nor put on administrative leave. Instead, he was moved off his squad to another supervisory position— as the F.B.I.'s drug-enforcement coordinator for the entire Northeastern United States, with unrestricted access to classified documents. He continued to hold that job after he informed the Bureau in a sworn statement that he was not amenable to a voluntary polygraph examination, and, incredibly, even after invoking his Fifth Amendment privilege and refusing to testify about his conduct as an F.B.I. supervisor at a hearing in May, 1996. No F.B.I. official—not even Louis Freeh or the New York chief, James Kallstrom—would comment on why a man being investigated for leaking information was kept in a post requiring top-security clearance. Douglas Grover, DeVecchio's lawyer, says it is because the Bureau had always understood what DeVecchio was doing to protect a valuable informant, and had approved of his actions. "Whatever Lin did, he did it as an agent of the institution, both literally and figuratively, acting on behalf of the F.B.I.," Grover says.

The confidential informant has been a staple of the F.B.I. for decades; J. Edgar Hoover exhorted agents to develop at least four such informants a year. Unlike cooperating witnesses—criminals who have been caught and have agreed to testify in exchange for leniency—confidential informants are not expected to take the witness stand. They function as undercover agents. From informants, the Bureau learns what phones to tap and what meetings to subject to surveillance. The top-echelon informant is that rare source high enough in a criminal enterprise to provide what the Bureau calls "singular" information, such as a detailed organization chart of the enterprise. Documents made public as a result of the investigation of DeVecchio show that Scarpa periodically supplied information of this kind. On one occasion, for instance, he gave up the names of three people proposed for membership in the Colombo family—including one who had been sponsored by Scarpa himself.

Criminal informants are often essential for making cases, and courts have long upheld the legality of their use. However, because they are practicing criminals they must be handled with extreme care, so that, in the words of the Justice Department guidelines, "the government itself does not become a violator of the law." The F.B.I. has repeatedly been accused of overprotecting its criminal sources. In 1985, federal prosecutors, unaware that the Teamsters boss Jackie Presser was a top-echelon F.B.I. informant, sought an indictment against him for putting two ghost employees on the payroll. The following year, three Cleveland F.B.I. agents were investigated for having blocked the indictment, allegedly by inventing an alibi for Presser. During an internal inquiry, one of those agents, Robert Friedrick, admitted to his role in creating the phony alibi. His statement was ruled inadmissible, however, and obstruction charges against him were dismissed; the other agents were never charged.

The F.B.I. had helped keep Presser on the street, but Presser, unlike Greg Scarpa, had never shown a penchant for violence. Scarpa had other qualities that made him a dangerous choice for informant: he was shrewd, and he had a proven ability to bend people to his will. "Greg was a true Machiavelli," Louis Diamond, a former attorney of his, says. "He was the puppeteer. He lived to manipulate people against people." Diamond adds that Scarpa was "one of the better gin-rummy players," and that the game showed off his "brilliance" and "ability to focus and plan." For thirty years, he adds, "Greg was able to keep the government on the schneider"—a cardplayer's term for preventing your opponent from scoring a point.

Scarpa was first officially opened by the F.B.I. on March 20, 1962, reputedly after agents seized him outside New York State for an armed robbery. It is not hard to see how his long relationship with the Bureau worked to his benefit. According to an associate, he "hated doing time," and, unlike most Mob figures, he seemed never to go to jail. During his three decades as an informant, his only incarceration, at Rikers Island for bribing two policemen, was thirty days in 1978—one of the years in which he was closed by the F.B.I. He had previously been arrested for bookmaking, assault with a lead pipe (twice), hijacking a tractor-trailer loaded with J. & B. Scotch, possession of stolen mail, and interstate transportation of stolen bonds. In each instance, the charges were dismissed.

Scarpa's ability to stay out of jail did not go unnoticed by his Mob associates, and periodically there were rumors that he was a snitch. But everyone in the family knew that the government did not ally itself with killers, and, as one associate pointed out about Scarpa, "He was crazy. He killed a lot. He was nuts." Lou Diamond adds, "Greg was an absolutely fearless man who enjoyed killing, and enjoyed vengeance. And enjoyed the subtlety. He would smile at a guy, take him out to dinner, and blow his brains out." After Scarpa became sick, he proposed that someone get him a wheelchair and roll him into a roomful of enemies with a machine gun hidden under his blanket. His associates gave him nicknames: the Mad Hatter, the Grim Reaper, General Schwarzkopf.

By the start of the Colombo war, Scarpa had murdered no fewer than eight people, and probably many more. One of his victims, according to a government document, was a Manhattan doctor named Eli Sckolnick. In the late seventies, Sckolnick lost his license to practice medicine and transferred title to a lucrative abortion clinic to a nurse who was on intimate terms with Scarpa. In the early eighties, Scarpa put a stop to Sckolnick's demands for money from the clinic by obtaining his address in Forest Hills and killing him. In 1984, it is alleged, Mary Bari, a young woman who was thought to know the whereabouts of a Colombo fugitive, was lured to a bar on the pretext of a job offer, was shot by Scarpa, and was tossed, dead, into the trunk of a car.

Scarpa was born in Brooklyn on May 8, 1928. He appears to have been drawn into the Colombo family—then called the Profaci family—by his older brother, Salvatore, who died in a shooting in 1987. In the early fifties, Scarpa married Connie Forrest; they had one daughter and three sons, including Gregory, Jr., who followed his father into the Mafia. By the time Scarpa separated from his wife, around 1973, he had had another son with a longtime girlfriend, Linda Schiro. Meanwhile, though he continued to live with Schiro, and had never divorced Forrest, he married Lili Dajani, a Palestinian-Israeli beauty queen, in 1975, in Las Vegas. Around 1978, Schiro began seeing a delivery boy named Larry Mazza; Scarpa permitted their love affair to continue, and, in the meantime, he inducted Mazza into his crew.

A number of crewmen answered to Scarpa's authority, but DeVecchio says that Scarpa never assumed the formal title of captain. He was what mafiosi call "a good earner." His income came from loan-sharking, bookmaking, the sale of marijuana and cocaine, securities and credit-card fraud, operating an auto-theft ring, and other forms of larceny. Simultaneously, he received money from the government: two hundred and fifty-three dollars a month in Social Security, and a total of at least a hundred and fifty thousand dollars in untaxed income—informant fees—from the F.B.I.

His early use by the Bureau went far beyond informant, and may have persuaded him that his violence—at least, when it was directed toward other bad guys—had the government's tacit approval. In the sixties, J. Edgar Hoover was criticized for the Bureau's failure to protect the civil rights of blacks in the Deep South. Consequently, the F.B.I. resorted to extreme measures in its war on the Ku Klux Klan. On January 10, 1966, the day after Vernon Dahmer, a black farmer and merchant in Forrest County, Mississippi, agreed to make his grocery store available as a place for blacks to pay poll tax, Klansmen set his house on fire, fatally searing his lungs and badly burning his ten-year-old daughter. Attorney General Nicholas Katzenbach promised to commit "the full resources of the Justice Department" to catching the perpetrators. On January 21st, the Jackson, Mississippi, office of the F.B.I. called the New York office and, as recorded in an internal memo, requested the use of informant NY-3461—Gregory Scarpa—for a special assignment.

One of the immediate suspects in the Dahmer homicide was Lawrence Byrd, the owner of Byrd's Radio & TV Service in Laurel, Mississippi, who held the post of senator in the Klan. One evening in late January, at around nine o'clock, as Byrd was about to close his shop, Scarpa and an F.B.I. agent agreed to buy a television from Byrd and asked him to help carry it to a car parked outside. Byrd was pistol-whipped, shoved into the back seat, forced to lie down, and driven, he believed, to Camp Shelby, a military base built on rural Mississippi swampland. There Scarpa beat a confession out of him. "Lawrence was a tough guy—a big, rawboned country boy—but he was beat up so bad he was never the same after that," says W. O. (Chet) Dillard, the local district attorney, who visited Byrd in the hospital immediately after the kidnapping. Byrd implored Dillard not to investigate the matter, and in early March he signed a twenty-two-page confession prepared by the F.B.I., in which he inculpated himself and seven other Klansmen. He got ten years for arson, and died early last year, having never learned that his brutal interrogator was a New York mafioso.

Lin DeVecchio plainly has a fascination with mobsters, and during two interviews conducted for this account he made no attempt to hide it.

He did not simply describe the wise guys he has known but mimicked them, down to their Brooklyn accents. He recalled a time when a fellow-agent introduced himself to an organized-crime figure stiffly, with a flash of his badge, "and the guy says to him, 'So whaddya want me to do—shit in my pants?'" DeVecchio laughed. His bad-guy imitations sometimes had an edge; at one point, he said he hoped that he would like this article, so that "I don't have to come looking for you some dark night."

DeVecchio spoke enthusiastically about how Mob figures had educated him to their way of looking at things. "It's a foreign culture to most of us," he said. "And you have to— 'Respect' is not the word, but you have to at least admire a guy who lives in an environment where every day he's looking over his shoulder. Scarpa used to tell me, 'I'd be called to meetings, and I'd leave my watch and valuables at home—I didn't know if I was coming back.' To survive in that milieu takes a special kind of person." After a pause, he added, "That doesn't mean Lin DeVecchio condones that way of life."

One thing that seemed to interest DeVecchio about organized-crime figures was their ability to kill in cold blood, and he went on, "I've asked a couple of wise guys about that, and they say the first couple of times it's hard but after that it's no big deal." He personally found that unfathomable, he said, but the mobsters taught him how "to talk, to act, as a true killer does"—a facility he used in undercover work. He created an alternative identity for himself—a hit man named Tony DeAngelo—and used it to good effect on a number of occasions. In 1983, a former C.I.A. agent, Edwin Wilson, in prison awaiting trial for illegally shipping weapons to Libya, was scouting for someone he could hire to murder two federal prosecutors and several potential witnesses. A fellow-inmate tipped off the authorities and then agreed to present DeVecchio to Wilson, in a visitors' room, as DeAngelo, the hit man. Days later, Wilson arranged for his son Erik to pay DeVecchio—unwittingly, it appeared—close to ten thousand dollars in a hotel men's room. Wilson was convicted of attempted murder.

DeVecchio, who is in his mid-fifties, is a husband and parent; he asked that no other details of his home life be disclosed. He spoke freely, however, about his late father, the Army colonel, who, as a finance officer, aided the Italian government in that country's postwar reconstruction. By the time DeVecchio was eighteen, he had lived in Italy, Japan, and Bermuda and in several American cities. He got an undergraduate degree in political science at George Washington University, and, in 1963, was about to accept a full commission in the military when the F.B.I. offered him a job as a clerk—an entrée into becoming an agent.

In March, 1966, having completed his agent training and passed an obligatory personal inspection by Hoover, DeVecchio was posted to upstate New York. He worked on routine crimes, such as bank robbery and car theft. In April, 1967, he was transferred to the New York City office, which was then on East Sixty-ninth Street; from that time forward, he specialized in organized crime. In less than a year, DeVecchio says, "I had my first informant under my belt." He also set about earning a master's degree in criminal justice from Long Island University.

DeVecchio found a kindred spirit and mentor on the organized-crime squad in Manhattan—an agent thirteen years his senior named Anthony Villano. "Tony had a very good way with wise guys," DeVecchio says. "I learned a lot of things by watching Tony." Villano, who died of heart failure in 1988, was an unorthodox agent—a tough Brooklynite, who once narrowly avoided arrest in a barroom brawl. He operated a number of informants, and one of them was Greg Scarpa. (DeVecchio says he learned this only after Villano quit the Bureau, in 1973.)

Villano left behind a blunt memoir of his F.B.I. career, written in 1977 with the author Gerald Astor and entitled "Brick Agent." (In Hoover's time, a street agent for the F.B.I. was said to be "on the bricks.") Astor says that two pseudonymous people in the book are actually Scarpa. The book recounts that Scarpa had had his first rift with the Bureau before Villano ever met him: he believed that the F.B.I. had welshed on a fifteen-hundred-dollar payment owed him for his work in the Deep South. Villano wrote that after finding Scarpa's name in the closed-informant file he got him the money but was unable to win his cooperation until he impressed the mobster, who was built like "an ox," by arm-wrestling him to a standoff.

Villano, who referred to developing a criminal informant as "getting married," came to regard Scarpa as "a friend," and repeatedly bent, or even broke, the law on his behalf. Often when Scarpa's information led to the recovery of stolen merchandise, Villano collected sizable reward money for him from insurance companies; and once, to make an illegal sports bet, Villano used Scarpa as his bookie. A more significant episode occurred when a criminal who could implicate Scarpa in acts of larceny offered to cooperate with the Bureau: Villano silenced the man by inventing the fiction that the Colombo family planned to kidnap his daughter if he talked. The man died in prison.

Although Scarpa tipped off the Bureau to a number of major heists, Villano wrote that all the time he himself worked with Scarpa "I had to reassure myself that our relationship was not the ultimate perversion of the whole law-enforcement idea. In my mind, what we did was justified on the grounds of the greatest good." Not everyone in the Bureau agreed. "I had a discussion with Tony that made me think that Scarpa thought he had a license to kill," one agent, now retired, recalls. "Around 1970, an informant for the Drug Enforcement Administration got blown away, and the D.E.A. heard that Scarpa was the triggerman. They wanted to interrogate Scarpa, and Tony did a tap dance to obstruct their investigation. Scarpa was not arrested or charged with that murder."

Scarpa was closed in 1975, two years after Villano left the Bureau. DeVecchio came across Scarpa's name in the closed-informant file, just as his ex-colleague had done, and in 1980 he got permission to try to reopen him. He says that he first called Villano for advice but can't now remember what he was told. One day that year, DeVecchio dressed casually, drove to Scarpa's residence, on Avenue J, in Brooklyn, and waited until Scarpa left the house alone. "I got out of the car and introduced myself," he recalls. "I said, 'I know you by reputation—you have a good reputation on the street.' I flattered him. I told him I worked the

Colombo family, and I said, 'I'm not looking for anything now, but one of these days I could use your help.'" Scarpa provided a phone number. A few days later, the two men went for a drive, and Scarpa explained why he'd been closed: he had had a shouting match with the assistant director of the F.B.I.'s New York office over what he termed a broken promise. "Scarpa said the guy was not a gentleman," DeVecchio recalls. "I just played dumb."

DeVecchio continued to meet with Scarpa for the next eleven and a half years. He acknowledges that he found Scarpa "very personable," and that he accepted a few small gifts from him—a bottle of wine, a pan of lasagna, and, in the early eighties, a Cabbage Patch doll for a friend's niece. "We got along," he says. He does not characterize Scarpa as having been a friend, however, nor does he distinguish him from the other top-echelon informants he worked with in the course of his career—five in all.

Although his squad had oversight of both the Colombo and the Bonanno families from the late eighties on, DeVecchio says he had no knowledge until 1992, after the Colombo war had ended, that Scarpa was a multiple murderer. But he does say, "The information we had for years and years on Scarpa was that he was a tough opponent on the street. He was a vicious, tough man. But, you know, when you talk to any organized-crime member you can almost take it to the bank that he's killed somebody."

DeVecchio says he never knew why Scarpa chose to cooperate with the F.B.I. "I think part of his motivation was he thought there was a quid pro quo—that I could be of some help to him sometime, one hand washing the other." He adds, "I think that's illusory." Earlier, he said, "A smart wise guy will talk to law enforcement in hopes—*in hopes*, not because it's gonna happen—that he'll derive some benefit from it. What does that mean? Does that mean a pass? He may think that. I'll tell you right now, I told Scarpa, as I did all my other T.E. informants, 'If you screw up, I'm not gonna help you out.'" The most he could ever do for an informant who'd been arrested, he says, was make his informant status known to the prosecution and the judge.

In practical terms, however, this could amount to a pass. In 1985, the Secret Service, unaware that Scarpa was anything other than a mobster suspected of dealing in counterfeit credit cards, sent an undercover agent to his principal hangout, the Wimpy Boys Athletic Club, in Brooklyn, where the agent sold Scarpa three hundred blank Master-Card and Visa cards. Scarpa was indicted the following year by the Brooklyn Organized Crime Strike Force, and he agreed to plead guilty. In July, 1986, the strike force sent the judge a lengthy letter detailing Scarpa's criminal history and penchant for violence, and urged that he be jailed and fined substantially. Then, with the permission of F.B.I. officials in Washington, DeVecchio conferred with members of the strike force, and he and Scarpa met with the judge. Scarpa drew a ten-thousand-dollar fine and five years' probation.

In August, 1986, while Scarpa was awaiting the outcome of the credit-card case, he developed bleeding ulcers and was admitted to Victory Memorial Hospital, in Brooklyn. When medication failed to stop the bleeding, he was told he would need transfusions. Scarpa did not want any of the hospital's blood in his veins—in the words of one of his attorneys, "Greg could never be accused of being racially liberal"—and he asked Linda Schiro to round up as many friends and relatives as she could. By the next day, almost thirty people had come to the hospital, and blood from some of them was administered to Scarpa without having been screened for H.I.V. One of the donors—Paul Mele, a weight lifter who served on Scarpa's crew—had contracted the virus, apparently from a steroid needle; six months after donating his blood, he was dead.

After the transfusions, Scarpa was taken to the operating room at Victory Memorial for emergency ulcer surgery. He seemed fine for a day or two, but then came down with a high fever, and began drifting in and out of consciousness. Linda Schiro claimed that the resident surgeon who had performed the operation, a Filipino named Angelito Sebollena, insisted that everything was all right, but she was unnerved one day when she caught him shaving Scarpa's face, in order to, as the doctor put it, "make him look nice." She had Scarpa transferred to Mt. Sinai Hospital, in Manhattan. There his stomach, which was hemorrhaging beyond repair, was removed. Scarpa finally went home in October, with the aid of a walker.

Scarpa blamed Sebollena for making a faulty incision, and Victory Memorial for exposing him to AIDS. He filed suit. Before long, Sebollena was in further trouble. In 1991, he injected two male patients with the drug Versed, a central-nervous-system depressant that leaves a person conscious but immobile, and performed oral sex on them. Gary Pillersdorf, the lawyer who represented Scarpa at the medical-malpractice trial, in August, 1992, recalls that on the morning of the opening statements the judge motioned him to the bench and said, "Let me get this straight. You're representing a hit man with AIDS against a doctor who sodomizes his patients. Am I on the right page?"

Scarpa made a superb witness in his own behalf. Choking back tears, he testified that he was afraid now to kiss his grandchildren, and he said that living with AIDS was like being "a person that's condemned to death and, each time he walks the corridor to the execution, he gets a reprieve." A black woman on the jury—an elementary-school principal, whose husband worked for the Brooklyn D.A.'s office— began to cry; she later described Scarpa as "a noble man." Several jurors later said they had been prepared to award Scarpa millions of dollars, but by August 28th he was too exhausted to continue with the trial, and agreed to a settlement of three hundred thousand dollars. He wanted the money in twenty-four hours, however, and in cash. The next morning, he sent a bodyguard, in a nylon jogging suit and heavy jewelry, to a Manhattan Citibank branch to collect it. Pillersdorf says that bank employees were nonplussed when the man tossed the cash into a duffelbag without counting it, and were "wide-eyed" when he told them, "I know who you guys are, if there's a problem."

While Scarpa was recuperating at home after his surgery, the family consigliere, Carmine Sessa, dropped in on him several times. Once or twice, Sessa handed Scarpa the phone and told him the caller was somebody named Mr. Dello, and he remembered hearing Scarpa once tell Dello, "But I already brought you up to date on that." Sessa, who later turned cooperator, said he had always figured that Scarpa had a friend in law enforcement—someone who protected him. Sessa also believed that Scarpa had an information source in the government. During the Colombo war, some of Scarpa's crewmen heard him refer to a source he called The Girlfriend, who was understood to be a man—not a lover, certainly, but someone Scarpa trusted deeply. Whenever The Girlfriend paged Scarpa, even if Scarpa was in a car on the highway, he got to a phone as quickly as possible. Scarpa seemed to have inside information about the enemy faction during the war, including rebels' addresses, and he told his crewmen that The Girlfriend was a mole in the enemy camp. At least one of those crewmen, Joey Ambrosino, didn't believe it; he later told the authorities that there was no way any rebel would trust someone as "vicious" as Greg Scarpa.

A number of Scarpa's associates had concluded that he had a law-enforcement source as early as 1987, because that year he had inside information about a drug case. Around that time, he had joined his son Greg, Jr., and nine of Greg, Jr.'s crewmen in a violent narcotics-and-extortion enterprise. Dealers who sold marijuana and other drugs in areas that Scarpa, Sr., considered to be his turf, which included, for example, the campus of the College of Staten Island, were required to make payoffs of as much as a thousand dollars a day or have their bones broken. With the help of a dealer who had been beaten with baseball bats, the Drug Enforcement Administration soon began to build a case against Greg, Jr., and his crew. The D.E.A. was unaware that Scarpa, Sr., was involved in the enterprise, but he knew all about the D.E.A. investigation. One day that summer, Greg, Jr., showed some of his crewmen a piece of paper that he had got from his father, which listed ten people, including Greg, Jr., who had been targeted for arrest. He said the list had been supplied by "a friend" of his father's, whom he also described as "an agent."

Scarpa, Sr., ordered that no one but Greg, Jr., attempt to flee—it is believed that he wanted to learn how strong a case the government had against his son—and the nine crewmen were arrested on November 12, 1987. Greg, Jr., could not be found. Valerie Caproni, the Brooklyn federal prosecutor handling the case, was angry. "This was going to be a big, expensive case to try, and our top defendant was in the wind," she recalls. He was not caught until August, 1988, after being featured on the television program "America's Most Wanted," by which time Caproni had convicted the nine crewmen. Though she subsequently convicted Greg, Jr., and he got twenty years, she complains that it was "not a lot of fun" to have to mount a second trial.

Caproni, a Southerner with a reputation for toughness, has since risen to chief of the criminal division of the Brooklyn United States Attorney's Office. In early 1994, she learned from two of the convicted crewmen, who had become cooperating witnesses, that in 1987 Greg, Jr., had obtained a list of all her defendants. She plainly suspects Lindley DeVecchio; in a court document she states that there is "some reason to believe" he leaked the list. DeVecchio vehemently denies doing so, but Caproni recalls that in the summer of 1987, while the D.E.A. case was being developed, she invited an F.B.I. agent named Michael Tabman to a planning meeting, and that Tabman took notes. Tabman later recalled, in a sworn statement, that sometime after the meeting he'd told DeVecchio about the D.E.A. case, and found him "very interested in this matter."

Caproni also finds some reason to believe that DeVecchio leaked another piece of confidential information to Scarpa in 1987— information that nearly got a man killed. She recalls saying at the summer meeting in Tabman's presence that one of the crewmen she planned to indict, Cosmo Catanzano, was "a weak link," who might cooperate if he was arrested. Tabman says he doesn't remember this. That same summer, Greg, Jr., informed one of his crewmen (who later cooperated with federal authorities) that his father's "agent source" had warned that Catanzano was "going to rat." Sometime after that, Scarpa, Sr., ordered that Catanzano be murdered and buried—and quickly, because the D.E.A. arrests were imminent. Two crewmen dug a grave for Catanzano in a secluded spot off the Arthur Kill Road, in Staten

Island, but Catanzano's execution was foiled by his arrest. He never did cooperate. DeVecchio denies ever mentioning Catanzano to Scarpa.

Caproni would not say anything about DeVecchio in an interview, but she lavishly praised an agent named Christopher Favo, who had worked under him, and who became DeVecchio's most vocal accuser. Favo, an attorney and a graduate of Notre Dame, joined the Bureau in 1983. "I think Chris Favo is an excellent agent," Caproni said. "He's an extremely hard worker. He's very bright. I have used him as a witness in a couple of cases, and find him to be easy to prepare. He has a good memory." During the Colombo war, Favo was, among other things, an information liaison between the F.B.I. and New York City police officers, who found him rather straitlaced—"like a young seminarian," one recalls. But that was all right: the cops had been given the job of trying to suppress the war by arresting people for carrying guns, and they believed that Favo could be trusted. The standard criticism of Favo was that he worked too hard—he seemed never to go home—and that he wanted to do everything himself and would not delegate responsibility.

DeVecchio doesn't share Caproni's high opinion of Favo. "Suffice it to say, he's not a favorite of mine," he says. "Everything's black-and-white for Chris Favo. If you were crossing the street and missed the crosswalk by a foot, he'd give you a ticket for jaywalking. And he's an egomaniac of the worst kind."

It was Favo who eventually reported DeVecchio to the Bureau. Though Favo was joined by three other agents when he voiced his suspicions, DeVecchio says those agents were "duped" by Favo. They all misinterpreted his actions, he says, because they all lacked street experience, and had "no clue" to what it took to operate a top-echelon source. "Favo used to say, 'I've got a lot of experience with cooperating witnesses.'" DeVecchio says. "So what? Anybody can make a deal with some guy who doesn't want to go to jail for the rest of his life. He never worked in the street covertly and developed an informant."

Favo's thoughts and actions during the Colombo war have been preserved in testimony, affidavits, memorandums, and a daily diary. He was the senior field agent investigating the war, and was one of the first agents on the scene on November 18, 1991, when its opening shots were fired—at Greg Scarpa.

Scarpa had been predicting a shooting war for some time—ever since it became apparent that the family's acting boss, Victor Orena, Sr., was trying to depose the jailed Carmine Persico and take over the family. From Scarpa, and from Scarpa's girlfriend's daughter, who was also named Linda, Favo learned what had happened. Scarpa was pulling out of his driveway in his car, and Linda, with her infant son, was pulling out in another car, when a van and a panel truck blocked their way. A group of men in ski masks jumped out of the van and opened fire with automatic weapons, leaving a row of bullet holes in the fender of Linda's car. Scarpa escaped by driving up onto the sidewalk, past the panel truck. (He later groused that for the gunmen to have even risked hitting Linda and her son showed that discipline was falling apart in the Mafia.) Favo took down the plate number of the truck, which had been left behind, and traced it to a rental office in Queens. He says he provided that information to DeVecchio, whom he had not yet begun to suspect of leaking information to Scarpa. He says he didn't learn until after the war, from a cooperator, that someone had told Scarpa where the truck had been rented.

Scarpa believed that the gunmen had been sent by William (Wild Bill) Cutolo, then reputedly the acting underboss. Scarpa made plans to disguise himself as a Hasidic Jew and mow down Wild Bill as he left his girlfriend's house on Thanksgiving Day, 1991, but that morning an article in the *Post* mentioned the snitch rumor about Scarpa, and he was forced to call off the hit so that he could assuage his confederates. Between December 3rd and January 7th, Scarpa did kill two other rebels, wounded a third, and accidentally shot and killed a Genovese family associate, who was blamed for his own death, because he was at a Colombo hangout at the time. There was no more talk of Scarpa being a snitch.

In a 1995 sworn statement DeVecchio denied ever deliberately leaking intelligence to Scarpa, but he said it was possible that Scarpa had inferred information from his questions, adding, "You cannot debrief a top-echelon source in a vacuum." Though the entire record is not available, it appears that much of the information that Scarpa was giving back during the war was worse than useless. F.B.I. documents show that he repeatedly pinned his wartime violence on other people; they also show that DeVecchio conferred with Scarpa on the very day Scarpa committed one of his murders.

As the war escalated, DeVecchio found it difficult to reach Scarpa by phone, and one time he dropped by Scarpa's house. Whenever DeVecchio met with an informant at home, he brought along one or two other agents, to make the visit look like an intrusion. He did not let his subordinates participate in the debriefing with Scarpa, however; he sat them down in Scarpa's living room, with the television turned on, while he spoke privately with his informant in the kitchen for about an hour.

Some of Scarpa's men later told federal authorities that during the war Scarpa was paged frequently by The Girlfriend. He was warned to be careful, and to watch out in particular for a rebel nicknamed Joe Waverly. In January, 1992, Scarpa and Waverly had a gunfight from adjacent cars, two feet apart, near Avenue U. Waverly shot out Scarpa's window, and Scarpa, whose Tec-9 had misfired, sped off with glass fragments in his hair. On February 26th, out on Avenue U, Scarpa shot Waverly in the stomach.

The following day, Favo appears to have formed his first suspicions about DeVecchio. That morning, a loan shark named Carmine Imbriale was arrested by the Brooklyn District Attorney's Office, and he told the authorities that he'd been at a dinner the evening before at which Scarpa had proposed a toast and bragged about shooting Waverly. The D.A.'s office alerted Favo, and he conveyed the news to DeVecchio. Favo says that DeVecchio then got a phone call from Scarpa, and told Scarpa that the Brooklyn D.A.'s office had Imbriale in temporary custody, adding, "I don't know what he's saying about you." Favo was concerned that DeVecchio had just endangered Imbriale's life.

And, in fact, that evening, according to a cooperator, Scarpa said, "It would be a good idea to kill Imbriale." Favo claims that he persuaded DeVecchio to call Scarpa the next day and warn him that if any harm came to Imbriale he would be held suspect. DeVecchio says that neither phone conversation with Scarpa about Imbriale took place, and that he has "no idea" why Favo would invent such a story.

A report that Scarpa had boasted about shooting someone was not sufficient evidence to arrest him, but it should have been cause, according to the Department of Justice guidelines on F.B.I. informants, to consider closing him. DeVecchio did not seem inclined to do so. Around the same time, however, DeVecchio's immediate supervisor, Donald North, to whom all the Mafia squads reported, became uneasy about Scarpa. North had been told by an agent not on DeVecchio's squad that Scarpa was conspiring to murder someone. (The intended victim's identity has not been revealed.) North has testified that he asked DeVecchio if he had reason to believe that Scarpa was committing crimes of violence. "He was adamant," North recalled. "He was convinced that Mr. Scarpa was not engaged in any violent activity." Nevertheless, North checked on the information about the murder conspiracy and found it credible, so, as of March 3, 1992, Scarpa was ordered closed, and DeVecchio was told to have no further contact with him. A month later, F.B.I. headquarters permitted DeVecchio to reopen Scarpa, after he attributed the murder-conspiracy charge against Scarpa to the "paranoia" among Colombo-family members which had been engendered by the war.

On May 22nd, Scarpa killed again. At about three-thirty in the morning, as the rebel soldier Larry Lampesi was locking the gate of his apartment building, Scarpa shot him with a rifle extended from his car window, then got out of the car with two of his crewmen and pumped some extra rounds into his body. The same morning, another Colombo rebel was wounded in a second incident.

A few hours later, Favo says he stopped by DeVecchio's office to report the two shootings. Twice in court, in the past two years, Favo has given a dramatic account of how he says DeVecchio reacted to the news. Favo said he and his fellow-agents believed that "every time there was a shooting or a murder it was a defeat for us"; but DeVecchio "laughed" and "got excited" at the report, and, with his open palm, slapped his desk and said, "We're going to win this thing!" Favo said DeVecchio "seemed to be a cheerleader for the Persico faction," and also testified, "A line had been blurred. . . . He was compromised. He had lost track of who he was." DeVecchio has acknowledged making "some statement to that effect," but thinks it was in front of "probably half a dozen agents," and that he obviously meant the F.B.I. was going to win in its efforts to fight organized crime. He adds, "If I'm siding with an organized-crime family, why would I tell that to my agents? What person in their right mind would do that?"

By late spring, the war was winding down. A number of the rebels had been arrested, including the faction leader, Victor Orena. In June, agents on DeVecchio's squad placed a microphone in a car belonging to Scarpa's crewman Joey Ambrosino, a Persico faction member. DeVecchio says he approved of the electronic surveillance—bolstering his contention that he was not playing sides in the war—though there is an odd passage in his sworn statement concerning its use. He wrote that "Scarpa, Sr., was astounded to learn that Ambrosino's car had been 'bugged' and that I had not told him of this situation." One is left to wonder why Scarpa would ever have expected to be told.

The bug was a productive one, and DeVecchio's agents began making arrests, starting with Ambrosino, who immediately elected to cooperate, and who connected Scarpa to at least one killing. Still, DeVecchio made no move to close Scarpa. "I saw this to be a dilemma," one of DeVecchio's agents later said, in a sworn statement. "I know if this was my source, I would have gone to the U.S. Attorney's to obtain a warrant for his arrest." Chris Favo had a plan to do exactly that: he asked a Brooklyn prosecutor if he could write up a murder-conspiracy complaint against Scarpa as soon as Favo gave the signal. He kept his plan a secret from DeVecchio. He has testified that by then "I believed that he was liable to say anything to Gregory Scarpa."

Meanwhile, the squad continued to make other arrests—so rapidly, in some cases, that DeVecchio was not notified in advance. In late June, agents arrested four Colombo suspects at an apartment in Point Pleasant, New Jersey. When the agents next saw DeVecchio, he was visibly agitated. One of them, Howard Leadbetter, a former Army officer who had worked in Special Operations, said in a sworn statement that he heard DeVecchio, "in a very forceful tone of voice," tell Favo, "'I've had it! You will not arrest another single individual without my specific approval!'" Leadbetter testified in court that he could not understand DeVecchio's agitation until sometime later, when he learned that Scarpa had been at the New Jersey apartment earlier that day and had narrowly avoided being arrested himself.

On the morning of August 31st, Favo dropped by DeVecchio's office, and told him that Scarpa was about to turn himself in to New York City police detectives on a gun charge. During the month that Scarpa had been closed by the F.B.I., he'd been seen tossing a loaded automatic from the window of his car. DeVecchio knew all about the gun arrest and, according to Favo, seemed unconcerned: it had been agreed beforehand that Scarpa would be arraigned and released. Only three days earlier, Scarpa had settled his medical-malpractice case, and had told a *Newsday* reporter that he was planning to celebrate with a vacation in Florida. Favo then sprang his surprise: he informed DeVecchio that immediately after the gun arraignment Scarpa was going to be arrested by two of DeVecchio's own agents and booked on federal murder-conspiracy charges. "DeVecchio was visibly upset" by that news, Favo says, and tried to alert Scarpa via the confidential hello line, but it was too late.

Even then, DeVecchio did not abandon his top-echelon source. He got in touch with prosecutors at the Brooklyn United States Attorney's Office to ask them to request bail for Scarpa. One prosecutor, Andrew Weissmann, later said he was "incredulous" that any agent would want Scarpa on the street, and, at a September bail hearing, before the federal magistrate John L. Caden, Weissmann argued vigorously for detention. Caden was not aware that Scarpa was an informant, and the attorney representing Scarpa at the hearing, Joseph Benfante, says he wasn't aware of it, either. "That would be tantamount to me thinking that Mother Teresa is assisting Saddam Hussein, because no F.B.I. informant goes out and engages in a Colombo war—it's insanity," Benfante says.

Benfante's motion for bail was made strictly on the ground of Scarpa's medical condition. By now, Scarpa had full-blown AIDS, with a T-cell count of zero (two thousand is normal), and at his malpractice trial in August his doctor had testified that he had between two and six months to live. Benfante says that Scarpa had also begun to show signs of AIDS dementia. During visits he paid to Scarpa in prison, he recalls, "He told me to make a list—he wants to give all the guards attaché cases, special cases of wine, and filet-mignon steaks. I told him, 'Greg, you can't have a steak in prison.' 'What do you mean!' He'd throw the chair. The next day, he'd be fine."

Judge Caden agreed to house arrest, with the stipulation that Scarpa wear an electronic anklet that would alert police if he left the house. All went well until December 29, 1992, when Scarpa's son by Linda Schiro, Joseph, got into a dispute over a drug transaction, and was said to have told his father that he had been spoken to disrespectfully. Scarpa rushed out of the house armed, went around the block, and got into a gun battle with two Bay Ridge drug dealers, one of whom he is believed to have killed. In the altercation, Scarpa's left eye was shot out. He is said to have walked back home, pressed a towel to his bleeding eye socket, drunk a glass of Scotch, and—because Schiro was hysterical—driven himself to Mt. Sinai Hospital. Joseph has since been killed in what was apparently a drug-related shooting.

Scarpa's house arrest was revoked. It was agreed that he would be sent to Rikers Island, a prison known for its superior AIDS facility, to serve a year on his gun charge. It seemed inconceivable that a man with a zero-T-cell count and no stomach, who had just had an eye shot out, would live anywhere near that long. The following spring, however, Scarpa was still alive, and on May 6, 1993, he appeared before federal Judge Jack B. Weinstein to plead guilty to three murders and conspiracy to murder several others.

Then, in October, at a meeting with prosecutors at the Brooklyn United States Attorney's Office, Scarpa offered, unsuccessfully, to become a cooperating witness for the government. He had asked his new attorney, a former prosecutor named Steven Kartagener, to make sure that DeVecchio attended. Kartagener recalls that at one point "Greg says, 'I've always been helpful to the government in the past—isn't that right, Mr. DeVecchio?'" and goes on to recount, "I assumed DeVecchio would say, 'What are you talking about? Stop being an asshole.' Instead, he says, 'Yes, that's true.' My jaw did a bounce off the tabletop." Two prosecutors recall hearing DeVecchio tell Favo at an earlier meeting that if there were "an O.P.R."—an Office of Professional Responsibility inquiry—into DeVecchio's handling of Scarpa "I'll have your ass."

Scarpa's sentencing for murder and murder conspiracy took place on December 15, 1993. Judge Weinstein asked Scarpa if he had anything to say, and was told no, "other than I expect to go home."

"You're not going to go home," Weinstein said. "You're going to go to prison."

"I tried to help, Your Honor," Scarpa said. "But it just didn't work out."

During Scarpa's final days in prison, his AIDS dementia took hold, and he was given to rambling. Occasionally, he spoke of the dirty work he claimed to have done for the government. He told one visitor how, after kidnapping a Mississippi man for the F.B.I., "he placed a gun in the guy's mouth, and started cutting his dick off with a razor" and demanded that the man tell him the location of "three kids that were missing"—lending credence to a report, first published in the *Daily News,* that Scarpa had led the F.B.I. to the buried bodies of the civil-rights workers Michael Schwerner, Andrew Goodman, and James Chaney, slain in Philadelphia, Mississippi, in 1964. He also spoke about a secret assignment in Costa Rica for the United States government in the sixties that involved murder. On June 8, 1994, Scarpa died, of complications from AIDS, at the Federal Medical Center in Rochester, Minnesota.

• • •

For a year and half after the Colombo war ended, Chris Favo kept quiet about DeVecchio. He says he was worried that if he accused a well-respected veteran like DeVecchio of leaking confidential information the F.B.I. brass "would take it about as well as I would take it if somebody came up to me and said my wife was unfaithful." By January, 1994, however, Favo and three agents on his squad felt compelled to come forward. Several of Scarpa's crewmen had begun to cooperate, and their accounts of Scarpa and his alleged law-enforcement source were disturbing. Most disturbing, Favo says, was that during the Colombo war he had given DeVecchio a partial address for the hideout of the rebel leader, Victor Orena, and a physical description—a white, two-family house, with aluminum siding—and an incorrect address for one of Orena's men. Now it appeared from statements made by a cooperator that Scarpa's crew had tried unsuccessfully to locate and kill those two rebels after Scarpa supplied them with the identical information.

Favo's diary records what happened when he and the three other agents—Raymond Andjich, Howard Leadbetter, and Jeffrey Tomlinson—came forward that month to voice their concerns to officials at the New York office. At first they were commended for taking action, and assured of confidentiality, but only two weeks later, Favo wrote in his diary, an F.B.I. official carelessly exposed him and Leadbetter as whistle-blowers; when he complained, he says, the official told him that he personally believed in DeVecchio's innocence, and that "we will have to live with the problems." A few days after that, Favo wrote, DeVecchio called a squad meeting, at which he angrily denied the charges and added that "anyone that did not believe him could go f— themselves." Before long, Favo had concluded that blowing the whistle on DeVecchio "was a mistake that would follow us for our careers."

By March, 1994, an internal O.P.R. investigation of DeVecchio was under way. He was eventually moved out of organized crime and into drug enforcement, and, in the meantime, his investigation was transferred from the Bureau to the Public Integrity Section of the Department of Justice. The investigation proceeded slowly, and was kept quiet, even as alleged participants in the Colombo war continued to go to trial for murder and assault.

It was not until the summer of 1994 that, largely through the efforts of the New York attorney Alan Futerfas and his associate, Ellen Resnick, the investigation came to light. Futerfas and Resnick had been retained by a number of defendants accused of participation in the Colombo war. They immediately recognized the DeVecchio controversy as a gold mine for the defense, and they used it to formulate what might be called the "comrades in arms" theory of the war. According to this theory, the F.B.I. had deliberately fed Scarpa information, to help foment the war, and to make certain that he would emerge victorious. Futerfas argues that when DeVecchio allegedly declared, "We're going to win this thing," he was expressing the hope that Scarpa would end up as a boss when it was all over, with a seat on the Mafia's ruling commission.

The comrades-in-arms theory, whatever its merits, has been an unqualified success with juries. There have been nine trials stemming from the Colombo war, and at two of them the judges have permitted evidence of DeVecchio's relationship with Scarpa to be introduced. At both trials, every defendant—fourteen in all, including Wild Bill Cutolo—was acquitted of all charges. At the conclusion of one trial, a juror told the *Daily News*, "If the F.B.I.'s like this, society is really in trouble." Some people who were convicted before the DeVecchio controversy became known made motions for new trials. It was at a hearing on one such motion that DeVecchio took the Fifth.

Despite its interest in winning convictions, the Brooklyn United States Attorney's Office has done nothing to make DeVecchio look good; the government has even conceded that DeVecchio "may have" disclosed confidential information to Scarpa, including, as Favo had charged, the whereabouts of people Scarpa was looking for. Douglas Grover, the lawyer for DeVecchio, blames the "rape" of his client by the Brooklyn United States Attorney's Office on Valerie Caproni, the head of the criminal division. He says that she continues to bear a grudge against DeVecchio in the mistaken belief that he leaked word of her

1987 drug indictment, causing Greg Scarpa, Jr., to flee. "A government prosecutor should be defending the government's actions, but Valerie wanted to get Lin," Grover says. Caproni disputes this. "I don't know what Mr. Grover would have had us do, given that evidence," she says.

Grover nevertheless had been predicting for some time that DeVecchio would be cleared. And on September 4, 1996, after two and a half years, the O.P.R. investigation ended abruptly with a two-sentence letter stating that prosecution of DeVecchio was "not warranted."

The Bureau continues to maintain its silence, and many questions about the DeVecchio matter remain unanswered. Though the F.B.I.'s long relationship with Scarpa appears to have shocked jurors, who found it sordid, it came as less of a surprise to people in other branches of law enforcement. They have long viewed the F.B.I. as an institution with its own agenda, obsessed with making successful cases even at the expense of upholding the law. There is nothing in the record to dispute DeVecchio's claim, echoed by his attorney, that "I didn't operate in a vacuum," and that key decisions concerning Scarpa, including the decision to reopen him during the war, were made with "the full knowledge of any number of people well above me in rank."

In October, 1996, Lin DeVecchio retired from the F.B.I., after thirty-three years of service. His retirement party was held at a seafood restaurant in lower Manhattan. About fifty well-wishers turned out. It was a crowd made up largely of F.B.I. retirees—"an old-timers' night," in the words of one guest—and, when speeches were made, the crowd got boisterous. The subject of DeVecchio's O.P.R was far from taboo, and as one retirement gift was handed to him somebody yelled, "Lin—it's a subpoena!" There was never any question, however, that the crowd was in DeVecchio's corner, and near the end of the evening the last speaker, a retired agent, broke down in sobs, and declared, "Lin DeVecchio is not corrupt! Lin DeVecchio did what he believed was right!"

How the crowd felt about Christopher Favo was no secret, either. One speaker presented DeVecchio with an infectious-agent clothing kit, in case he should ever come in contact again with "the viral, infectious agent who started all this." James Kossler, a retired supervisor to whom DeVecchio had once reported, expressed his views about DeVecchio's accuser before the party: "The trouble with Chris Favo is that Chris Favo has a very high opinion of himself. He works sixteen hours a day, seven days a week, and you lose all objectivity when that happens. You see things you can't relate to or understand. This whole thing was a travesty, and Lin's reputation has been destroyed. Why wasn't Favo stopped? If I'd been there, I would have cut his nuts off."

Favo remains an F.B.I. agent, but recently he was transferred from New York to a regional office in the Midwest. The three other agents who reported DeVecchio to the Bureau continue to work in New York; one of them recently testified that Favo had "taken the brunt of a lot of this." Valerie Caproni says of Favo, "The fact that he's no longer working organized-crime cases in New York is to me just a horrible fallout of this whole thing," and adds, "It's been a very difficult situation, as it always is for a whistle-blower." Reached by phone recently, Favo said he'd be happy to comment on how he ended up in the Midwest, or answer any other question, pending permission from the F.B.I., which, as he guessed correctly, was denied.

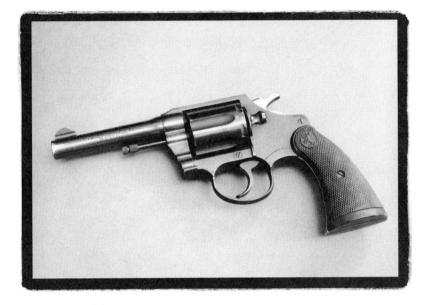

from **Killer**

by Joey with David Fisher

A mob killer known to readers as Joey wrote this 1973 autobiography with the help of David Fisher (born 1946). Like Nicholas Pileggi's Wise Guy, *which came 12 years later,* Killer *offers a convincing and instructive look at gangster methods and motives. Here's Joey's seminar on how to administer a hit.*

've dabbled in just about every area of crime, but my specialty, the thing I do best, is kill people. I am to mob rubouts what Leonard Bernstein is to music. I am one of the most feared killers in the United States today. I'm proud of that reputation; I've worked long hours and in dangerous places to earn it.

I don't make that claim braggingly, but truthfully. I have sent 38 deserving men to their early graves. I can remember each man that I hit. I can give you the order. The details. Even the weather on the day I made the hit. Number 18, for example, was a gambler who was discovered informing on the mob. He had been arrested quietly and made a deal in order to keep himself out of a jackpot. Certain things began to kick back, and some people checked and found out my man was the source, so he had to go. I caught him in a small bar and I just walked in and blasted him with a .38. It was dark, and I was wearing a dark shirt and dark pants and when I started shooting everybody scrambled for cover. I remember him. I remember them all. You never really forget.

But it doesn't bother me, not one bit. This is my job. It is my business. I shoot people and that's it. I never think in terms of morality, although that may be hard for a lot of people to believe. I know the difference between right and wrong. By most standards of morality what I do would be considered wrong. But this doesn't bother me. I also know the difference between eating and starving. Between having a new pair of shoes and stuffing newspapers in an old pair to keep my feet from freezing. Believe me, I know.

So I don't worry about it. Because I have the ability to pull the trigger I can do what I like to do, go where I want to go, live comfortably, eat well, be what I want to be. I have no second thoughts. No recriminations. I don't even think about it because, if I did, and if I was an emotional person, I could not live with it. It would destroy me. So I do my job like a guy lays brick, a guy tends bar, a guy cuts hair.

At home, I'm not really that much different from your average bricklayer, bartender or barber. I take out the garbage four nights a week, worry about my wife when she's out alone at night, clean the outside windows every few months and complain about those ridiculously high telephone bills. Believe it or not, I'm a human being. I laugh at funny jokes, I love children around the house and I can spend hours playing with my mutt. Only one thing, I never cry during sad movies. I've only cried for one person in my life, my first wife. The day I found out she had been killed, I cried. Then I changed. So my eyes weren't even damp at the end of *Love Story*.

I've had my chances to get out of the business. One night, in I think 1966, my wife and I were driving back from spending the weekend with some relatives and there was a car pulled over to the side of the road. Regardless of my profession, when I see somebody in trouble, I stop. I pulled over, took my cannon out of the glove compartment and handed it to my wife. "If there's anything wrong," I said, "just pull the trigger."

There was a woman sitting alone in the front seat, and her husband, who turned out to be a well-known, very wealthy businessman, was sitting in back with his leg in a cast. He had broken it so he was helpless, and she didn't know the first thing about cars. I couldn't get their car going, so we drove them back to town. This guy asked for my phone number and, when I told him I didn't give it out, he gave me his card and asked me to call him.

About three days later I did call, and he invited me to his club for lunch. We really got along well, and when he asked me what I did for a living I told him straight out. "You're too nice a guy to be in that business," he told me. "How would you like to work for me?" He offered me good money, and I almost said yes. But I finally turned him down because I knew I would go out of my mind. So I stayed in the old business, doing the same old thing, killing people.

There are three things you need to kill a man: the gun, the bullets and the balls. A lot of people will point a gun at you, but they haven't got the courage to pull the trigger. It's as simple as that. I would give you odds on almost anybody you name that, if I put a gun in his hand, he would not pull the trigger. I mean, some people will go ape for one minute and shoot, but there are very few people who are capable of thinking about, planning and then doing it. To carry out an execution with the cold knowledge of what you're doing, you have to believe in nothing but yourself. That I do.

I killed my first man when I was 16 years old. The hit was offered to me by a mob guy who protected the numbers organization I worked for. The thought of killing a man had never occurred to me before. I had been a violent person and I had laid guys out, but actually killing a man just hadn't entered my mind. I was sitting on a stoop one day, and he walked over and sat down next to me. Very casually, without even looking at me, he asked if I was interested in making a hit.

I stared at him and said, "You got to be kidding." He said he was serious. I said, "You must have fifty guys that can do the same job."

He nodded. "We understand that. Just let me know tonight."

At some point you become a man or you fade. For me, this was the point. I had to make the decision whether I wanted to be dirt or accomplish something. I was very young, but I decided I wasn't going to be a piece of shit. I wasn't going to let people walk all over me. I was going to be a man.

So when he came back that night I told him okay. I had no idea what the guy I was going to kill had done. I was handed a gun, and this guy was pointed out to me. He could have been anybody; once I made the decision I knew I would stick to it. I had to plan the job myself and I wasn't too damned thorough. I waited for him one night. When I saw him on the street I just walked up behind him and blew the top of his head off. He was dead before he hit the sidewalk. Then I turned and walked away. I didn't run, I walked.

I had to get rid of the gun, but I didn't know exactly how. The first thing I did was go back to my apartment and get a little saw and I sawed the gun barrel into four quarters. Then I took the gun and the shells and got on the subway. I rode it all the way down into lower Manhattan, the Wall Street area, and I started throwing the shells down the sewers. I wasn't taking any chances, one shell to one sewer. When I finished doing that I went over to the river and heaved the pieces of the gun as far as I could. Then I went home and went to bed.

I never really got to sleep. I just tossed and turned for a few hours, going over the whole thing in my mind about a hundred times, making sure I didn't make any mistakes. I held my breath for about two days until I was positive there were no witnesses. Nothing happened.

Then the realization came to me that I was a made individual. I was a force to be reckoned with. A lot of people who had looked at me as being a snot-nosed wise-ass kid would now be speaking to me in different tones. The job paid $5000. Five thousand dollars! It seemed like a billion. My older brother was working ten hours a day in a warehouse and bringing home $24 a week. Five thousand dollars, that's how it started.

Contrary to legend, there is no great celebration after you make your first hit. I mean, nobody throws a party for you or anything. But you are made. The word is out very quickly that you are a capable individual. That you are a heavyweight, a gunsel, a torpedo, a cannon, a hit man, a boy who will do the job. In *The Godfather* they said, "Make your bones." Now I never heard that before, but it has the same meaning.

After this first hit my career was interrupted by the army, which taught me the proper way to handle a gun—I beg your pardon, a weapon. They taught us this rhyme I remember. You had to hold your rifle and point one finger at your prick and repeat, "This is my weapon [the rifle], this is my gun [the prick], one is for shooting, one is for fun." My only problem was I never could figure out which was for which.

After I got separated from the service I kicked around in New York for a while and then went out to California and began working for Jack Dragna. Jack knew I was a wild man, but he didn't know how wild. He wanted to test me and offered me a hit.

"Sure," I told him, "why not?" After my experience in Korea I figured what difference would another guy or two make. I never did find out what number two had done either. Jack just showed me his picture and handed me a gun. He told me what kind of car this guy drove, gave me his license-plate number and explained that the guy always collected some payoffs in a certain shopping center on Monday afternoons.

The following Monday afternoon I drove over there in a stolen car and found his car parked towards the back of the parking lot. I found a spot almost directly across from his car and pulled in. I got out and sat on the trunk of my car for almost three hours, doing nothing but watching for him and listening to a transistor radio. Nobody paid any attention to me; for all anybody knew I was waiting for my wife. Finally I saw him walking down the aisle toward his car. I looked around and there wasn't another person within 70 yards. Lucky for me—unlucky for him. If I had seen anybody else I would have got in my car and trailed him and waited for another opportunity. I waited until he started to edge between his car and the car parked next to him, then I took a few steps across the driving lane and hit him. Nobody saw him go down. I put three bullets in him, then I got in my own car and drove away.

There are many reasons an individual is killed: He may be a stool pigeon, he may be too greedy, the man he is working for might suspect he is taking too much, the man he is working for might think he is too ambitious, he might be blown away because he has not lived up to an agreement he made, the job might be planned by an underling trying to take over from a boss, the target could be a mob member who has become a junkie and is therefore unreliable, it might be part of a gang war and it could even be payment for an attempted double cross. There is always a good reason and it always involves doing something you shouldn't be doing as a member of organized crime.

Innocent people, civilians, are very rarely hit. You recently saw the reason for that in New York City. You had half a battalion of mob guys killed after the Colombo-Gallo business and nobody did much of anything. But when two innocent meat salesmen in a restaurant were mistaken for mob men and killed accidentally, the commissioner almost declared martial law.

We leave civilians alone. We don't hurt them and we don't work for them. As a matter of fact, if a civilian wants to buy a hit he might be able to get someone who has done a few, but I doubt he could get anyone connected with the mob. Chances are, whoever he got, the civilian would just be taken for his money. The hit will never be made. What's he gonna do about it? Who's he gonna complain to?

Mob guys very rarely take outside work because they can't trust civilians. The police lean on a civilian and he is going to fold. He has never been battered by questions, he has never been mentally assaulted, so he's gonna quit on you. The police are experts, they can turn you up one side and down the other with their questions. And who needs to depend on a civilian?

Not me. And not any professional hit man that I know. I just don't want to mess with your so-called honest citizens. As a rule you just can't trust them.

I did come close once. Tony Bender asked me to see a civilian about doing a job for him. Tony had done me some favors, so I said I would. The civilian was a wealthy New York City socialite type. I figured maybe somebody was leaning on him businesswise. Generally civilians want other civilians hit to settle personal scores, and I certainly don't want to get involved in that. But this guy didn't want that, he wanted a broad hit in the head. I found it very unusual for a man to want a girl killed so I asked him about it. He said he had been shacking up with her and things were getting complicated.

Before giving him an answer I started doing a little investigating on my own. I found out the reason he wanted her hit in the head was that she had the nerve to get pregnant on him. I figured maybe she wanted a lot of money, but I was wrong. All she wanted was to make sure the kid was properly cared for. She didn't want no big amount of money, she wasn't looking to shake him down and she didn't want to get involved with the Social Register. Two hundred fifty dollars a month for the kid was what she wanted. My blueblooded friend was terrified someone would find out about the baby and it would embarrass his family. After considering the facts I decided I did not like this socialite's idea of the proper way to treat children.

I went back and I told the guy, "I am going to give you some very bad news. For one, you're gonna give this girl friend of yours one hundred thousand dollars. And then you're gonna give her two hundred fifty a month until that kid is old enough to take care of itself. And if you don't, motherfucker, I'm gonna put a bullet in your head and I'm gonna let the whole world know why you got killed." He went running to see Tony Bender. Tony told him he couldn't interfere. Actually he could've, but he didn't want to. This guy finally gave her the money. She eventually found out the story and what I did for her. After that she left town and had the kid. Today she is married and lives out in the Midwest. I heard from her a couple of times, but I'm a part of her life she would rather forget.

But you see the problem you get into when you deal with civilians. I like to stick to my own. It's easier.

Every hit begins with a contract. If you're working independently, as I usually do, the people who need your services get in touch with you. A meeting is set up, and details are discussed. I'm told what the job entails and how much it pays and occasionally what the beef is. I'm not told who the party is, but that's not important. The details will probably give me a good idea who he might be, but I will very rarely ask for a name until I decide to take the job. If I figure I might know the man, or the people he hangs with, I'll probably say "pass." If I figure it's okay I'll do business. On certain jobs I'm told who it is right away, like with Joey Gallo, for instance, because the word was out all over anyway.

There is no set price for a hit. It depends on who the man is, how difficult the job and what the results (who will gain what) will be. It usually averages anywhere between $10,000 and $25,000 and could go higher. The largest contract I've ever heard of was an open offer of $250,000 payable to anyone who could get to Joe Valachi. But nobody would take the job. If the mob could have gotten to Valachi nobody would ever talk to the police again because it would have completely destroyed the confidence of anybody who thought about becoming an informer. (There's a story that Valachi was causing problems in prison and word was sent to Attorney General Bobby Kennedy. "Tell him to stop it," Kennedy supposedly said, "or we'll let him go.") The most I've ever been offered was $50,000 and I've been offered that a few times. That was the price I was quoted on Joey Gallo.

A contract is always a verbal agreement, but these contracts are as strong as any written agreement in the world. You don't have to sign a paper, you're guaranteeing it with your own life.

The money is paid in advance. The full amount. After the contract is out, the man who put it out can rescind it, but none of his money will be returned. Once I take your money I'm going to make the hit—unless you tell me you've changed your mind. That's fine, but you pay the full amount for that privilege.

There is a guarantee in the contract covering the unlikely situation that I'm caught. I will not talk. Not a word. Not a sound. Not a peep. In order to ensure that, the party with whom I've made my deal must pay all legal fees, support my family the entire time I'm in jail, and have something waiting for me the day I get out. When I came out of the Tombs (that's the Manhattan House of Detention) after sitting there for almost a full year, I was handed $50,000 for keeping my mouth shut.

That may sound like a lot of money, but it's worth it to the mob. Knowing my family is being supported and I'm earning while I'm sitting, there's no reason for me to talk. The only alternative the mob has is to try to kill me and that's stupid because, if they did, no professional would ever work for them again. Amateurs, like Jerome Johnson who shot Joe Colombo, don't get this sort of deal because no one has any doubts that, when caught, they would reveal everything. Their payment is inevitably a bullet in the head. But amateurs are very rarely used.

If you happen to be a full-time employee of a particular organization, rather than a free-lancer, the contract procedure is a little different. If you're on salary and they tell you somebody has got to go, he goes. Makes no difference who he is and how close the two of you might be. He's gone. A new soldier for that big organization in the sky.

Under any circumstances, if I take your money the job is going to be done unless you decide differently. Once I take a penny, I've guaranteed that contract will be fulfilled. And so I want to make sure it gets done quickly and correctly. That's where experience comes in.

Planning a hit is not difficult. There are only a few simple rules you have to be aware of: You do not kill a man in his own home; you do not kill a man in front of his own family; you do not harm his family; you do not hit him in a church or near a church or any other place of worship; you do not torture a man (we're not his judges, just his executioners); and you do not rob him. Other than that, he's all yours.

There are three basic ways to plan a hit. The hit man will be given his intended's routine, or he'll study the man and pick up his routine himself, or the party will be brought to him at a preselected spot. I like to do as much as possible myself. I like being in total control and I'll spend as much time as necessary making sure everything is exactly the way I want it. I once clocked a man for ten days before I hit him. This guy was a numbers controller who was fingering other controllers to be robbed. He used to park his car in a gas station overnight, and I decided that the gas station would be the place. I waited in my car, which I parked in a shadow, until he showed up. When he did I walked up to his car. He didn't realize what was about to happen until I pulled the cannon. Then he realized—I'm gonna die. He started to beg, but I didn't give him a chance to get five words out of his mouth. He knew why, and it wasn't my job to sit there and give him a lecture. That gas station was the perfect spot: closed, quiet and dark.

The safest way is to have the party brought to you. If I'm told the hit is being set up this way, I get to the location early and check it out carefully. If I'm not completely satisfied with it I may not do the job. After all, it's my head in the noose. I got sent to St. Louis once on a loan. They had the thing all lined up and needed an outside gun. When I got there, I said, "You guys don't mind if I take a couple of days and see if I go along with the plan, do you?" I wouldn't care if the FBI had checked it out in advance, I wanted to check it myself. They agreed, and I found their schedule was perfect and the spot they picked likewise. Only then did I agree to pull the trigger.

After you're satisfied that the proper plans have been made you can begin the execution. There are actually very few preparations that have to be made. I normally get the gun I'm going to use as soon as I agree to take the job. The gun can come from anywhere. It might be stolen off the docks or I might get a hot gun from a friend. There is a tremendous market in hot guns. Wherever I get it, the first thing I'll do is file the serial number off to make it as untraceable as possible.

If there is any chance people will see me leaving after I've done the job, I'll use a stolen car. I'll steal the car myself two or three days before the day I'm going to make the hit and just stash it away. I'll check it over carefully to make sure it's going to start when I need it to start, and if the battery looks the slightest bit worn I'll put a new one in.

Up until the time I intend to make the actual hit, my day will be very normal. I'll give you an example.

A mob guy dealing narcotics had started using them himself. He had turned himself into an addict, and the man he worked for wanted him eliminated. I agreed to do the job.

His boss gave me a pretty good idea of what his schedule was like, and I followed him for a few days just to verify my information and pick the spot. He did different things each night but always ended up at this girl's apartment. She lived in a brownstone way over in the West Forties, which is a good area to make a hit because it's dark and, in the winter, when this all took place, there are few people on the street late at night. He also parked his car in front of the same fire hydrant every night.

I got up about 11:30 the morning the job was going to be done. I made myself some coffee, and my wife and I sat down to watch the television program "Jeopardy," which is one of my favorite shows. If they would let me go on as a contestant I could win a lot of money. The only categories my wife can beat me in are "show business" and "literature."

After "Jeopardy" ended I went to a pool hall and spent most of the afternoon shooting with a buddy of mine. My days aren't what you call structured. I really never know what I'm going to be doing; it depends on what I feel like. I might go to the track, go bowling, play cards, visit some friends, see a broad. I might even stay home. But it was cold outside, so I stayed in and shot pool.

From there I went to a small Italian restaurant in the East Village named Sonny's and had dinner with some friends. I left there about 9:30 and just drove around the city till about midnight. I went over the plan in my mind a few times, but I didn't really concentrate on it. Sometimes when I've got a job to do I'll spend the night at home watching television or even go to a movie, but this night I just felt like driving. I did stop in a few different places to say hello to some friends, but I didn't stay anywhere very long.

Finally I drove up to this block and parked about three car lengths behind the fire hydrant. I looked for his car and it wasn't there, so I knew he hadn't shown up early. I have had people do that on me, which earns them an extra night of living. The only things I brought with me were a transistor radio, a thermos of coffee and a blanket. I use the transistor because I don't want to run down the battery of the car. I rarely mind the cold because it keeps you awake and alert, but the blanket is there in case it really freezes up.

This guy showed up right on time. I saw him coming in my rear-view mirror and I kind of laid down across the front seat so he wouldn't see me. While he was parking I slid out of my car and hid so he didn't see me and take off. When he turned his engine off I began the casual walk toward his car. I hit him in the head as he started to get out. Two bullets. I knew he was dead.

I walked back to my car and drove home. I was asleep within a half hour.

I usually work alone, but when you're just starting out in this line of work a backup man is normally sent along to make sure everything goes correctly. Once you're established you go out by yourself or, at worst, with a single driver. The only exception is when you're hitting someone in a crowded area and you think there is a chance you might be chased. Then you use a getaway car and a crash car. The crash car is set up to block traffic after the job is done and, if somebody tries to follow you, to "accidentally" crash into them. Under any circumstances you're only going to use the getaway car to go a few blocks. Then, depending on where you are, you're going to get out of your vehicle and lose yourself as quickly as you can in a crowd, or take some public transportation, or ride a cab, or even take another car that you have waiting.

The most important thing is to try to isolate your victim. I may be sitting in his car waiting for him and as soon as he gets in I'll blast him, or I may have made arrangements for him to be picked up by someone he trusts and brought to a destination where I'll be waiting. If possible, it's best to catch him late at night. But catching him alone is really the important thing because, if you don't, innocent people might get hurt and you don't want that, no way.

I've never had a problem with innocent people because I've always been very careful about picking my spots. But if I was on a job and an innocent person got in the way, he would have to go. I know I wouldn't feel too good about doing it, but I know I'd kill him anyway. It's part of being a professional. Other people don't take as much care as I do. Little Augie Pisano, for example, was with a girl when he received a phone call and was told to come to a meeting. The jerk brought the girl with him. Now it is a clear violation of the rules to bring a civilian with you to any business meeting. So, when he showed up, his killers were waiting for him. They had no choice—the girl had to go too. And she did.

Sometimes, though, it's almost impossible to get a guy alone. Maybe he has too many bodyguards, or maybe he's very careful. Then you have to hit him in public. On a job like this the important thing is to be cool. If you're careful there is actually very little to worry about. I've walked into restaurants in which my man was sitting and I've calmly walked over and calmly pulled the trigger and then I turned around and calmly walked out. I didn't run. I just make sure, in a situation like this, that I use a gun that's going to make a lot of noise because I want everybody in that place diving under tables. I was fortunate enough to see the police report on number 14, which I did in a restaurant. I was described by 11 different people in 11 different ways . . . and not one of them was totally accurate.

Like every professional hit man I've ever known, I've always used a gun. Always. All 38 times. I am a good shot and I know where I'm going to hit you and you are going to die. No one has lived yet. I have steady hands, a sharp eye—I don't wear glasses—and a great amount of confidence.

I prefer to use a .38 revolver whenever possible because it's not too big and I know it's not going to jam unless I have a bad cartridge in there or the hammer's busted, and I always check to make sure this is not the case. If I catch the guy by himself I use a silencer. That way the gun doesn't make any loud noises, just a small pfffttt. You always try to catch a guy in the head with your first shot because that ends the argument quickly.

A magnum, which is a very big gun, is nice to have around if you're putting down a revolution, but you're not going to use it in my work because it's too heavy and you need fluidity when you're doing a job. It's also not that accurate a weapon because, when you pull the trigger, you get a severe kickback. If you hold it at hip level when you fire, by the time you get through you'll be pointing at the sky.

At one point drowning was a popular way of killing people, but no more. Why go through all the trouble of taking somebody and dragging them to a spot where there is water and then drowning them when you can shoot them much more easily? Because you want it to look like an accident? Bullshit! You *don't* want it to look like an accident! You want people to know why a guy was hit. It serves as a warning to others.

The weapon I carry every day was especially made for me by a friend who is an excellent mechanic. (A mechanic is our term used to describe anybody who is great at anything.) It's a "gun" about two and one-half inches in length and about an inch wide. It's about half an inch thick and, in general, looks just like a cigarette lighter. It is actually a trigger mechanism. I have buckshot cartridges that have been designed for this weapon. I simply screw the cartridges in and pull the trigger and, at 30 feet or less, I can make a long-division problem out of you. I can have cartridges made up for any bullet I want. As far as I know there are only about five weapons like this in existence, all made by my friend. They're great guns because there is absolutely no recoil and no markings are left on the slug or shot.

I've heard of people who have used knives, hatchets and icepicks, who'll strangle you and garrotte you, and every once in a while someone'll use something exotic like a blowtorch. I've also heard of one guy who uses garlic. He rubs the bullets he's going to use with it. This guarantees that his target is going to die—if the bullets don't get him, the garlic will cause a slow, agonizing death by blood poisoning. I've also been told of one guy left hanging on a meat hook for three days until he died, and another guy who was heated slowly with an iron, but I don't go in for anything like that. I don't want to spend that much time with my targets, I don't want to watch them suffer. That's not my job. Of course, some people have different tastes. A midwestern hit man used alcohol and a truck. His target was a stool pigeon, and the organization did not want the police to know they were on to this guy. The guy was a heavy drinker to begin with, so the hit man and his driver kidnapped him and brought him to a small apartment. They put a gun at his head and a glass of whiskey in his hand. "Drink," the hit man said, and the target did. He kept drinking until he was completely drunk. Then they brought him down to the highway, parked his car nearby and pushed him in front of a truck. Even if the police suspected anything there was nothing they could prove.

Lately I've been hearing about a new weapon. It's a certain type of gas that you spray in someone's face. Not only does it kill him immediately, it leaves the same aftereffects as a heart attack. I got a hunch the two men who were involved in the trial of Newark Mayor Hugh Addonizio were killed this way. It's very strange that two important witnesses should die of heart attacks behind the wheel of their cars within a short time of each other.

I'm a traditionalist. I like using a gun. I feel comfortable with it. I doubt I would ever use anything else because I don't like to get too close to my man. I'm not looking to be sophisticated, I'm looking to do a job and not get caught, and so I never get closer than two or three feet.

Hell, if I'm within two or three feet of him, he's dead. It's important to set it up so the guy never really has a chance to move or try to protect himself or run away. The furthest I've ever had to chase a guy was about 30 yards and that was someone else's fault. This guy was brought out to a field in the middle of nowhere. He thought he was going to a business meeting. The idiot driver let him get out of the car before I was ready; he saw me and took off. I chased him on foot and, when I got close enough, I pumped four bullets into him. End of story.

He was one of the few who had that much time. Very few of the 38 ever knew what was about to hit them. I was the last thing they ever saw. I never said a word to any of them. What am I going to say? A lot of times you'll get ready to hit a man and he'll realize briefly what's happening and make the sign of the cross, or he'll start screaming, "No!" But before he can get too much of anything out it's usually all over.

Let me give you an example of a perfect hit. Number 27. At the time I was working for a particular organization, and it was decided that a man was going to die because he had become too ambitious. He was trying to move up too quickly. I was contacted and told there was a contract I was to fulfill. I had no choice in the matter. The price, I was told over pizza, was $20,000.

"Do I set up my own deal or do you set it up for me?" I asked. My employer told me I was on my own, and I began studying my man. I took about a week and by the end of it I knew what time he left his house, where he went, who he saw, what business he conducted on what days and, finally, who he was sleeping with. I noticed that this man continually drove through an isolated area and I studied this area carefully, trying to find a good quiet spot where I could pick him off. I couldn't find exactly what I wanted so I looked for another place.

I discovered he had a girl friend who he visited on the nights he made his gambling collections, and I picked one of these nights. I used a driver but I made sure he parked about a block away so he couldn't actually see what I was doing. That way he couldn't testify to a single thing. He wasn't about to hear the shots because I was working with a silencer.

When my target came out of his girl friend's house about six in the morning, I was standing there leaning against a lamppost. I hit him as he walked to his car. Three shots and he went down. I walked over and put another one in the back of his head. My driver dropped me off at my own car and I got in and drove home. The first thing I did that morning was get rid of the gun.

Most professional hits are similar to that one. The only time it's really different, as I said, is when a boss is involved. There are two ways to kill a boss. The easy way is to get to his bodyguard or the top man in his organization and make a deal with him.

Now the tougher way. If the bodyguard does not agree to the hit he has to go too. I was working for Meyer Lansky at one point, and some representatives of Vito Genovese invited me to a meeting. They had decided that Meyer was to be hit. An offer was made and I said no thank you. Maybe some people don't, but I believe in being loyal to an individual who helps you earn. But by saying no I made myself a target.

The only reason I wasn't killed right on the spot, after I turned them down, was because I had a gun in my hand. Whenever I go to meet somebody on business I always wear a pair of pants in which the pocket has been cut out and I can reach through to a gun I have strapped to the inside of my leg. In this particular instance we were sitting in a restaurant, me with my back to the wall. After I said no the guy said, "I'm sorry to hear that."

I pulled my cannon out and laid it on the table. "Now why is that?" I asked. He said, "We'll be seeing you," and got up and left. I made one mistake after that—I didn't tell Meyer. It almost cost me my life, but I thought I could handle it.

I couldn't. I was coming out of a bank in Miami Beach and three guys opened up on me. It's a very strange thing to be hit by a bullet. For a second there is a tremendous burning sensation, then shock takes over. Then you go into what I would call limbo—everything moves in sort of slow motion. You can feel the impact, but not the pain, when you're hit again, but you're not exactly sure what you're doing. That's when your reflexes take complete control. The next thing I remember, I had a gun in my hand and I was using it. I remember hitting one guy and seeing his head explode. I remember shooting the second guy. I never saw the third guy, he took off.

The lawyer I had gone to the bank with managed to get me into a cab. The next thing I knew I was lying on a slab in a warehouse and a doctor was cutting bullets out of me. One week later I was on a boat to Brazil where I stayed, well supported, for almost a year. So they didn't get me and they didn't get Meyer.

A few years later I was sitting in an Italian restaurant and a man walked up to me and said, "You don't know me, but I was almost your executioner." This was the third man. We talked about it. I understood. Business is business.

Normally a boss is very careful where he goes and rarely travels without a bodyguard. One mistake is all any good hit man needs. I'll give you an example. I was out in California recently and I went to visit a friend of mine who has a bakery shop. Whenever I'm out there I go see him because he's probably the only person west of the Mississippi who makes good cannoli. Of course, I'm not the only guy who knows this.

We talked in his back room for a little while, and then I got up to leave. As I walked out from the back of the place who's standing by himself at the counter but one of the biggest mob bosses in the country. He took one look at me and his face went white. His eyes opened to about the size of a silver dollar. I looked at him and smiled. "Take it easy, babe," I said. "If I was here to see you, you wouldn't have seen me." Then I reached under the counter, handed him a chocolate-chip cookie and walked out. I guarantee you he won't go to the bathroom by himself for the next five years.

In any case, whoever the victim, the first thing you do after making a hit is dispose of the weapon. Once the weapon is out of your hands, and can't be traced back to you, it's almost impossible to get pinned with a crime. No weapon, no murder raps. I break up every gun that I don't leave on the spot. I have a friend who has a little machine shop and he takes the gun and melts it down. Or I'll bring it to a junkyard and flip it into one of the compressors. Good-bye, gun. As soon as the barrel is destroyed you're safe. Once that's gone there is no way of matching the bullet to the gun.

As I said, sometimes I leave the gun right on the spot. I'll do this if it's a stolen weapon and it's completely clean. There's really nothing to worry about. The handle of the gun has ridges and won't pick up fingerprints (unless you're stupid enough to use something like a pearl-handled revolver and if you do you deserve to get caught). The hammer has ridges too, and there is always a line right down the middle of the trigger. Sometimes I'll wipe the gun anyway, just to be certain, because fingerprints can kill you. One guy blasted a target with a shotgun and left the shotgun there. Fine, except he also left fingerprints on it, so his employers decided he had to go too. Can't have him being traced back and caught, because then it gets too hot for the people who hired him.

After I make a hit, and get rid of the gun, I follow my regular schedule. I remember going directly from a hit to a wedding reception. I just forget about it.

One thing I never do is plan an alibi in advance. To me that is really stupid because, by planning, you've got to get other people involved. If you ask them to front for you they know you're going to be doing something. But if I do the job right, who's gonna know I'm there? If I have to I can always set up an alibi. I can get 18 guys to swear they were playing cards with me. Or I can get the owner of some restaurant or movie theater who owes me a favor to swear I was there. No problems.

The police don't usually bother you too much. Number one, a cop is not going to knock his brains out on a mob hit because history shows they are not going to be able to get corroborating testimony, even if they know who did the job, which they do in a lot of so far "unsolved" cases. Don't underestimate the police. They do a good job. But when a mob guy is hit by another mob guy . . . well, let's say they're not overly disappointed and don't work as hard as they might under other circumstances.

You can almost forget about witnesses. There have been very few people willing to testify in cases involving organized-crime members. Not so much because they tend to disappear, but because your average individual is a family person and he is terrified someone in his family will get hurt if he gets involved. And, second, he's just not that socially conscious. They think just like the cops, what the hell, he only killed another gangster, what's the difference. Let 'em all kill one another.

Who can blame them? The newspapers, television, movies, magazines and books have done our job for us. The newspapers in particular love to turn simple rubouts into full-scale pitched battles. I personally never check the papers after I've done a job. There is no reason for me to, I'm not interested in the publicity, and I decided a long time ago it would be a poor idea for me to keep a scrapbook. Besides, the event the papers report is not going to have too much in common with the one I remember. I quit looking after my fourth hit. It was simple and quick, I just put three bullets in the guy from close range. The papers made it sound like a whole platoon of hit men had ventilated him with submachine guns. They didn't even have the number of bullets right.

All that the communications media have succeeded in doing is scaring the hell out of people. Let me ask you a question: After seeing *The Godfather*, would you testify against Don Corleone? Shit. After seeing *The Godfather*, would you even testify against Marlon Brando?

Even when the occasional silly soul comes along and claims he has seen a crime being committed, he usually changes his thinking before the trial begins. That is exactly what happened to me—but before the witnesses realized their mistake I spent almost a year in the Tombs in New York.

The district attorney claimed he had two witnesses who had seen me pull the trigger. They were a man and a woman in their late twenties and they had been parked in the shadows near the docks making out.

Four cops came to my door to arrest me. They stood right there in the hallway and read me my constitutional rights. My wife didn't take the whole thing very seriously at first. "Now what have you done?" she kind of scolded.

"Nothing," I said. "I don't know what these gentlemen are talking about." The only person I ever discussed this with was my attorney. I sat in the Tombs for almost a year, and we finally went to trial. Amazingly enough, the DA couldn't produce his witnesses. He asked the judge for 24 hours to produce them.

The next day he came into court and he was fuming. "Your honor, the witnesses have disappeared. But the state believes the defendant had something to do with their disappearance!"

"Your honor," my attorney protested, "my client has been sitting in jail for almost one full year. He could not possibly have had anything to do with the disappearance of the DA's alleged witnesses. We're ready to go to trial. If the state isn't ready to proceed, after all this time, we ask that you dismiss the charges." Case dismissed.

I don't know what happened to the witnesses. All I can guess is they had a sudden attack of honesty and decided to go on a long vacation.

Witnesses sometimes need help to understand that things aren't always what they appear to be. In 1963 I was hired to provide that help.

A man claimed he had seen a member of a particular organization shoot down a guy in cold blood. The police put him under full protection: a squad car outside his apartment building, a cop in the lobby and a third cop in his living room. I was offered $20,000 to prove to him that the cops couldn't protect him.

I watched his place for a few days and made my move one night.

Dark, no moon. I didn't want to use the fire escape because I couldn't take the chance on making noise and having someone look out their window. So I went to the roof of another building on the block and climbed across to his roof. I brought a rope—with plenty of knots tied in it to rest my feet on—and a grappling hook. I dug that hook into the roof and lowered myself down. It was only two stories.

This was in the middle of the summer and his window was wide open. I climbed in very quietly. Then I put one hand over his mouth and put my gun in my other hand, and shook him gently. "Don't make a move or a sound," I said. "There's a cop right outside your door and if he comes in here you're both gonna die. All I want to do is show you that the cops can't stop us. Wherever you go, whatever you do, we're gonna find you. We don't want to hurt you, but we think you should consider it carefully before you squeal on our mutual friend. Just do the right thing by him and you won't get hurt, I promise you. Now I'm gonna leave you. You go back to sleep. If you make a sound and I get caught, you're dead." Then I climbed back up the rope and went home.

We didn't want to kill him because that would have created a lot of heat for us. It worked out very well, he just had a sudden loss of memory. I made $20,000 and I didn't even have to pull the trigger.

Neither witnesses nor informers are hurt unless they have to be. Abe Reles, who informed on Murder, Inc., had to be. He just knew too much. He was supposedly under police protection when he "fell" out of a window and was killed. The story was that he had tried to get away from the police by tying sheets together and climbing out. The mob got to somebody and he was thrown right out the window. I assume the police who were supposedly guarding him were paid a great deal of money.

One stool pigeon who died was Arnold Shuster, the kid who fingered Willie Sutton. Arnold just had a case of bad luck. Nobody cared about Sutton, he was a free-lance bank robber and meant nothing to the organization. But one day Albert Anastasia happened to turn on the television and some sort of interview was on. He looked at Shuster and said, "Kill that motherfucker. I hate stool pigeons," and a few days later Shuster was blown away. If Anastasia had not turned the television set on, Shuster would never have been hit. As it turned out his death served as a warning to other potential informers, but it also led to Anastasia's death. It was a totally unnecessary killing and it brought a lot of heat down on the mob. The other bosses never forgave Anastasia for this.

About the only thing you have to think about, after the gun, the witnesses and the police, is the body. Most of the time it's best to leave it where it falls, but some people prefer to have victims simply disappear off the face of the earth. No body, no police. What the hell, they're paying for it. One organization brings its leftovers to a junkyard that has a compressor and makes them part of next year's Lincolns. Another uses a furnace in the backyard of a New Jersey estate. And there are still some undiscovered farms with lots of shallow graves fertilizing the plants. I suppose the most popular places are construction sites. The organization finds an area where concrete is about to be poured and they put the body in there. Some guy comes to work the next morning and, what does he know, he pours the concrete. Here's a helpful hint, though—always pour lime over the body or, when it starts decomposing, it's going to smell just terrible.

This point was proven just a few years ago by some people in the Canarsie section of Brooklyn. They had the bodies of two recently departed individuals on their hands and they did not want them discovered by the police. These victims had been linked to a business everyone thought was legitimate, and the mob didn't need that. So they made an early deposit in what was going to be a bank. They showed up one night in February and stuck the bodies in the foundation. Unfortunately, they neglected to cover them with lime. This was fine in the winter, because the bodies froze and nobody knew they were there. But by the time the bank opened in August the bodies were decomposing and nobody could walk in or out of that place without losing lunch.

I've only broken one rule in my career. I have killed three men for revenge—and I made them suffer when I did it. Normally you're supposed to get permission, but I didn't bother. When I think back on it, it seems like a plot for a bad motion picture. I remember in *Nevada Smith,* Steve McQueen tracked down the three guys who killed his parents and, when he found the third one, he just couldn't kill him. That's the difference between real life and pictures. There wasn't a man on this planet who could've stopped me.

It was 1958 and I had made a private deal to bring narcotics into the country from Mexico. My cut was supposed to be $40,000, but instead of paying me the party thought it would be a great deal cheaper to kill me. Unfortunately, when he sent his goons to my house I wasn't there. My wife was there and four months pregnant at the time. They came into the house looking for me and when they realized I wasn't home they got abusive. One of them kicked my wife in the stomach and they left her lying on the kitchen floor. She started hemorrhaging. She was dead by the time our neighbors got her to the hospital.

They caught up to me in Reno, Nevada. I had just come out of one of the casinos—at this point I didn't know what happened to my wife—and I started to cut through this alley over by some railroad tracks. The lights blanked out. I was smashed over the head with a blunt instrument.

Ten days later I came to, paralyzed from the neck down, in the Washoe Medical Center. The doctor manipulated my vertebrae and managed to restore some feeling in my body. The next day some friends came by and they told me what had happened to my wife.

That was the day I stopped caring whether I lived or died. That was the day I lost all fear of death. All I had within me was hatred. I would not have gone after the three men for what they did to me—business was business—and I would have simply settled with the head man. But they were dead the moment they kicked my wife.

We had only been married a few months. When we got married I didn't know if I was going to stay in this business or not. I certainly never would've stayed in as a hit man if she had lived; I even like to think I would have quit. You talk about your life changing around because of a woman . . . mine did. She was a real clean kid. And she was mine. For the first time in my life I had found someone who made me completely happy. Until that point, I didn't know what happiness was. All my life I had been a taker, everything I owned I had had to grab. Finally I had found someone who was willing to give simply because she liked me. There were never any threats, any wild shows, any violence; she liked me just because I was me.

Then my whole world exploded. It just came apart. It changed me radically. Before this I was sometimes wild and crazy, but I just wasn't mean. This made me mean. As soon as I could move I got on the telephone and called the guy who had set the whole thing up. He picked up the phone. All I said was, "You made a mistake, fuck. I'm still alive."

I laid in the hospital for eight months, and one day the doctor walked in and said I could either lie there like a vegetable for the rest of my life or risk an operation. I asked him what my chances were.

"Even," he said. "You'll either walk out or be carried out." I didn't give a damn either way, so I told him to start cutting. Seven months later I walked out of that place. And went after the three men who had killed my wife.

I started to hunt them down. I carried .22 long-range flat-nosed bullets because I wanted them to suffer. At short range they won't kill you, but they will smash your bones and make you bleed. I found the first one in California. I killed him very slowly. I had trapped him in a garbage-filled alley and he started swearing he had nothing to do with it. There was no way I was going to listen. I just started to pump bullets into him methodically. First into his legs so he couldn't move. Then into his rib cage so he would bleed. Then into his shoulders and then I shot his ears off. I just kept reloading the gun; I was having a good time. Then I left him there to die.

I found the second one in Mexico and killed him the same way. I had never known anything as sweet as these killings. They were wonderful sights. And I could smell the fear. If you've ever wondered why an animal attacks someone who's afraid of him, it's because the fear just pours out of him and creates an odor. I saw it. I smelled it. I loved it.

I had to chase the third one completely across the country. He knew

I was after him and he tried to hide. It took me almost a year to find him, but I did, in New York City. He went down just like the first two. Then I got on the phone to the boss. I said two words, "You're next," and then I hung up. But before I could get him he was arrested on a narcotics charge. That bust saved his life. I guarantee it. And, if he lives through it, the day he walks out I will be standing there waiting for him. I swear it.

Why do I do it? Why do I kill people? There are a number of reasons. Obviously, the money. I like money. I like what money can buy, what it can bring you. I remember when I didn't have it.

I like the status it brings. I'm somebody. Straight people like to associate with me. They like to be able to brag that they know a real live killer, or that this guy can "do things" for people. And girls, when they meet me, they want to find out what it's like to be with an individual who has killed people. They want to go to bed with you. Don't ask me why, but they do. They feel you're going to be different than anybody else. You're not, and they're disappointed when they find out, but the idea of being with an animal really appeals to a lot of people. Believe it or not, there are "hit man groupies." I like women being attracted to me. I didn't have what you would call a normal social life when I was younger; I didn't do too much dating. And I know I'm not the best-looking guy in the world either, so if it's being the tough killer that turns women on, I'll play that role. I'll be as tough as they want. Usually, though, after they ball you, they get sick. They feel they've corrupted themselves.

I also see killing as a test of loyalty and courage.

In business terms the ability to pull the trigger is vitally important. If you expect to progress in the organization you have to be able to do it. I would say almost every man who has ever become a boss has pulled it somewhere along the line.

And, finally, I guess I do it because I enjoy it. I like having the power of knowing that I am it, that I can make the final decision of whether someone lives or dies. It is an awesome power.

Don't try to analyze me or any other hit man either. I would guess there are maybe 1000 men still working at it throughout the country. But except in New York there hasn't been much work lately, so I guess you could call us a dying breed. The thing about hit men that is so unusual is that they are so usual. A man that is sadistic, that is crazy-wild, that is a troublemaker, that has strange habits or stands out in a crowd, he can't make it. He'll be disposed of.

Hit men differ in a thousand ways. Some are friendly, some moody, some tall, some short, some bald, and, lately, some even have long hair. You would never be able to pick one out of a crowd but, then again, you won't have to. A hit man is only known to those people who have to know who he is.

What makes a good hit man? Pride and confidence. A good hit man goes out, does his job, comes home to his family and can sit down and eat his dinner without any problems. After all, no one likes to bring his work home with him.

from Legs
by William Kennedy

William Kennedy's (born 1928) 1975 novel about bootlegger Jack "Legs" Diamond is part of his celebrated Albany Cycle novels. The books draw upon Albany, New York and its environs and history to create a fictional world populated by drifters and hustlers, who often come up short in the face of life's indignities and their own incompetence.

K iki lay naked on the bed that was all hers and which stood where Alice's had stood before Jack had it taken out and bought the new one. She was thinking of the evening being unfinished, of the fudge that hadn't hardened the last time she touched it, and of Jack lying asleep in his own room, his heavy breathing audible to Kiki, who could not sleep and who resented the uselessness of her nakedness.

They had been together in her bed at early evening, hadn't eaten any supper because they were going to have dinner out later. The fudge was already in the fridge then. Jack was naked too, lying on his back, smoking and staring at the wall with the prints of the Michelangelo sketches, the punishment of Tityus and the head of a giant, prints Jack told her he bought because Arnold Rothstein liked them and said Michelangelo was the best artist who ever brushed a stroke. Jack said Kiki should look at the pictures and learn about art and not be so stupid about it. But the giant had an ugly head and she didn't like the one with the bird in it either, so she looked at Jack instead of dopey pictures. She wanted to touch him, not look at him, but she knew it wouldn't be right because there was no spark in him. He was collapsed and he had tried but wasn't in the mood. He started out in the mood, but the mood left him. He needed a rest, maybe.

He wouldn't look at her. She kept looking at him but he wouldn't look back, so she got up and said, "I'm going downstairs and see if that fudge is hard yet."

"Put something on."

"I'll put my apron on."

"Take a housecoat. There may be somebody on the porch."

"They're all out in the cottage playing pool or in the car watching the road. I know they are."

"I don't want you showing off your ass to the hired help."

She put on one of Alice's aprons, inside out so it wouldn't look too familiar to Jack, and went downstairs. She looked in the mirror and knew anybody could see a little bit of her tail if there was anybody to see it, but there wasn't. She didn't want clothes on. She didn't want to start something and then have to take the clothes off in a hurry and maybe lose the spark, which she would try to reignite when she went back upstairs. She wanted Jack to see as much of her as he could as often as he could, wanted to reach him with all she could reach him with. She had the house now. She had beaten Alice. She had Jack. She did not plan to let go of him.

The fudge was still soft to her touch. She left another fingerprint in it. She had made it for Jack, but it wasn't hardening. It had been in the fridge twenty-eight hours, and it wasn't any harder now than it was after the first hour.

"What do you like—chocolate or penuche?" she had asked him the day before.

"Penuche's the white one with nuts, right?"

"Right."

"That's the one."

"That's the one I like too."

"How come you know so much about fudge?"

"It's the only thing I ever learned how to cook from my mother. I haven't made it in five or six years, but I want to do it for you."

The kitchen had all the new appliances, Frigidaire, Mixmaster, chrome orange juice squeezer, a machine for toasting two slices of bread. But, for all its qualities, Kiki couldn't find the ingredients she remembered from her mother's recipe. So she used two recipes, her own and one out of Alice's *Fanny Farmer Cook Book*, mixed them up together and cooked them and poured it all into a tin pie plate and set it on the top shelf of the fridge. But it didn't harden. She tasted it and it was sweet and delicious, but it was goo after an hour. Now it was still goo.

"It's all goo," she told Jack when she went back upstairs. She stood alongside him and took off her apron. He didn't reach for her.

"Let's go out," he said, and he rolled across the bed, away from her, and stood up. He put on his robe and went into his own room to dress. Even when Alice was there he had had his own room. Even at the hotel he had kept his own room to go to when he and Kiki had finished making love.

"Are you angry because the fudge didn't harden?"

"For crissakes, no. You got other talents."

"Do you wish I could cook?"

"No. I cook good enough for both of us."

And he did, too. Why Jack made the best chicken cacciatore Kiki ever ate, and he cooked a roast of lamb with garlic and spices that was fantastic. Jack could do anything in life. Kiki could only do about three things. She could dance a little and she could love a man and she could be pretty. But she could do those things a thousand times better than most women. She knew about men, knew what men told her. They told her she was very good at love and that she was pretty. They also liked to talk about her parts. They all (and Jack too) told her she was lovely everyplace. So Kiki didn't need to learn about cooking. She wasn't going to tie in with anybody as a kitchen slave and a fat mommy. She wore an apron, but she wore it her way, with nothing underneath it. If Jack wanted a cook, he wouldn't have got rid of Alice.

Kiki would just go on being Kiki, somebody strange. She didn't know how she was strange. She knew she wasn't smart enough to understand the reasons behind that sort of thing. I mean I know it already, she said to herself. I don't have to figure it out. I know it and I'm living it.

Kiki thought about these things as she was lying naked in her bed wishing the fudge would harden. Earlier in the night, after Jack had rolled out of her bed, they'd gone out, had eaten steaks at the New York Restaurant in Catskill, one of the best, then had drinks at Sweeney's club, a good-time speakeasy. It was on the way home that everything was so beautiful and quiet. She felt strange then. She and Jack were in the back seat and Fogarty was driving. She was holding Jack's hand, and they were just sitting there a little glassy-eyed from the booze, yes, but that wasn't the reason it was so beautiful. It was beautiful because they were together as they deserved to be and because they didn't have to say anything to each other.

She remembered looking ahead on the road and looking out the window she'd rolled down and feeling the car was moving without a motor. She couldn't hear noise, couldn't see anything but the lights on the road and the darkened farmhouses and the open fields that were all so brightly lighted by the new moon. The stars were out too, on this silent, this special night. It was positively breathtaking, is how Kiki later described the scene and the mood that preceded the vision of the truck.

That damn truck.

Why did it have to be there ahead of them?

Why couldn't Joe have taken another road and not seen it?

Oh, jeez, wouldn't everything in her whole life have been sweet if they just hadn't seen that truck?

When he saw the old man in the truck, got a good look and saw the side of his face with its bumpkin stupid smile, Jack felt his heart leap up. When Fogarty said, "Streeter from Cairo—he hauls cider, but we never caught him with any," Jack felt the flush in his neck. He had no pistol with him, but he opened the gun rack in the back of the front seat and unclipped one of the .38's. He rolled down the window on his side, renewed.

"Jack, what's going to happen?" Kiki asked.

"Just a little business. Nothing to get excited about."

"Jack, don't get, don't get me, don't get . . ."

"Just shut up and stay in the car."

They were on Jefferson Avenue, heading out of Catskill when the trucker saw Jack's pistol pointing at him. Fogarty cruised at equal speed with the truck until Streeter pulled to the side of the road across from a cemetery. Jack was the first out, his pistol pointed upward. He saw the barrels on the truck and quick-counted more than fifteen. Son of a bitch. He saw the shitkicker's cap, country costume, and he hated the man for wearing it. Country son of a bitch, where Jack had to live.

"Get down out of that truck."

Streeter slid off the seat and stepped down, and Jack saw the second head, another cap on it, sliding across the seat and stepping down, a baby-faced teenager with a wide forehead, a widow's peak, and a pointy chin that gave his face the look of a heart.

"How many more you got in there?" Jack said.

"No more. Just me and the boy."

"Who is he?"

"Bartlett, Dickie Bartlett."

"What's he to you?"

"A helper."

Streeter's moon face was full of rotten teeth and a grin.

"So you're Streeter, the wise guy from Cairo," Jack said.

Streeter nodded, very slightly, the grin stayed in place and Jack punched it, cutting the flesh of the cheekbone.

"Put your hands up higher or I'll split your fucking head."

Jack poked Streeter's chest with the pistol barrel. The Bartlett boy's hands shot up higher than Streeter's. Jack saw Fogarty with a pistol in his hand.

"What's in the barrels?"

"Hard cider," said Streeter through his grin.

"Not beer or white?"

"I don't haul beer, or white either. I ain't in the booze business."

"You better be telling the truth, old man. You know who I am?"

"Yes, I know."

"I know you too. You been hauling too many barrels."

"Haulin's what I do."

"Hauling barrels is dangerous business when they might have beer or white in them."

"Nothing but cider in them barrels."

"We'll see. Now move."

"Move where?"

"Into the car, goddamn it," Jack said, and he slapped Streeter on the back of the head with his gun hand. He knocked off the goddamn stinking cap. Streeter bent to pick it up and turned to Jack with his grin. He couldn't really be grinning.

"Where you taking that cider?"

"Up home, and some over to Bartlett's."

"The kid?"

"His old man."

"You got a still yourself?"

"No."

"Bartlett got a still?"

"Not that I know of."

"What's all the cider for then?"

"Drink some, make vinegar, bottle some, sell some of that to stores up in the hollow, sell what's left to neighbors. Or anybody."

"Where's the still?"

"Ain't no still I know of."

"Who do you know's got a still?"

"Never hear of nobody with a still."

"You heard I run the only stills that run in this county? You heard that?"

"Yes siree, I heard that."

"So who runs a still takes that much cider?"

"Ain't that much when you cut it up."

"We'll see how much it is," Jack said. He told Kiki to sit in front and he put Streeter and Bartlett in the back seat. He pulled their caps down over their eyes and sat in front with Kiki while Fogarty drove the truck inside the cemetery entrance. Fogarty was gone ten minutes, which passed in silence, and when he came back, he said, "Looks like it's all hard cider. Twenty-four barrels." And he slipped behind the wheel. Jack rode with his arm over the back seat and his pistol pointed at the roof. No one spoke all the way to Acra, and Streeter and Bartlett barely moved. They sat with their hands in their laps and their caps over their eyes. When they got out of the car inside the garage, Jack made them face the wall and tied their hands behind them. Fogarty backed the car out, closed the door, and took Kiki inside the house. Jack sat Streeter and Bartlett on the floor against a ladder.

Shovels hung over the old man's head like a set of assorted guillotines. Jack remembered shovels on the wall of the cellar in The Village where the Neary mob took him so long ago when they thought he'd hijacked a load of their beer—and he had. They tied him to a chair with wire around his arms and legs, then worked him over. They got weary and left him, bloody and half conscious, to go to sleep. He was fully awake and moved his arms back and forth against the wire's twist until he ripped his shirt. He sawed steadily with the wire until it ripped the top off his right bicep and let him slip his arm out of the bond. He climbed up a coal chute and out a window, leaving pieces of the bicep on the twist of wire, and on the floor: skin, flesh, plenty of blood. Bled all the way home. Bicep flat now. Long, rough scar there now. Some Nearys paid for that scar.

He looked at the old man and saw the ropes hanging on the wall behind him, can of kerosene in the corner, paintbrushes soaking in turpentine. Rakes, pickax. Old man another object. Another tool. Jack hated all tools that refused to yield their secrets. Jack was humiliated before the inanimate world. He hated it, kicked it when it affronted him. He shot a car once that betrayed him by refusing to start. Blew holes in its radiator.

The point where the hanging rope bellied out on the garage wall looked to Jack like the fixed smile on Streeter's face. Streeter was crazy to keep smiling. He wasn't worth a goddamn to anybody if he was crazy. You can kill crazies. No loss. Jack made ready to kill yet another man. Wilson, the first one he killed. Wilson, the card cheat. Fuck you, cheater, you're dead. I'm sorry for your kids.

In the years after he dumped Wilson in the river Jack used Rothstein's insurance connections to insure family men he was going to remove from life. He made an arrangement with a thieving insurance salesman, sent him around to the family well in advance of the removal date. When the deal was sealed, give Jack a few weeks, then bingo!

"You got any insurance, old man?"

"No."

"You got any family?"

"Wife."

"Too bad. She's going to have to bury you best she can. Unless you tell me where that still is you got hid."

"Ain't got no still hid nowheres, mister. I told you that."

"Better think again, old man. You know where the still is, kid?" Dickie Bartlett shook his head and turned to the wall. Only a kid. But if Jack killed one, he would have to kill two. Tough break, kid.

"Take off your shoes."

Streeter slowly untied the rawhide laces of his high shoe-boots without altering his grin. He pulled off one shoe and Jack smelled his foot, his sweaty white wool sock, his long underwear tucked inside the sock. Country leg, country foot, country stink. Jack looked back at the grin, which seemed as fixed as the shape of the nose that hovered above it. But you don't fix a grin permanently. Jack knew. That old son of a bitch is defying me, is what he thought. He hasn't got a chance and yet he's defying Jack Diamond's law, Jack Diamond's threat, Jack Diamond himself. That grinning façade is a fake and Jack will remove it. Jack knows all there is to know about fake façades. He remembered his own grin in one of the newspapers as he went into court in Philadelphia. Tough monkey, smilin' through. They won't get to me. And then in the courtroom he knew how empty that smile was, how profoundly he had failed to create the image he wanted to present to the people of Philadelphia, not only on his return but all his life, all through boyhood, to live down the desertion charge in the Army, and, worse, the charge that he stole from his buddies. Not true. So many of the things they said about Jack were untrue and yet they stuck.

He was a nobody in the Philadelphia court. Humiliated. Arrested coming in, then kicked out. And stay out, you bum. I speak for the decent people of this city in saying that Philadelphia doesn't want you any more than Europe did. Vomit. Puke, puke. Vomit. Country feet smelled like vomit. Jack's family witnessing it all in the courtroom. Jack always loved them in his way. Jack dumped about eight cigarettes out of his Rameses pack and pocketed them. He twisted the pack and lit it with a loose match, showed the burning cellophane and paper to Streeter, who never lost his grin. Jack said, "Where's the still?"

"Jee-zus, mister, I ain't seen no still. I ain't and that's a positive fact, I tell you."

Jack touched the fire to the sock and then to the edge of the underwear. Streeter shook it and the fire went out. Jack burned his own hand, dropped the flaming paper and let it burn out. Fogarty came back in then, pistol in hand.

"Kneel on him," Jack said, and with pistol pointed at Streeter's head, Fogarty knelt on the old man's calf. The pistol wasn't loaded, Fogarty said later. He was taking no chances shooting anybody accidentally. It had been loaded when they stopped Streeter's truck because he felt when he traveled the roads with Jack he was bodyguard as well as chauffeur, and he would stand no chance of coping with a set of killers on wheels if his gun was empty. But now he wasn't a bodyguard anymore.

"He's a tough old buzzard," Jack said.

"Why don't you tell him what he wants to know?" Fogarty said conspiratorially to Streeter.

"Can't tell what I don't know," Streeter said. The grin was there. The flame had not changed it. Jack knew now he would remove that grin with flame. Finding the still was receding in importance, but such a grin of defiance is worth punishing. Asks for punishing. Will always get what it asks for. The Alabama sergeant who tormented Jack and other New York types in the platoon because of their defiance. "New Yoahk mothahfucks." Restriction. Punishment. KP over and over. Passes denied. And then Jack swung and got the son bitch in the leg with an iron bar. Had to go AWOL after that, couldn't even go back. That was when they got him, in New Yoahk. Did defiance win the day for Jack? It was satisfying, but Jack admits it did not win the day. Should have shot the son bitch in some ditch off-post. Let the rats eat him.

"Where's that still, you old son bitch?"

"Hey, mister, I'd tell you if I knew. You think I'd keep anythin' back if I knew? I dunno, mister, I just plain dunno."

Jack lit the sock, got it flaming this time, and the old man yelled, shook his whole leg again and rocked Fogarty off it. The flame went out again. Jack looked, saw the grin. The old man is totally insane. Should be bugged. Crazy as they make 'em. Crazy part of a man that takes any kind of punishment, suffers all humiliations. No pride.

"You old son bitch, ain't you got no pride? Tell me the goddamn answer to my question. Ain't you got no sense? I'm gonna hang your ass off a tree you don't tell me what I want to know."

But you can't really punish a crazy like that, Jack. He loves it. That's why he's sitting there grinning. Some black streak across his brain makes him crazier than a dog with his head where his ass oughta be. He's making you crazy now, Jack. Got you talking about hanging. You can't be serious, can you?

"All right, old man, get up. Speed, get that rope."

"What you got in mind, Jack?"

"I'm gonna hang his Cairo country ass from that maple tree outside."

"Hey," said Streeter, "you ain't really gonna hang me?"

"I'm gonna hang you like a side of beef," Jack said. "I'm gonna pop your eyes like busted eggs. I'm gonna make your tongue stretch so far out you'll be lickin' your toes."

"I ain't done nothin' to nobody, mister. Why you gonna hang me?"

"Because you're lyin' to me, old man."

"No, sir, I ain't lyin'. I ain't lyin'."

"How old are you right now?"

"Fifty."

"You ain't as old as I thought, but you ain't gonna be fifty-one. You're a stubborn buzzard, but you ain't gonna be fifty-one. Bring him out."

Fogarty led the old man outside with only one shoe, and Jack threw the rope over the limb of the maple. He tied a knot, looped the rope through the opening in the knot—a loop that would work like an animal's choker chain—and slipped it over Streeter's neck. Jack pulled open a button, one down from the collar, to give the rope plenty of room.

"Jack," Fogarty said, shaking his head. Jack tugged the rope until he took up all the slack and the rope rose straight up from Streeter's neck.

"One more chance," Jack said. "Where is that goddamn still you were headed for?"

"Jee-zus Keh-ryst, mister, there just ain't no still, you think I'm kiddin' you? You got a rope around my neck. You think I wouldn't tell you anything I knew if I knew it? Jee-zus, mister, I don't want to die."

"Listen, Jack. I don't think we ought to do this." Fogarty was trembling. The poor goddamn trucker. Like watching a movie and knowing how it ends, Fogarty said later.

"Shitkicker!" Jack yelled. "Where is it? SHITKICKER! SHITKICKER!"

Before the old man could answer, Jack tugged at the rope and up went Streeter. But he had worked one hand loose and he made a leap as Jack tugged. He grabbed the rope over his head and held it.

"Retie the son of a bitch," Jack said, and Fogarty knew then he was party to a murder. Full accomplice now and the tied-up Bartlett kid a witness. There would be a second murder on this night. Fogarty, how far you've come under Jack's leadership. He tied the old man's hands, and Jack then wound the rope around both his own arms and his waist so it wouldn't slip, and he jerked it again and moved backward. The old man's eyes bugged as he rose off the ground. His tongue came out and he went limp. The Bartlett kid yelled and then started to cry, and Jack let go of the rope. The old man crumpled.

"He's all right," Jack said. "The old son of a bitch is too miserable to die. Hit him with some water."

Fogarty half-filled a pail from an outside faucet and threw it on Streeter. The old man opened his eyes.

"You know, just maybe he's telling the truth," Fogarty said.

"He's lying."

"He's doing one hell of a good job."

Jack took Fogarty's pistol and waved it under Streeter's nose. *At least he can't kill him with that,* Fogarty thought.

"It's too much work to hang you," Jack said to Streeter, "so I'm gonna blow your head all over the lawn. I'll give you one more chance."

The old man shook his head and closed his eyes. His grin was gone. I finally got rid of that, is what Jack thought. But then he was suddenly enraged again at the old man. You made me do this to you, was the nature of Jack's accusation. You turned me into a goddamn sadist because of your goddamn stinking country stubbornness. He laid the barrel of the pistol against the old man's head and then he thought: *Fogarty.* And he checked the cylinder. No bullets. He gave Fogarty a look of contempt and handed him back the empty pistol. He took his own .38 from his coat pocket, and Streeter, watching everything, started to tremble, his lip turned down now. Smile not only gone, but that face unable even to remember that it had smiled even once in all its fifty years. Jack fired one shot. It exploded alongside Streeter's right ear. The old man's head jerked and Jack fired again, alongside the other ear.

"You got something to tell me now, shitkicker?" Jack said.

The old man opened his eyes, saucers of terror. He shook his head. Jack put the pistol between his eyes, held it there for seconds of silence. Then he let it fall away with a weariness. He stayed on his haunches in front of Streeter, just staring. Just staring and saying nothing.

"You win, old man," he finally said. "You're a tough monkey."

Jack stood up slowly and pocketed his pistol. Fogarty and one of the porch guards drove Streeter and Bartlett back to their truck. Fogarty ripped out their ignition wires and told them not to call the police. He drove back to Acra and slept the sleep of a confused man.

When Speed had brought her from the car into the house, Kiki had said to him, "What's going to happen with those men?"

"I don't know. Probably just some talk."

"Oh, God, Joe, don't let him hurt them. I don't want to be mixed up in that kind of shit again, please, Joe."

"I'll do what I can do, but you know Jack's got a mind of his own."

"I'll go and see him. Or maybe you could tell him to come in. Maybe if I asked him not to do anything, for me, don't do it for me, he wouldn't do it."

"I'll tell him you said it."

"You're a nice guy, Joe."

"You go to bed and stay upstairs. Do what I tell you."

Kiki was thinking that Joe really and truly was a nice guy and that maybe she could make it with him if only she wasn't tied up with Jack. Of course, she wouldn't do anything while she was thick with Jack. But it was nice to think about Joe and his red hair and think about how nice he would be to play with. He was nicer than Jack, but then she didn't love Jack because he was nice.

She worried whether Jack had killed the two men when she later heard the two shots and the screaming. But she had thought the worst at the Monticello, thought Jack had killed *those* men when they had really tried to kill him. She didn't want to think bad things about Jack again. But she lived half an hour with uncertainty. Then Jack came into her room and said the men were gone and nobody got hurt.

"Did you get the information you wanted?" she asked.

"Yeah, I don't want to talk about it."

"Oh, good. Are you done now?"

"All done."

"Then we can finish the evening the way we intended."

"It's finished."

"I mean really finished."

"And I mean really finished."

He kissed her on the cheek and went to his bedroom. He didn't come back to see her or ask her to come to him. She tried to sleep, but she kept wanting to finish the evening, continue from where she and Jack had left off in the car in the silence and the chilliness and the brightness of the new moon on the open fields. She wanted to lie alongside Jack and comfort him because she knew from the way he was behaving that he had the blues. If she went in and loved him, he would feel better. Yet she felt he didn't really want that, and she rolled over and tossed and turned, curled and uncurled for another hour before she decided: Maybe he really does want it. So then, yes, she ought to do it. She got up and very quietly tiptoed into Jack's room and stood naked alongside his bed. Jack was deeply asleep. She touched his ear and ran her fingers down his cheek, and all of a sudden she was looking down the barrel of his .38 and he was bending her fingers back so far she was screaming. Nobody came to help her. She thought of that later. Jack could have killed her and nobody would have tried to stop him. Not even Joe.

"You crazy bitch! What were you trying to do?"

"I just wanted to love you."

"Never, never wake me up that way. Don't ever touch me. Call me and I'll hear it, but don't touch me."

Kiki was weeping because her hand hurt so much. She couldn't bend her fingers. When she tried to bend them, she fainted. When she came to, she was in a chair and Jack was all white in the face, looking at her. He was slapping her cheek lightly just as she came out of it.

"It hurts an awful lot."

"We'll go get a doctor. I'm sorry, Marion, I'm really sorry I hurt you."

"I know you are, Jack."

"I don't want to hurt you."

"I know you don't."

"I love you so much I'm half nuts sometimes."

"Oh, Jackie, you're not nuts, you're wonderful and I don't care if you hurt me. It was an accident. It was all my fault."

"We'll go get the doc out of bed."

"He'll fix me up fine, and then we can come back and finish the evening."

"Yeah, that's a swell idea."

The coroner was Jack's doctor, and they got him out of bed. He bandaged her hand and said she'd have to have a cast made at the hospital next day, and he gave her pills for her pain. She told him she'd been rehearsing her dance steps and had fallen down. He didn't seem to believe that, but Jack didn't care what he believed, so she didn't either. After the doctor's they went back home. Jack said he was too tired to make love and that they'd do it in the morning. Kiki tossed and turned for a while and then went down to the kitchen and checked the fudge again, felt it with the fingers of her good hand. It was still goo, so she put it out on the back porch for the cat.

Clem Streeter told his story around Catskill for years. He was a celebrity because of it, stopped often by people and asked for another rendition. I was being shaved in a Catskill barber chair the year beer came back, and Jack was, of course, long gone. But Clem was telling the story yet again for half a dozen locals.

"The jedge in Catskill axed me what I wanted the pistol *permit* for," he said, "and I told him 'bout how that Legs Diamond feller burned my feet and hung me from a sugar maple th' other night up at his garage. 'That so?' axed the jedge. 'I jes told you it were,' I said. People standin' 'round the courthouse heard what we was sayin' and they come over to listen better. 'You made a complaint yet against this Diamond person?' the jedge axes me. But I tell him, only complaint I made so far was to the wife. That jedge he don't know what to do with hisself he's so took out by what I'm sayin'. I didn't mean to upset the jedge. But he says, 'I guess we better get the sheriff on this one and maybe the DA,' and they both of 'em come in after a little bit and I tell 'em my story, how they poked guns outen the winders of their car and we stopped the truck, me and Dickie Bartlett. They made us git down, but I didn't git fast enough for Diamond, so he hit me with his fist and said, 'Put up your hands or I'll split your effin' head.' Then they hauled us up to Diamond's place with our caps pulled down so we wouldn't know where we was goin', but I see the road anyway out under the side of the cap and I know that place of his with the lights real well. Am I sure it was Diamond, the jedge axes. 'Acourse I'm sure. I seen him plenty over at the garage in Cairo. He had a woman in the car with him, and I recognized the other feller who did the drivin' 'cause he stopped my truck another night I was haulin' empty barrels 'bout a month back.' 'So this here's Streeter, the wise guy from Cairo,' Diamond says to me and he cuffs me on the jaw with his fist, just like that, afore I said a word. Then up in the garage they tried to burn me up. 'What'd they do that for?' the jedge axes me, and I says,' 'Cause he wants to know where there's a still I'm s'posed to know about. But I told Diamond I don't know nothin' 'bout no still.' And the jedge says, 'Why'd he think you did?' And I says, 'Cause I'm haulin' twenty-four barrels of hard cider I'd picked up down at Post's Cider Mill.' 'Who for?' says the jedge. 'For me,' I says. 'I like cider. Drink a bunch of it.' 'Cause I ain't about to tell no jedge or nobody else 'bout the still me and old Cy Bartlett got between us. We do right nice business with that old still. Make up to a hundred, hundred and thirty dollars apiece some weeks off the fellers who ain't got no stills and need a little 'jack to keep the blood pumpin.' That Diamond feller, he surely did want to get our still away from us. I knew that right off. Did me a lot of damage, I'll say. But sheeeeee. Them fellers with guns is all talk. Hell, they don't never kill nobody. They just like to throw a scare into folks so's they can get their own way. Son of a bee if I was gonna give up a hundred and thirty dollars a week for some New York feller."

Gangland Style: The Transcript
by Bruce McCall

Mobsters' wiretapped conversations often are a mind-numbing blend of vulgarity, self-pity, greed, grandiosity and sentimentality. Humorist Bruce McCall's (born 1935) fictional encounter between a group of wiseguys and their image consultant reads a little like the real thing.

(Inaudible)

Gangland Style is . . . All they see is, you know, like cement wing tips. Period.

(Expletive) media.

Or whacking somebody. That's what everybody thinks Gangland Style is. Just whacking a guy. Stuffing him face up in the trunk of his own Lincoln Town Car.

Whereas, it's so much more.

Right. But to them, it's like, midnight dinners for twenty-eight in bad Italian restaurants where nobody pays the check, and somebody never gets to eat dessert. *(Laughter)*

Yeah, well, it's our own *(expletive)* fault. We keep letting those other *(expletive)* define us.

So maybe we open a theme park. Gangland. Why not? Know what I'm . . . Go public! We got this dump on Staten Island that . . .

Like, the Last Ride. The Money Laundry . . . Crush 'em in a mangle. . . .

Exactly wrong, *(expletive)*-face. Listen what I'm talking, *(expletive)*. This here is Mr. Buncombe. Image consultant. We checked him out. He's all right. Mr. Buncombe, here, is gonna help us turn our *(expletive)* image right around. Make room, make room.

Thanks, thanks a lot, gentlemen. I'm, uh, thrilled to be here today. *(Inaudible)* . . . won't go through all these charts *(inaudible)*. In a nutshell, preliminary focus-group research pretty much backs up your gut feel vis-à-vis your current image. Very skewed toward what we call "ultimate negatives." Record-high scores, in fact.

That's like . . .

Death, things of that nature—correct. But don't, heh heh, kill the messenger quite yet, heh heh, because . . . But look at this chart, please.

(Expletive!)

Exactly! In short, fifty-two per cent of those interviewed say they fantasize at least some of the time about the Gangland experience. With males only, seventy-nine per cent. Very high among the young males, of course, but here's a surprise . . . numbers for income earners over a hundred thousand annually.

(Expletive) daydreaming . . .

Right, and that's the key. Even they secretly want to be . . . you know, like you. Frankly, this excites the hell out of us. We see it as what we call your "hidden positive." And it's leverage to turn Gangland Style from a P.R. nightmare into a marketing bonanza.

You mean, money?

Strictly legit. Not even the RICO laws could touch us. Gentlemen, imagine a provocative new line of Ravenite Social Club men's fragrances, as redolent of Gangland Style as a punch in the nose. Sir, smell this.

Hmm. *(Expletive)* nice!

That's Cutler. An intimidating blend of Canarsie dock-walloper burliness and the suavity of a six-hundred-dollar-an-hour uptown lawyer, with just that piquant hint of marinara sauce. Gunmetal packaging, the works. Now you, sir. Smell this.

Kinda like, um, lavender and gunpowder?

Perfect. That's Made Man. Makes ladies swoon and men cross to the other side of the street. We've already roughed out an ad campaign. Then, I have here . . . Look at this. Try it on.

A *(expletive)* bathrobe?

Not dust another bathrobe. Gangland Style leisure wear, branded The 247 Mulberry Street Collection, by Vincent the Chin. Believe me, this will take Sutton Place and Greenwich by storm.

Who's hungry? Wanna order out?

Don't bother, sir. Over here *(inaudible)* . . . Gangland Style Mean Cuisine.

I'll be *(expletive)*!

Quick-cooking, microwave-ready tubs of your favorite linguini, tortellini, spaghetti, with all the fixin's. Enough per serving to feed a whole Family, so to speak, heh heh. Sorry. Just a little . . .

I got it! "Gangland Style—a whole new way of life, for those who live on the edge!"

Excellent! We could make a move on the self-improvement category. Books and cassettes. "Improve Your Confidence, Gangland Style." "A Thousand and One Ways to Beat the Tax Man, Gangland Style." Weekend seminars. A thousand bucks a pop.

"Gangland Style. It ain't just cops 'n' robbers anymore!"

Now you're talking. Video games. Ladies' fashion wear . . . Why not? Sky's the *(expletive)* limit.

This here Mr. Buncombe's given us a lot to think about. Somebody . . . You—give him a ride home. You know what I'm saying?

from The Godfather
by Mario Puzo

Mario Puzo's (1920–1999) scripts for the first two Godfather *movies won Oscars, and his 1969 novel that inspired those films is still a great read. Here, Don Corleone—the Godfather himself—has been critically wounded by rival mobsters in a dispute over mafia policy. His son Michael—a freshly-minted veteran of World War II, who has avoided involvement in the family's criminal activities—visits his father in the hospital.*

When Michael Corleone went into the city that night it was with a depressed spirit. He felt that he was being enmeshed in the Family business against his will and he resented Sonny using him even to answer the phone. He felt uncomfortable being on the inside of the Family councils as if he could be absolutely trusted with such secrets as murder. And now, going to see Kay, he felt guilty about her also. He had never been completely honest with her about his family. He had told her about them but always with little jokes and colorful anecdotes that made them seem more like adventurers in a Technicolor movie than what they really were. And now his father had been shot down in the street and his eldest brother was making plans for murder. That was putting it plainly and simply but that was never how he would tell it to Kay. He had already said his father being shot was more like an "accident" and that all the trouble was over. Hell, it looked like it was just beginning. Sonny and Tom were off-center on this guy Sollozzo, they were still underrating him, even though

Sonny was smart enough to see the danger. Michael tried to think what the Turk might have up his sleeve. He was obviously a bold man, a clever man, a man of extraordinary force. You had to figure him to come up with a real surprise. But then Sonny and Tom and Clemenza and Tessio were all agreed that everything was under control and they all had more experience than he did. He was the "civilian" in this war, Michael thought wryly. And they'd have to give him a hell of a lot better medals than he'd gotten in World War II to make him join this one.

Thinking this made him feel guilty about not feeling more sympathy for his father. His own father shot full of holes and yet in a curious way Michael, better than anyone else, understood when Tom had said it was just business, not personal. That his father had paid for the power he had wielded all his life, the respect he had extorted from all those around him.

What Michael wanted was out, out of all this, to lead his own life. But he couldn't cut loose from the family until the crisis was over. He had to help in a civilian capacity. With sudden clarity he realized that he was annoyed with the role assigned to him, that of the privileged noncombatant, the excused conscientious objector. That was why the word "civilian" kept popping into his skull in such an irritating way.

When he got to the hotel, Kay was waiting for him in the lobby. (A couple of Clemenza's people had driven him into town and dropped him off on a nearby corner after making sure they were not followed.)

They had dinner together and some drinks. "What time are you going to visit your father?" Kay asked.

Michael looked at his watch. "Visiting hours end at eight-thirty. I think I'll go after everybody has left. They'll let me up. He has a private room and his own nurses so I can just sit with him for a while. I don't think he can talk yet or even know if I'm there. But I have to show respect."

Kay said quietly, "I feel so sorry for your father, he seemed like such a nice man at the wedding. I can't believe the things the papers are printing about him. I'm sure most of it's not true."

Michael said politely, "I don't think so either." He was surprised to find himself so secretive with Kay. He loved her, he trusted her, but he would never tell her anything about his father or the Family. She was an outsider.

"What about you?" Kay asked. "Are you going to get mixed up in this gang war the papers are talking about so gleefully?"

Michael grinned, unbuttoned his jacket and held it wide open. "Look, no guns," he said. Kay laughed.

It was getting late and they went up to their room. She mixed a drink for both of them and sat on his lap as they drank. Beneath her dress she was all silk until his hand touched the glowing skin of her thigh. They fell back on the bed together and made love with all their clothes on, their mouths glued together. When they were finished they lay very still, feeling the heat of their bodies burning through their garments. Kay murmured, "Is that what you soldiers call a quickie?"

"Yeah," Michael said.

"It's not bad," Kay said in a judicious voice.

They dozed off until Michael suddenly started up anxiously and looked at his watch. "Damn," he said. "It's nearly ten. I have to get down to the hospital." He went to the bathroom to wash up and comb his hair. Kay came in after him and put her arms around his waist from behind. "When are we going to get married?" she asked.

"Whenever you say," Michael said. "As soon as this family thing quiets down and my old man gets better. I think you'd better explain things to your parents though."

"What should I explain?" Kay said quietly.

Michael ran the comb through his hair. "Just say that you've met a brave, handsome guy of Italian descent. Top marks at Dartmouth. Distinguished Service Cross during the war plus the Purple Heart. Honest. Hard-working. But his father is a Mafia chief who has to kill bad people, sometimes bribe high government officials and in his line of work gets shot full of holes himself. But that has nothing to do with his honest hard-working son. Do you think you can remember all that?"

Kay let go his body and leaned against the door of the bathroom. "Is he really?" she said. "Does he really?" She paused. "Kill people?"

Michael finished combing his hair. "I don't really know," he said. "Nobody really knows. But I wouldn't be surprised."

Before he went out the door she asked, "When will I see you again?"

Michael kissed her. "I want you to go home and think things over in that little hick town of yours," he said. "I don't want you to get mixed up in this business in any way. After the Christmas holidays I'll be back at school and we'll get together up in Hanover. OK?"

"OK," she said. She watched him go out the door, saw him wave before he stepped into the elevator. She had never felt so close to him, never so much in love and if someone had told her she would not see Michael again until three years passed, she would not have been able to bear the anguish of it.

When Michael got out of the cab in front of the French Hospital he was surprised to see that the street was completely deserted. When he entered the hospital he was even more surprised to find the lobby empty. Damn it, what the hell were Clemenza and Tessio doing? Sure, they never went to West Point but they knew enough about tactics to have outposts. A couple of their men should have been in the lobby at least.

Even the latest visitors had departed, it was almost ten-thirty at night. Michael was tense and alert now. He didn't bother to stop at the information desk, he already knew his father's room number up on the fourth floor. He took the self-service elevator. Oddly enough nobody stopped him until he reached the nurses' station on the fourth floor. But he strode right past her query and on to his father's room. There was no one outside the door. Where the hell were the two detectives who were supposed to be waiting around to guard and question the old man? Where the hell were Tessio and Clemenza's people? Could there be someone inside the room? But the door was open. Michael went in. There was a figure in the bed and by the December moonlight straining through the window Michael could see his father's face. Even now it was impassive, the chest heaved shallowly with his uneven breath. Tubes hung from steel gallows beside the bed and ran into his nose. On the floor was a glass jar receiving the poisons emptied from his stomach by other tubes. Michael stayed there for a few moments to make sure his father was all right, then backed out of the room.

He told the nurse, "My name is Michael Corleone, I just want to sit with my father. What happened to the detectives who were supposed to be guarding him?"

The nurse was a pretty young thing with a great deal of confidence in the power of her office. "Oh, your father just had too many visitors, it interfered with the hospital service," she said. "The police came and made them all leave about ten minutes ago. And then just five minutes ago I had to call the detectives to the phone for an emergency alarm from their headquarters, and then they left too. But don't worry, I look in on your father often and I can hear any sound from his room. That's why we leave the doors open."

"Thank you," Michael said. "I'll sit with him for a little while. OK?"

She smiled at him. "Just for a little bit and then I'm afraid you'll have to leave. It's the rules, you know."

Michael went back into his father's room. He took the phone from its cradle and got the hospital operator to give him the house in Long Beach, the phone in the corner office room. Sonny answered. Michael whispered, "Sonny, I'm down at the hospital, I came down late. Sonny, there's nobody here. None of Tessio's people. No detectives at the door. The old man was completely unprotected." His voice was trembling.

There was a long silence and then Sonny's voice came, low and impressed, "This is Sollozzo's move you were talking about."

Michael said, "That's what I figured too. But how did he get the cops to clear everybody out and where did they go? What happened to Tessio's men? Jesus Christ, has that bastard Sollozzo got the New York Police Department in his pocket too?"

"Take it easy, kid." Sonny's voice was soothing. "We got lucky again with you going to visit the hospital so late. Stay in the old man's room. Lock the door from the inside. I'll have some men there inside of fifteen minutes, soon as I make some calls. Just sit tight and don't panic. OK, kid?"

"I won't panic," Michael said. For the first time since it had all started he felt a furious anger rising in him, a cold hatred for his father's enemies.

He hung up the phone and rang the buzzer for the nurse. He decided to use his own judgment and disregard Sonny's orders. When the nurse came in he said, "I don't want you to get frightened, but we have to move my father right away. To another room or another floor. Can you disconnect all these tubes so we can wheel the bed out?"

The nurse said, "That's ridiculous. We have to get permission from the doctor."

Michael spoke very quickly. "You've read about my father in the papers. You've seen that there's no one here tonight to guard him. Now I've just gotten word some men will come into the hospital to kill him. Please believe me and help me." He could be extraordinarily persuasive when he wanted to be.

The nurse said, "We don't have to disconnect the tubes. We can wheel the stand with the bed."

"Do you have an empty room?" Michael whispered.

"At the end of the hall," the nurse said.

It was done in a matter of moments, very quickly and very efficiently. Then Michael said to the nurse, "Stay here with him until help comes. If you're outside at your station you might get hurt."

At that moment he heard his father's voice from the bed, hoarse but full of strength, "Michael, is it you? What happened, what is it?"

Michael leaned over the bed. He took his father's hand in his. "It's Mike," he said. "Don't be afraid. Now listen, don't make any noise at all, especially if somebody calls out your name. Some people want to kill you, understand? But I'm here so don't be afraid."

Don Corleone, still not fully conscious of what had happened to him the day before, in terrible pain, yet smiled benevolently on his youngest son, wanting to tell him, but it was too much effort, "Why should I be afraid now? Strange men have come to kill me ever since I was twelve years old."

● ● ●

The hospital was small and private with just one entrance. Michael looked through the window down into the street. There was a curved courtyard that had steps leading down into the street and the street was empty of cars. But whoever came into the hospital would have to come through that entrance. He knew he didn't have much time so he ran out of the room and down the four flights and through the wide doors of the ground floor entrance. Off to the side he saw the ambulance yard and there was no car there, no ambulances either.

Michael stood on the sidewalk outside the hospital and lit a cigarette. He unbuttoned his coat and stood in the light of a lamppost so that his features could be seen. A young man was walking swiftly down from Ninth Avenue, a package under his arm. The young man wore a combat jacket and had a heavy shock of black hair. His face was familiar when he came under the lamplight but Michael could not place it. But the young man stopped in front of him and put out his hand, saying in a heavy Italian accent, "Don Michael, do you remember me? Enzo, the baker's helper to Nazorine the Paniterra; his son-in-law. Your father saved my life by getting the government to let me stay in America."

Michael shook his hand. He remembered him now.

Enzo went on, "I've come to pay my respects to your father. Will they let me into the hospital so late?"

Michael smiled and shook his head. "No, but thanks anyway. I'll tell the Don you came." A car came roaring down the street and Michael was instantly alert. He said to Enzo, "Leave here quickly. There may be trouble. You don't want to get involved with the police."

He saw the look of fear on the young Italian's face. Trouble with the police might mean being deported or refusal of citizenship. But the young man stood fast. He whispered in Italian. "If there's trouble I'll stay to help. I owe it to the Godfather."

Michael was touched. He was about to tell the young man to go away again, but then he thought, why not let him stay? Two men in front of the hospital might scare off any of Sollozzo's crew sent to do a job. One man almost certainly would not. He gave Enzo a cigarette and lit it for him. They both stood under the lamppost in the cold December night. The yellow panes of the hospital, bisected by the greens of Christmas decorations, twinkled down on them. They had almost finished their cigarettes when a long low black car turned into 30th Street from Ninth Avenue and cruised toward them, very close to the curb. It almost stopped. Michael peered to see their faces inside, his body flinching involuntarily. The car seemed about to stop, then speeded forward. Somebody had recognized him. Michael gave Enzo another cigarette and noticed that the baker's hands were shaking. To his surprise his own hands were steady.

They stayed in the street smoking for what was no more than ten minutes when suddenly the night air was split by a police siren. A patrol car made a screaming turn from Ninth Avenue and pulled up in front of the hospital. Two more squad cars followed right behind it. Suddenly the hospital entranceway was flooded with uniformed police and detectives. Michael heaved a sigh of relief. Good old Sonny must have gotten through right away. He moved forward to meet them.

Two huge, burly policemen grabbed his arms. Another frisked him. A massive police captain, gold braid on his cap, came up the steps, his men parting respectfully to leave a path. He was a vigorous man for his girth and despite the white hair that peeked out of his cap. His face was beefy red. He came up to Michael and said harshly, "I thought I got all you guinea hoods locked up. Who the hell are you and what are you doing here?"

One of the cops standing beside Michael said, "He's clean, Captain."

Michael didn't answer. He was studying this police captain, coldly searching his face, the metallic blue eyes. A detective in plain clothes said, "That's Michael Corleone, the Don's son."

Michael said quietly, "What happened to the detectives who were supposed to be guarding my father? Who pulled them off that detail?"

The police captain was choleric with rage. "You fucking hood, who the hell are you to tell me my business? I pulled them off. I don't give a shit how many dago gangsters kill each other. If it was up to me, I wouldn't lift a finger to keep your old man from getting knocked off. Now get the hell out of here. Get out of this street, you punk, and stay out of this hospital when it's not visiting hours."

Michael was still studying him intently. He was not angry at what this police captain was saying. His mind was racing furiously. Was it possible that Sollozzo had been in that first car and had seen him standing in front of the hospital? Was it possible that Sollozzo had then called this captain and said, "How come the Corleones' men are still around the hospital when I paid you to lock them up?" Was it possible that all had been carefully planned as Sonny had said? Everything fitted in. Still cool, he said to the captain, "I'm not leaving this hospital until you put guards around my father's room."

The captain didn't bother answering. He said to the detective standing beside him, "Phil, lock this punk up."

The detective said hesitantly, "The kid is clean, Captain. He's a war hero and he's never been mixed up in the rackets. The papers could make a stink."

The captain started to turn on the detective, his face red with fury. He roared out, "Goddamn it, I said lock him up."

Michael, still thinking clearly, not angry, said with deliberate malice, "How much is the Turk paying you to set my father up, Captain?"

The police captain turned to him. He said to the two burly patrolmen, "Hold him." Michael felt his arms pinned to his sides. He saw the captain's massive fist arching toward his face. He tried to weave away but the fist caught him high on the cheekbone. A grenade exploded in his skull. His mouth filled with blood and small hard bones that he realized were his teeth. He could feel the side of his head puff up as if it were filling with air. His legs were weightless and he would have fallen if the two policemen had not held him up. But he was still conscious. The plainclothes detective had stepped in front of him to keep the captain from hitting him again and was saying, "Jesus Christ, Captain, you really hurt him."

The captain said loudly, "I didn't touch him. He attacked me and he fell. Do you understand that? He resisted arrest."

Through a red haze Michael could see more cars pulling up to the curb. Men were getting out. One of them he recognized as Clemenza's lawyer, who was now speaking to the police captain, suavely and surely. "The Corleone Family has hired a firm of private detectives to guard Mr. Corleone. These men with me are licensed to carry firearms, Captain. If you arrest them, you'll have to appear before a judge in the morning and tell him why."

The lawyer glanced at Michael. "Do you want to prefer charges against whoever did this to you?" he asked.

Michael had trouble talking. His jaws wouldn't come together but he managed to mumble. "I slipped," he said. "I slipped and fell." He saw the captain give him a triumphant glance and he tried to answer that glance with a smile. At all costs he wanted to hide the delicious icy chilliness that controlled his brain, the surge of wintry cold hatred that pervaded his body. He wanted to give no warning to anyone in this world as to how he felt at this moment. As the Don would not. Then he felt himself carried into the hospital and he lost consciousness.

When he woke up in the morning he found that his jaw had been wired together and that four of his teeth along the left side of his mouth were missing. Hagen was sitting beside his bed.

"Did they drug me up?" Michael asked.

"Yeah," Hagen said. "They had to dig some bone fragments out of your gums and they figured it would be too painful. Besides you were practically out anyway."

"Is there anything else wrong with me?" Michael asked.

"No," Hagen said. "Sonny wants you out at the Long Beach house. Think you can make it?"

"Sure," Michael said. "Is the Don all right?"

Hagen flushed. "I think we've solved the problem now. We have a firm of private detectives and we have the whole area loaded. I'll tell you more when we get in the car."

Clemenza was driving, Michael and Hagen sat in the back. Michael's head throbbed. "So what the hell really happened last night, did you guys ever find out?"

Hagen spoke quietly. "Sonny has an inside man, that Detective Phillips who tried to protect you. He gave us the scoop. The police captain, McCluskey, is a guy who's been on the take very heavy ever since he's been a patrolman. Our Family has paid him quite a bit. And he's greedy and untrustworthy to do business with. But Sollozzo must have paid him a big price. McCluskey had all Tessio's men around and in the hospital arrested right after visiting hours. It didn't help that some of them were carrying guns. Then McCluskey pulled the official guard detectives off the Don's door. Claimed he needed them and that some other cops were supposed to go over and take their place but they got their assignments bollixed. Baloney. He was paid off to set the Don up. And Phillips said he's the kind of guy who'll try it again. Sollozzo must have given him a fortune for openers and promised him the moon to come."

"Was my getting hurt in the papers?"

"No," Hagen said. "We kept that quiet. Nobody wants that known. Not the cops. Not us."

"Good," Michael said. "Did that boy Enzo get away?"

"Yeah," Hagen said. "He was smarter than you. When the cops came he disappeared. He claims he stuck with you while Sollozzo's car went by. Is that true?"

"Yeah," Michael said. "He's a good kid."

"He'll be taken care of," Hagen said. "You feeling OK?" His face was concerned. "You look lousy."

"I'm OK," Michael said. "What was that police captain's name?"

"McCluskey," Hagen said. "By the way, it might make you feel better to know that the Corleone Family finally got up on the scoreboard. Bruno Tattaglia, four o'clock this morning."

Michael sat up. "How come? I thought we were supposed to sit tight."

Hagen shrugged. "After what happened at the hospital Sonny got hard. The button men are out all over New York and New Jersey. We made the list last night. I'm trying to hold Sonny in, Mike. Maybe you can talk to him. This whole business can still be settled without a major war."

"I'll talk to him," Michael said. "Is there a conference this morning?"

"Yeah," Hagen said. "Sollozzo finally got in touch and wants to sit down with us. A negotiator is arranging the details. That means we win. Sollozzo knows he's lost and he wants to get out with his life." Hagen paused. "Maybe he thought we were soft, ready to be taken, because we didn't strike back. Now with one of the Tattaglia sons dead he knows we mean business. He really took an awful gamble bucking the Don. By the way, we got the confirmation on Luca. They killed him the night before they shot your father. In Bruno's nightclub. Imagine that?"

Michael said, "No wonder they caught him off guard."

At the houses in Long Beach the entrance to the mall was blocked by a long black car parked across its mouth. Two men leaned against the hood of the car. The two houses on each side, Michael noticed, had opened windows on their upper floors. Christ, Sonny must really mean business.

Clemenza parked the car outside the mall and they walked inside it. The two guards were Clemenza's men and he gave them a frown of greeting that served as a salute. The men nodded their heads in acknowledgment. There were no smiles, no greetings. Clemenza led Hagen and Michael Corleone into the house.

The door was opened by another guard before they rang. He had obviously been watching from a window. They went to the corner office and found Sonny and Tessio waiting for them. Sonny came to Michael, took his younger brother's head in his hands and said kiddingly, "Beautiful. Beautiful." Michael knocked his hands away, and went to the desk and poured himself some scotch, hoping it would dull the ache in his wired jaw.

The five of them sat around the room but the atmosphere was different from their earlier meetings. Sonny was gayer, more cheerful, and Michael realized what that gaiety meant. There were no longer any doubts in his older brother's mind. He was committed and nothing would sway him. The attempt by Sollozzo the night before was the final straw. There could no longer be any question of a truce.

"We got a call from the negotiator while you were gone," Sonny said to Hagen. "The Turk wants a meeting now." Sonny laughed. "The balls on that son of a bitch," he said admiringly. "After he craps out last night he wants a meeting today or the next day. Meanwhile we're supposed just to lay back and take everything he dishes out. What fucking nerve."

Tom asked cautiously, "What did you answer?"

Sonny grinned. "I said sure, why not? Anytime he says, I'm in no hurry. I've got a hundred button men out on the street twenty-four hours a day. If Sollozzo shows one hair on his asshole he's dead. Let them take all the time they want."

Hagen said, "Was there a definite proposal?"

"Yeah," Sonny said. "He wants us to send Mike to meet him to hear his proposition. The negotiator guarantees Mike's safety. Sollozzo doesn't ask us to guarantee his safety; he knows he can't ask that. No point. So the meeting will be arranged on his side. His people will pick Mike up and take Mike to the meeting place. Mike will listen to Sollozzo and then they'll turn him loose. But the meeting place is secret. The promise is the deal will be so good we can't turn it down."

Hagen asked, "What about the Tattaglias? What will they do about Bruno?"

"That's part of the deal. The negotiator says the Tattaglia Family has agreed to go along with Sollozzo. They'll forget about Bruno Tattaglia. He pays for what they did to my father. One cancels out the other." Sonny laughed again. "The nervy bastards."

Hagen said cautiously, "We should hear what they have to say."

Sonny shook his head from side to side. "No, no, *Consigliere*, not this time." His voice held a faint trace of Italian accent. He was consciously mocking his father just to kid around. "No more meetings. No more discussions. No more Sollozzo tricks. When the negotiator gets in touch with us again for our answer I want you to give him one message. I want Sollozzo. If not, it's all-out war. We'll go to the mattresses and we'll put all the button men out on the street. Business will just have to suffer."

"The other Families won't stand for an all-out war," Hagen said. "It puts too much heat on everybody."

Sonny shrugged. "They have a simple solution. Give me Sollozzo. Or fight the Corleone Family." Sonny paused, then said roughly, "No more advice on how to patch it up, Tom. The decision is made. Your job is to help me win. Understand?"

Hagen bowed his head. He was deep in thought for a moment. Then he said, "I spoke to your contact in the police station. He says that Captain McCluskey is definitely on Sollozzo's payroll and for big money. Not only that, but McCluskey is going to get a piece of the drug operation. McCluskey has agreed to be Sollozzo's bodyguard. The Turk doesn't poke his nose out of his hole without McCluskey. When he meets Mike for the conference, McCluskey will be sitting beside him. In civilian clothes but carrying his gun. Now what you have to understand, Sonny, is that while Sollozzo is guarded like this, he's invulnerable. Nobody has ever gunned down a New York police captain and gotten away with it. The heat in this town would be unbearable what with the newspapers, the whole police department, the churches, everything. That would be disastrous. The Families would be after you. The Corleone Family would become outcasts. Even the old man's political protection would run for cover. So take that into consideration."

Sonny shrugged. "McCluskey can't stay with the Turk forever. We'll wait."

Tessio and Clemenza were puffing on their cigars uneasily, not daring to speak, but sweating. It would be their skins that would go on the line if the wrong decision was made.

Michael spoke for the first time. He asked Hagen, "Can the old man be moved out of the hospital onto the mall here?"

Hagen shook his head. "That's the first thing I asked. Impossible. He's in very bad shape. He'll pull through but he needs all kinds of attention, maybe some more surgery. Impossible."

"Then you have to get Sollozzo right away," Michael said. "We can't wait. The guy is too dangerous. He'll come up with some new idea. Remember, the key is still that he gets rid of the old man. He knows that. OK, he knows that now it's very tough so he's willing to take defeat for his life. But if he's going to get killed anyway, he'll have another crack at the Don. And with that police captain helping him who knows what the hell might happen. We can't take that chance. We have to get Sollozzo right away."

Sonny was scratching his chin thoughtfully. "You're right, kid," he said. "You got right to the old nuts. We can't let Sollozzo get another crack at the old man."

Hagen said quietly, "What about Captain McCluskey?"

Sonny turned to Michael with an odd little smile. "Yeah, kid, what about that tough police captain?"

Michael said slowly, "OK, it's an extreme. But there are times when the most extreme measures are justified. Let's think now that we have to kill McCluskey. The way to do it would be to have him heavily implicated so that it's not an honest police captain doing his duty but a crooked police official mixed up in the rackets who got what was coming to him, like any crook. We have newspaper people on our payroll we can give that story to with enough proof so that they can back it up. That should take some of the heat off. How does that sound?" Michael looked around deferentially to the others. Tessio and Clemenza had gloomy faces and refused to speak. Sonny said with the same odd smile, "Go on, kid, you're doing great. Out of the mouths of infants, as the Don always used to say. Go ahead, Mike, tell us more."

Hagen was smiling too a little and averting his head. Michael flushed. "Well, they want me to go to a conference with Sollozzo. It will be me, Sollozzo and McCluskey all on our own. Set up the meeting for two days from now, then get our informers to find out where the meeting will be held. Insist that it has to be a public place, that I'm not going to let them take me into any apartments or houses. Let it be a restaurant or a bar at the height of the dinner hour, something like that, so that I'll feel safe. They'll feel safe too. Even Sollozzo won't figure that we'll dare to gun the captain. They'll frisk me when I meet them so I'll have to be clean then, but figure out a way you can get a weapon to me while I'm meeting them. Then I'll take both of them."

All four heads turned and stared at him. Clemenza and Tessio were gravely astonished. Hagen looked a little sad but not surprised. He started to speak and thought better of it. But Sonny, his heavy Cupid's face twitching with mirth, suddenly broke out in loud roars of laughter. It was deep belly laughter, not faking. He was really breaking up. He pointed a finger at Michael, trying to speak through gasps of mirth. "You, the high-class college kid, you never wanted to get mixed up in the Family business. Now you wanta kill a police captain and the Turk just because you got your face smashed by McCluskey. You're taking it personal, it's just business and you're taking it personal. You wanta kill these two guys just because you got slapped in the face. It was all a lot of crap. All these years it was just a lot of crap."

Clemenza and Tessio, completely misunderstanding, thinking that Sonny was laughing at his young brother's bravado for making such an offer, were also smiling broadly and a little patronizingly at Michael. Only Hagen warily kept his face impassive.

Michael looked around at all of them, then stared at Sonny, who still couldn't stop laughing. "*You'll* take both of them?" Sonny said. "Hey, kid, they won't give you medals, they put you in the electric chair. You know that? This is no hero business, kid, you don't shoot people from a mile away. You shoot when you see the whites of their eyes like we got taught in school, remember? You gotta stand right next to them and blow their heads off and their brains get all over your nice Ivy League suit. How about that, kid, you wanta do that just because some dumb cop slapped you around?" He was still laughing.

Michael stood up. "You'd better stop laughing," he said. The change in him was so extraordinary that the smiles vanished from the faces of Clemenza and Tessio. Michael was not tall or heavily built but his presence seemed to radiate danger. In that moment he was a reincarnation of Don Corleone himself. His eyes had gone a pale tan and his face was bleached of color. He seemed at any moment about to fling himself on his older and stronger brother. There was no doubt that if he had had a weapon in his hands Sonny would have been in danger. Sonny stopped laughing, and Michael said to him in a cold deadly voice, "Don't you think I can do it, you son of a bitch?"

Sonny had got over his laughing fit. "I know you can do it," he said. "I wasn't laughing at what you said. I was just laughing at how funny things turn out. I always said you were the toughest one in the Family, tougher than the Don himself. You were the only one who could stand off the old man. I remember you when you were a kid. What a temper you had then. Hell, you even used to fight me and I was a lot older than you. And Freddie had to beat the shit out of you at least once a week. And now Sollozzo has you figured for the soft touch in the Family because you let McCluskey hit you without fighting back and you wouldn't get mixed up in the Family fights. He figures he got nothing to worry about if he meets you head to head. And McCluskey too, he's got you figured for a yellow guinea." Sonny paused and then said softly, "But you're a Corleone after all, you son of a bitch. And I was the only one who knew it. I've been sitting here waiting for the last three days, ever since the old man got shot, waiting for you to crack out of that Ivy League, war hero bullshit character you've been wearing. I've been waiting for you to become my right arm so we can kill those fucks that are trying to destroy our father and our Family. And all it took was a sock on the jaw. How do you like that?" Sonny made a comical gesture, a punch, and repeated, "How do you like that?"

The tension had relaxed in the room. Mike shook his head. "Sonny, I'm doing it because it's the only thing to do. I can't give Sollozzo another crack at the old man. I seem to be the only one who can get close enough to him. And I figured it out. I don't think you can get anybody else to knock off a police captain. Maybe you would do it, Sonny, but you have a wife and kids and you have to run the Family business until the old man is in shape. So that leaves me and Freddie. Freddie is in shock and out of action. Finally that leaves just me. It's all logic. The sock on the jaw had nothing to do with it."

Sonny came over and embraced him. "I don't give a damn what your reasons are, just so long as you're with us now. And I'll tell you another thing, you're right all the way. Tom, what's your say?"

Hagen shrugged. "The reasoning is solid. What makes it so is that I don't think the Turk is sincere about a deal. I think he'll still try to get at the Don. Anyway on his past performance that's how we have to figure him. So we try to get Sollozzo. We get him even if we have to get the police captain. But whoever does the job is going to get an awful lot of heat. Does it have to be Mike?"

Sonny said softly, "I could do it."

Hagen shook his head impatiently. "Sollozzo wouldn't let you get within a mile of him if he had ten police captains. And besides you're the acting head of the Family. You can't be risked." Hagen paused and said to Clemenza and Tessio, "Do either one of you have a top button man, someone really special, who would take on this job? He wouldn't have to worry about money for the rest of his life."

Clemenza spoke first. "Nobody that Sollozzo wouldn't know, he'd catch on right away. He'd catch on if me or Tessio went too."

Hagen said, "What about somebody really tough who hasn't made his rep yet, a good rookie?"

Both *caporegimes* shook their heads. Tessio smiled to take the sting out of his words and said, "That's like bringing a guy up from the minors to pitch the World Series."

Sonny broke in curtly, "It has to be Mike. For a million different reasons. Most important they got him down as faggy. And he can do the job, I guarantee that, and that's important because this is the only shot we'll get at that sneaky bastard Turk. So now we have to figure out the best way to back him up. Tom, Clemenza, Tessio, find out where Sollozzo will take him for the conference, I don't care how much it costs. When we find that out we can figure out how we can get a weapon into his hands. Clemenza, I want you to get him a really 'safe' gun out of your collection, the 'coldest' one you got. Impossible to trace. Try to make it short barrel with a lot of blasting power. It doesn't have to be accurate. He'll be right on top of them when he uses it. Mike, as soon as you've used the gun, drop it on the floor. Don't be caught with it on you. Clemenza, tape the barrel and the trigger with that special stuff you got so he won't leave prints. Remember, Mike, we can square everything, witnesses, and so forth, but if they catch you with the gun on you we can't square that. We'll have transportation and protection and then we'll make you disappear for a nice long vacation until the heat wears off. You'll be gone a long time, Mike, but I don't want you saying good-bye to your girl friend or even calling her. After it's all over and you're out of the country I'll send her word that you're OK. Those are orders." Sonny smiled at his brother. "Now stick with Clemenza and get used to handling the gun he picks out for you. Maybe even practice a little. We'll take care of everything else. Everything. OK, kid?"

Again Michael Corleone felt that delicious refreshing chilliness all over his body. He said to his brother, "You didn't have to give me that crap about not talking to my girl friend about something like this. What the hell did you think I was going to do, call her up to say good-bye?"

Sonny said hastily, "OK, but you're still a rookie so I spell things out. Forget it."

Michael said with a grin, "What the hell do you mean, a rookie? I listened to the old man just as hard as you did. How do you think I got so smart?" They both laughed.

Hagen poured drinks for everyone. He looked a little glum. The statesman forced to go to war, the lawyer forced to go to law. "Well, anyway, now we know what we're going to do," he said.

Captain Mark McCluskey sat in his office fingering three envelopes bulging with betting slips. He was frowning and wishing he could decode the notations on the slips. It was very important that he do so. The envelopes were the betting slips that his raiding parties had picked up when they had hit one of the Corleone Family bookmakers the night before. Now the bookmaker would have to buy back the slips so that players couldn't claim winners and wipe him out.

It was very important for Captain McCluskey to decode the slips because he didn't want to get cheated when he sold the slips back to the bookmaker. If there was fifty grand worth of action, then maybe he could sell it back for five grand. But if there were a lot of heavy bets and the slips represented a hundred grand or maybe even two hundred grand, then the price should be considerably higher. McCluskey fiddled with the envelopes and then decided to let the bookie sweat a little bit and make the first offer. That might tip off what the real price should be.

McCluskey looked at the station house clock on the wall of his office. It was time for him to pick up that greasy Turk, Sollozzo, and take him to wherever he was going to meet the Corleone Family. McCluskey went over to his wall locker and started to change into his civilian clothes. When he was finished he called his wife and told her he would not be home for supper that night, that he would be out on the job. He never confided in his wife on anything. She thought they lived the way they did on his policeman's salary. McCluskey grunted with amusement. His mother had thought the same thing but he had learned early. His father had shown him the ropes.

His father had been a police sergeant, and every week father and son had walked through the precinct and McCluskey Senior had introduced his six-year-old son to the storekeepers, saying, "And this is my little boy."

The storekeepers would shake his hand and compliment him extravagantly and ring open their cash registers to give the little boy a gift of five or ten dollars. At the end of the day, little Mark McCluskey would have all the pockets of his suit stuffed with paper money, would feel so proud that his father's friends liked him well enough to give him a present every month they saw him. Of course his father put the money in the bank for him, for his college education, and little Mark got at most a fifty-cent piece for himself.

Then when Mark got home and his policemen uncles asked him what he wanted to be when he grew up and he would lisp childishly, "A policeman," they would all laugh uproariously. And of course later on, though his father wanted him to go to college first, he went right from high school to studying for the police force.

He had been a good cop, a brave cop. The tough young punks terrorizing street corners fled when he approached and finally vanished from his beat altogether. He was a very tough cop and a very fair one. He never took his son around to the storekeepers to collect his money presents for ignoring garbage violations and parking violations; he took the money directly into his own hand, direct because he felt he earned it. He never ducked into a movie house or goofed off into restaurants when he was on foot patrol as some of the other cops did, especially on winter nights. He always made his rounds. He gave his stores a lot of protection, a lot of service. When winos and drunks filtered up from the Bowery to panhandle on his beat he got rid of them so roughly that they never came back. The tradespeople in his precinct appreciated it. And they showed their appreciation.

He also obeyed the system. The bookies in his precinct knew he would never make trouble to get an extra payoff for himself, that he was content with his share of the station house bag. His name was on the list with the others and he never tried to make extras. He was a fair cop who took only clean graft and his rise in the police department was steady if not spectacular.

During this time he was raising a large family of four sons, none of whom became policemen. They all went to Fordham University and since by that time Mark McCluskey was rising from sergeant to lieutenant and finally to captain, they lacked for nothing. It was at this time that McCluskey got the reputation for being a hard bargainer. The bookmakers in his district paid more protection money than the bookmakers in any other part of the city, but maybe that was because of the expense of putting four boys through college.

McCluskey himself felt there was nothing wrong with clean graft. Why the hell should his kids go to CCNY or a cheap Southern college just because the Police Department didn't pay its people enough money to live on and take care of their families properly? He protected all these people with his life and his record showed his citations for gun duels with stickup men on his beat, strong-arm protection guys, would-be pimps. He had hammered them into the ground. He had kept his little corner of the city safe for ordinary people and he sure as hell was entitled to more than his lousy one C note a week. But he wasn't indignant about his low pay, he understood that everybody had to take care of themselves.

Bruno Tattaglia was an old friend of his. Bruno had gone to Fordham with one of his sons and then Bruno had opened his night-club and whenever the McCluskey family spent an infrequent night on the town, they could enjoy the cabaret with liquor and dinner—on the house. On New Year's Eve they received engraved invitations to be guests of the management and always received one of the best tables. Bruno always made sure they were introduced to the celebrities who performed in his club, some of them famous singers and Hollywood stars. Of course sometimes he asked a little favor, like getting an employee with a record cleared for a cabaret work license, usually a pretty girl with a police dossier as a hustler or roller. McCluskey would be glad to oblige.

McCluskey made it a policy never to show that he understood what other people were up to. When Sollozzo had approached him with the proposition to leave old man Corleone uncovered in the hospital, McCluskey didn't ask why. He asked price. When Sollozzo said ten grand, McCluskey knew why. He did not hesitate. Corleone was one of the biggest Mafia men in the country with more political connections than Capone had ever had. Whoever knocked him off would be doing the country a big favor. McCluskey took the money in advance and did the job. When he received a call from Sollozzo that there were still two of Corleone's men in front of the hospital he had flown into a rage. He had locked up all of Tessio's men, he had pulled the detective guards off the door of Corleone's hospital room. And now, being a man of principle, he would have to give back the ten grand, money he had already earmarked to insure the education of his grandchildren. It was in that rage that he had gone to the hospital and struck Michael Corleone.

But it had all worked out for the best. He had met with Sollozzo in the Tattaglia nightclub and they had made an even better deal. Again McCluskey didn't ask questions, since he knew all the answers. He just made sure of his price. It never occurred to him that he himself could be in any danger. That anyone would consider even for a moment killing a New York City police captain was too fantastic. The toughest hood in the Mafia had to stand still if the lowliest patrolman decided to slap him around. There was absolutely no percentage in killing cops. Because then all of a sudden a lot of hoods were killed resisting arrest or escaping the scene of a crime, and who the hell was going to do anything about that?

McCluskey sighed and got ready to leave the station house. Problems, always problems. His wife's sister in Ireland had just died after many years of fighting cancer and that cancer had cost him a pretty penny. Now the funeral would cost him more. His own uncles and aunts in the old country needed a little help now and then to keep their potato farms and he sent the money to do the trick. He didn't begrudge it. And when he and his wife visited the old country they were treated like a king and queen. Maybe they would go again this summer now that the war was over and with all this extra money coming in. McCluskey told his patrolman clerk where he would be if he was needed. He did not feel it necessary to take any precautions. He could always claim Sollozzo was an informer he was meeting. Outside the station house he walked a few blocks and then caught a cab to the house where he would meet with Sollozzo.

It was Tom Hagen who had to make all the arrangements for Michael's leaving the country, his false passport, his seaman's card, his berth on an Italian freighter that would dock in a Sicilian port. Emissaries were sent that very day by plane to Sicily to prepare a hiding place with the Mafia chief in the hill country.

Sonny arranged for a car and an absolutely trustworthy driver to be waiting for Michael when he stepped out of the restaurant where the meeting would be held with Sollozzo. The driver would be Tessio himself, who had volunteered for the job. It would be a beat-up-looking car but with a fine motor. It would have phony license plates and the car itself would be untraceable. It had been saved for a special job requiring the best.

Michael spent the day with Clemenza, practicing with the small gun that would be gotten to him. It was a .22 filled with soft-nosed bullets that made pinpricks going in and left insulting gaping holes when they exited from the human body. He found that it was accurate up to five of his steps away from a target. After that the bullets might go any-where. The trigger was tight but Clemenza worked on this with some tools so that it pulled easier. They decided to leave it noisy. They didn't want an innocent bystander misunderstanding the situation and inter-fering out of ignorant courage. The report of the gun would keep them away from Michael.

Clemenza kept instructing him during the training session. "Drop the gun as soon as you've finished using it. Just let your hand drop to your side and the gun slip out. Nobody will notice. Everybody will think you're still armed. They'll be staring at your face. Walk out of the place very quickly but don't run. Don't look anybody directly in the eye but don't look away from them either. Remember, they'll be scared of you, believe me, they'll be scared of you. Nobody will interfere. As soon as you're outside Tessio will be in the car waiting for you. Get in and leave the rest to him. Don't be worried about accidents. You'd be surprised how well these affairs go. Now put this hat on and let's see how you look." He clapped a gray fedora on Michael's head. Michael, who never wore a hat, grimaced. Clemenza reassured him. "It helps against identification, just in case. Mostly it gives witnesses an excuse to change their identification when we make them see the light. Remember, Mike, don't worry about prints. The butt and trigger are fixed with special tape. Don't touch any other part of the gun, remember that."

Michael said, "Has Sonny found out where Sollozzo is taking me?"

Clemenza shrugged. "Not yet. Sollozzo is being very careful. But don't worry about him harming you. The negotiator stays in our

hands until you come back safe. If anything happens to you, the negotiator pays."

"Why the hell should he stick his neck out?" Michael asked.

"He gets a big fee," Clemenza said. "A small fortune. Also he is an
important man in the Families. He knows Sollozzo can't let anything
happen to him. Your life is not worth the negotiator's life to Sollozzo.
Very simple. You'll be safe all right. We're the ones who catch hell
afterwards."

"How bad will it be?" Michael asked.

"Very bad," Clemenza said. "It means an all-out war with the
Tattaglia Family against the Corleone Family. Most of the others will
line up with the Tattaglias. The Sanitation Department will be
sweeping up a lot of dead bodies this winter." He shrugged. "These
things have to happen once every ten years or so. It gets rid of the bad
blood. And then if we let them push us around on the little things they
wanta take over everything. You gotta stop them at the beginning. Like
they shoulda stopped Hitler at Munich, they should never let him get
away with that, they were just asking for big trouble when they let him
get away with that."

Michael had heard his father say this same thing before, only in
1939 before the war actually started. If the Families had been running
the State Department there would never have been World War II, he
thought with a grin.

They drove back to the mall and to the Don's house, where Sonny
still made his headquarters. Michael wondered how long Sonny could
stay cooped up in the safe territory of the mall. Eventually he would
have to venture out. They found Sonny taking a nap on the couch. On
the coffee table was the remains of his late lunch, scraps of steak and
bread crumbs and a half-empty bottle of whiskey.

His father's usually neat office was taking on the look of a badly
kept furnished room. Michael shook his brother awake and said, "Why
don't you stop living like a bum and get this place cleaned up?"

Sonny yawned. "What the hell are you, inspecting the barracks?
Mike, we haven't got the word yet where they plan to take you, those

bastards Sollozzo and McCluskey. If we don't find that out, how the hell are we going to get the gun to you?"

"Can't I carry it on me?" Michael asked. "Maybe they won't frisk me and even if they do maybe they'll miss it if we're smart enough. And even if they find it—so what. They'll just take it off me and no harm done."

Sonny shook his head. "Nah," he said. "We have to make this a sure hit on that bastard Sollozzo. Remember, get him first if you possibly can. McCluskey is slower and dumber. You should have plenty of time to take him. Did Clemenza tell you to be sure to drop the gun?"

"A million times," Michael said.

Sonny got up from the sofa and stretched. "How does your jaw feel, kid?"

"Lousy," Michael said. The left side of his face ached except those parts that felt numb because of the drugged wire holding it together. He took the bottle of whiskey from the table and swigged directly from it. The pain eased.

Sonny said, "Easy, Mike, now is no time to get slowed up by booze."

Michael said, "Oh, Christ, Sonny, stop playing the big brother. I've been in combat against tougher guys than Sollozzo and under worse conditions. Where the hell are his mortars? Has he got air cover? Heavy artillery? Land mines? He's just a wise son of a bitch with a big-wheel cop sidekick. Once anybody makes up their mind to kill them there's no other problem. That's the hard part, making up your mind. They'll never know what hit them."

Tom Hagen came into the room. He greeted them with a nod and went directly to the falsely listed telephone. He called a few times and then shook his head at Sonny. "Not a whisper," he said. "Sollozzo is keeping it to himself as long as he can."

The phone rang. Sonny answered it and he held up a hand as if to signal for quiet though no one had spoken. He jotted some notes down on a pad, then said, "OK, he'll be there," and hung up the phone.

Sonny was laughing. "That son of a bitch Sollozzo, he really is something. Here's the deal. At eight tonight he and Captain McCluskey pick up Mike in front of Jack Dempsey's bar on Broadway. They go someplace to talk, and get this. Mike and Sollozzo talk in Italian so that the Irish cop don't know what the hell they are talking about. He even tells me, don't worry, he knows McCluskey doesn't know one word in Italian unless it's 'soldi' and he's checked you out, Mike, and knows you can understand Sicilian dialect."

Michael said dryly, "I'm pretty rusty, but we won't talk long."

Tom Hagen said, "We don't let Mike go until we have the negotiator. Is that arranged?"

Clemenza nodded. "The negotiator is at my house playing pinochle with three of my men. They wait for a call from me before they let him go."

Sonny sank back in the leather armchair. "Now how the hell do we find out the meeting place? Tom, we've got informers with the Tattaglia Family, how come they haven't given us the word?"

Hagen shrugged. "Sollozzo is really damn smart. He's playing this close to the vest, so close that he's not using any men as a cover. He figures the captain will be enough and that security is more important than guns. He's right too. We'll have to put a tail on Mike and hope for the best."

Sonny shook his head. "Nah, anybody can lose a tail when they really want to. That's the first thing they'll check out."

By this time it was five in the afternoon. Sonny, with a worried look on his face, said, "Maybe we should just let Mike blast whoever is in the car when it tries to pick him up."

Hagen shook his head. "What if Sollozzo is not in the car? We've tipped our hand for nothing. Damn it, we have to find out where Sollozzo is taking him."

Clemenza put in, "Maybe we should start trying to figure why he's making it such a big secret."

Michael said impatiently, "Because it's the percentage. Why should he let us know anything if he can prevent it? Besides, he smells danger. He must be leery as hell even with that police captain for his shadow."

Hagen snapped his fingers. "That detective, that guy Phillips. Why don't you give him a ring, Sonny? Maybe he can find out where the hell the captain can be reached. It's worth a try. McCluskey won't give a damn who knows where he's going."

Sonny picked up the phone and dialed a number. He spoke softly into the phone, then hung up. "He'll call us back," Sonny said.

They waited for nearly another thirty minutes and then the phone rang. It was Phillips. Sonny jotted something down on his pad and then hung up. His face was taut. "I think we've got it," he said. "Captain McCluskey always has to leave word on where he can be reached. From eight to ten tonight he'll be at the Luna Azure up in the Bronx. Anybody know it?"

Tessio spoke confidently. "I do. It's perfect for us. A small family place with big booths where people can talk in private. Good food. Everybody minds their own business. Perfect." He leaned over Sonny's desk and arranged stubbed-out cigarettes into map figures. "This is the entrance. Mike, when you finish just walk out and turn left, then turn the corner. I'll spot you and put on my headlights and catch you on the fly. If you have any trouble, yell and I'll try to come in and get you out. Clemenza, you gotta work fast. Send somebody up there to plant the gun. They got an old-fashioned toilet with a space between the water container and the wall. Have your man tape the gun behind there. Mike, after they frisk you in the car and find you're clean, they won't be too worried about you. In the restaurant, wait a bit before you excuse yourself. No, better still, ask permission to go. Act a little in trouble first, very natural. They can't figure anything. But when you come out again, don't waste any time. Don't sit down again at the table, start blasting. And don't take chances. In the head, two shots apiece, and out as fast as your legs can travel."

Sonny had been listening judiciously. "I want somebody very good, very safe, to plant that gun," he told Clemenza. "I don't want my brother coming out of that toilet with just his dick in his hand."

Clemenza said emphatically, "The gun will be there."

"OK," Sonny said. "Everybody get rolling."

Tessio and Clemenza left. Tom Hagen said, "Sonny, should I drive Mike down to New York?"

"No," Sonny said. "I want you here. When Mike finishes, then our work begins and I'll need you. Have you got those newspaper guys lined up?"

Hagen nodded. "I'll be feeding them info as soon as things break."

Sonny got up and came to stand in front of Michael. He shook his hand. "OK, kid," he said, "you're on. I'll square it with Mom your not seeing her before you left. And I'll get a message to your girl friend when I think the time is right. OK?"

"OK," Mike said. "How long do you think before I can come back?"

"At least a year," Sonny said.

Tom Hagen put in, "The Don might be able to work faster than that, Mike, but don't count on it. The time element hinges on a lot of factors. How well we can plant stories with the newsmen. How much the Police Department wants to cover up. How violently the other Families react. There's going to be a hell of a lot of heat and trouble. That's the only thing we can be sure of."

Michael shook Hagen's hand. "Do your best," he said. "I don't want to do another three-year stretch away from home."

Hagen said gently, "It's not too late to back out, Mike, we can get somebody else, we can go back over our alternatives. Maybe it's not necessary to get rid of Sollozzo."

Michael laughed. "We can talk ourselves into any viewpoint," he said. "But we figured it right the first time. I've been riding the gravy train all my life, it's about time I paid my dues."

"You shouldn't let that broken jaw influence you," Hagen said. "McCluskey is a stupid man and it was business, not personal."

For the second time he saw Michael Corleone's face freeze into a mask that resembled uncannily the Don's. "Tom, don't let anybody kid you. It's all personal, every bit of business. Every piece of shit every man has to eat every day of his life is personal. They call it business. OK. But it's personal as hell. You know where I learned that from? The Don. My old man. The Godfather. If a bolt of lightning hit a friend of his the old man would take it personal. He took my going into the Marines personal. That's what makes him great. The Great Don. He takes everything personal. Like God. He knows every feather that falls from the tail of a sparrow or however the hell it goes. Right? And you know something? Accidents don't happen to people who take accidents as a personal insult. So I came late, OK, but I'm coming all the way. Damn right, I take that broken jaw personal; damn right, I take Sollozzo trying to kill my father personal." He laughed. "Tell the old man I learned it all from him and that I'm glad I had this chance to pay him back for all he did for me. He was a good father." He paused and then he said thoughtfully to Hagen, "You know, I can never remember him hitting me. Or Sonny. Or Freddie. And of course Connie, he wouldn't even yell at her. And tell me the truth, Tom, how many men do you figure the Don killed or had killed."

Tom Hagen turned away. "I'll tell you one thing you didn't learn from him: talking the way you're talking now. There are things that have to be done and you do them and you never talk about them. You don't try to justify them. They can't be justified. You just do them. Then you forget it."

Michael Corleone frowned. He said quietly, "As the *Consigliere*, you agree that it's dangerous to the Don and our Family to let Sollozzo live?"

"Yes," Hagen said.

"OK," Michael said. "Then I have to kill him."

Michael Corleone stood in front of Jack Dempsey's restaurant on Broadway and waited for his pickup. He looked at his watch. It said five minutes to eight. Sollozzo was going to be punctual. Michael had made sure he was there in plenty of time. He had been waiting fifteen minutes.

All during the ride from Long Beach into the city he had been trying to forget what he had said to Hagen. For if he believed what he said, then his life was set on an irrevocable course. And yet, could it be otherwise after tonight? He might be dead after tonight if he didn't stop all this crap, Michael thought grimly. He had to keep his mind on the business at hand. Sollozzo was no dummy and McCluskey was a very tough egg. He felt the ache in his wired jaw and welcomed the pain, it would keep him alert.

Broadway wasn't that crowded on this cold winter night, even though it was near theater time. Michael flinched as a long black car pulled up to the curb and the driver, leaning over, opened the front door and said, "Get in, Mike." He didn't know the driver, a young punk with slick black hair and an open shirt, but he got in. In the back seat were Captain McCluskey and Sollozzo.

Sollozzo reached a hand over the back of the seat and Michael shook it. The hand was firm, warm and dry. Sollozzo said, "I'm glad you came, Mike. I hope we can straighten everything out. All this is terrible, it's not the way I wanted things to happen at all. It should never have happened."

Michael Corleone said quietly, "I hope we can settle things tonight, I don't want my father bothered any more."

"He won't be," Sollozzo said sincerely. "I swear to you by my children he won't be. Just keep an open mind when we talk. I hope you're not a hothead like your brother Sonny. It's impossible to talk business with him."

Captain McCluskey grunted. "He's a good kid, he's all right." He leaned over to give Michael an affectionate pat on the shoulder. "I'm sorry about the other night, Mike. I'm getting too old for my job, too grouchy. I guess I'll have to retire pretty soon. Can't stand the aggravation, all day I get aggravation. You know how it is." Then with a doleful sigh, he gave Michael a thorough frisk for a weapon.

Michael saw a slight smile on the driver's lips. The car was going west with no apparent attempt to elude any trailers. It went up on to the West Side Highway, speeding in and out of traffic. Anyone following would have had to do the same. Then to Michael's dismay it took the exit for the George Washington Bridge, they were going over to New Jersey. Whoever had given Sonny the info on where the meeting was to be held had given him the wrong dope.

The car threaded through the bridge approaches and then was on it, leaving the blazing city behind. Michael kept his face impassive. Were they going to dump him into the swamps or was it just a last-minute change in meeting place by the wily Sollozzo? But when they were nearly all the way across, the driver gave the wheel a violent twist. The heavy automobile jumped into the air when it hit the divider and bounced over into the lanes going back to New York City. Both McCluskey and Sollozzo were looking back to see if anyone had tried doing the same thing. The driver was really hitting it back to New York and then they were off the bridge and going toward the East Bronx. They went through the side streets with no cars behind them. By this time it was nearly nine o'clock. They had made sure there was no one on their tail. Sollozzo lit up a cigarette after offering his pack to McCluskey and Michael, both of whom refused. Sollozzo said to the driver, "Nice work. I'll remember it."

Ten minutes later the car pulled up in front of a restaurant in a small Italian neighborhood. There was no one on the streets and because of the lateness of the hour only a few people were still at dinner. Michael had been worried that the driver would come in with them, but he stayed outside with his car. The negotiator had not mentioned a driver, nobody had. Technically Sollozzo had broken the agreement by bringing him along. But Michael decided not to mention it, knowing they would think he would be afraid to mention it, afraid of ruining the chances for the success of the parley.

The three of them sat at the only round table, Sollozzo refusing a booth. There were only two other people in the restaurant. Michael wondered whether they were Sollozzo plants. But it didn't matter. Before they could interfere it would be all over.

McCluskey asked with real interest, "Is the Italian food good here?"

Sollozzo reassured him. "Try the veal, it's the finest in New York." The solitary waiter had brought a bottle of wine to the table and uncorked it. He poured three glasses full. Surprisingly McCluskey did not drink. "I must be the only Irishman who don't take the booze," he said. "I seen too many good people get in trouble because of the booze."

Sollozzo said placatingly to the captain, "I am going to talk Italian to Mike, not because I don't trust you but because I can't explain myself properly in English and I want to convince Mike that I mean well, that it's to everybody's advantage for us to come to an agreement tonight. Don't be insulted by this, it's not that I don't trust you."

Captain McCluskey gave them both an ironic grin. "Sure, you two go right ahead," he said. "I'll concentrate on my veal and spaghetti."

Sollozzo began speaking to Michael in rapid Sicilian. He said, "You must understand that what happened between me and your father was strictly a business matter. I have a great respect for Don Corleone and would beg for the opportunity to enter his service. But you must understand that your father is an old-fashioned man. He stands in the way of progress. The business I am in is the coming thing, the wave of the future, there are untold millions of dollars for everyone to make. But your father stands in the way because of certain unrealistic scruples. By doing this he imposes his will on men like myself. Yes, yes, I know, he says to me, 'Go ahead, it's your business,' but we both know that is unrealistic. We must tread on each other's corns. What he is really telling me is that I cannot operate my business. I am a man who respects himself and cannot let another man impose his will on me so what had to happen did happen. Let me say that I had the support, the silent support of all the New York Families. And the Tattaglia Family became my partners. If this quarrel continues, then the Corleone Family will stand alone against everyone. Perhaps if your father were well, it could be done. But the eldest son is not the man the Godfather is, no disrespect intended. And the Irish *Consigliere*, Hagen, is not the man Genco Abbandando was, God rest his soul. So I propose a peace, a truce. Let us cease all hostilities until your father is well again and can take part in these bargainings. The Tattaglia Family agrees, upon my persuasions and my indemnities, to forgo justice for their son Bruno. We will have peace. Meanwhile, I have to make a living and will do a little trading in my business. I do not ask your cooperation but I ask you, the Corleone Family, not to interfere. These are my proposals. I assume you have the authority to agree, to make a deal."

Michael said in Sicilian, "Tell me more about how you propose to start your business, exactly what part my Family has to play in it and what profit we can take from this business."

"You want the whole proposition in detail then?" Sollozzo asked.

Michael said gravely, "Most important of all I must have sure guarantees that no more attempts will be made on my father's life."

Sollozzo raised his hand expressively. "What guarantees can I give you? I'm the hunted one. I've missed my chance. You think too highly of me, my friend. I am not that clever."

Michael was sure now that the conference was only to gain a few days' time. That Sollozzo would make another attempt to kill the Don. What was beautiful was that the Turk was underrating him as a punk kid. Michael felt that strange delicious chill filling his body. He made his face look distressed. Sollozzo asked sharply, "What is it?"

Michael said with an embarrassed air, "The wine went right to my bladder. I've been holding it in. Is it all right if I go to the bathroom?"

Sollozzo was searching his face intently with his dark eyes. He reached over and roughly thrust his hand in Michael's crotch, under it and around, searching for a weapon. Michael looked offended. McCluskey said curtly, "I frisked him. I've frisked thousands of young punks. He's clean."

Sollozzo didn't like it. For no reason at all he didn't like it. He glanced at the man sitting at a table opposite them and raised his eyebrows toward the door of the bathroom. The man gave a slight nod that he had checked it, that there was nobody inside. Sollozzo said reluctantly, "Don't take too long." He had marvelous antenna, he was nervous.

Michael got up and went into the bathroom. The urinal had a pink bar of soap in it secured by a wire net. He went into the booth. He really had to go, his bowels were loose. He did it very quickly, then reached behind the enamel water cabinet until his hand touched the small, blunt-nosed gun fastened with tape. He ripped the gun loose, remembering that Clemenza had said not to worry about leaving prints on the tape. He shoved the gun into his waistband and buttoned his jacket over it. He washed his hands and wet his hair. He wiped his prints off the faucet with his handkerchief. Then he left the toilet.

Sollozzo was sitting directly facing the door of the toilet, his dark eyes blazing with alertness. Michael gave a smile. "Now I can talk," he said with a sigh of relief.

Captain McCluskey was eating the plate of veal and spaghetti that had arrived. The man on the far wall had been stiff with attention, now he too relaxed visibly.

Michael sat down again. He remembered Clemenza had told him not to do this, to come out of the toilet and blaze away. But either out of some warning instinct or sheer funk he had not done so. He had felt that if he had made one swift move he would have been cut down. Now he felt safe and he must have been scared because he was glad he was no longer standing on his legs. They had gone weak with trembling.

Sollozzo was leaning toward him. Michael, his belly covered by the table, unbuttoned his jacket and listened intently. He could not understand a word the man was saying. It was literally gibberish to him. His mind was so filled with pounding blood that no word registered. Underneath the table his right hand moved to the gun tucked into his waistband and he drew it free. At that moment the waiter came to take their order and Sollozzo turned his head to speak to the waiter. Michael thrust the table away from him with his left hand and his right hand shoved the gun almost against Sollozzo's head. The man's coordination was so acute that he had already begun to fling himself away at Michael's motion. But Michael, younger, his reflexes sharper, pulled the trigger. The bullet caught Sollozzo squarely between his eye and his ear and when it exited on the other side blasted out a huge gout of blood and skull fragments onto the petrified waiter's jacket. Instinctively Michael knew that one bullet was enough. Sollozzo had turned his head in that last moment and he had seen the light of life die in the man's eyes as clearly as a candle goes out.

Only one second had gone by as Michael pivoted to bring the gun to bear on McCluskey. The police captain was staring at Sollozzo with phlegmatic surprise, as if this had nothing to do with him. He did not seem to be aware of his own danger. His veal-covered fork was suspended in his hand and his eyes were just turning on Michael. And the expression on his face, in his eyes, held such confident outrage, as if now he expected Michael to surrender or to run away, that Michael smiled at him as he pulled the trigger. This shot was bad, not mortal. It caught McCluskey in his thick bull-like throat and he started to choke loudly as if he had swallowed too large a bite of the veal. Then the air seemed to fill with a fine mist of sprayed blood as he coughed it out of his shattered lungs. Very coolly, very deliberately, Michael fired the next shot through the top of his white-haired skull.

The air seemed to be full of pink mist. Michael swung toward the man sitting against the wall. This man had not made a move. He seemed paralyzed. Now he carefully showed his hands on top of the table and looked away. The waiter was staggering back toward the kitchen, an expression of horror on his face, staring at Michael in disbelief. Sollozzo was still in his chair, the side of his body propped up by the table. McCluskey, his heavy body pulling downward, had fallen off his chair onto the floor. Michael let the gun slip out of his hand so that it bounced off his body and made no noise. He saw that neither the man against the wall nor the waiter had noticed him dropping the gun. He strode the few steps toward the door and opened it. Sollozzo's car was parked at the curb still, but there was no sign of the driver. Michael turned left and around the corner. Headlights flashed on and a battered sedan pulled up to him, the door swinging open. He jumped in and the car roared away. He saw that it was Tessio at the wheel, his trim features hard as marble.

"Did you do the job on Sollozzo?" Tessio asked.

For that moment Michael was struck by the idiom Tessio had used. It was always used in a sexual sense, to do the job on a woman meant seducing her. It was curious that Tessio used it now. "Both of them," Michael said.

"Sure?" Tessio asked.

"I saw their brains," Michael said.

There was a change of clothes for Michael in the car. Twenty minutes later he was on an Italian freighter slated for Sicily. Two hours later the freighter put out to sea and from his cabin Michael could see the lights of New York City burning like the fires of hell. He felt an enormous sense of relief. He was out of it now. The feeling was familiar and he remembered being taken off the beach of an island his Marine division had invaded. The battle had been still going on but he had received a slight wound and was being ferried back to a hospital ship. He had felt the same overpowering relief then that he felt now. All hell would break loose but he wouldn't be there.

from Casino

by Nicholas Pileggi

Nicholas Pileggi published Casino *in 1995. The book drew upon the experience of Frank "Lefty" Rosenthal, the Mob's main man in Las Vegas, to describe mafia influence in that city's casino industry. The Mob's influence in part reflected its ability to funnel financial backing to people such as fledgling real estate developer Allen Glick, who in 1974 set out to buy the struggling Stardust Casino. Glick soon found himself deeply involved with people who terrified him.*

n 1971, when Frank Rosenthal went to work at the Stardust, the hotel-casino was for sale. "It was owned by the Recrion Corporation, which also owned the Fremont," said Dick Odessky, who was the director of public relations at the Stardust, "and the big shareholders were looking to sell it. They'd run the price of the stock way up, and they were all looking to get out. But the Securities and Exchange Commission had gotten suspicious and forced them to sign a consent decree not to sell their shares.

"It was like sitting there with a great big steak and not being able to eat it. If anybody tried to sell stock he would have been in big trouble with the court. So the only way the shareholders could get their money out was to sell the entire company.

"Del Coleman [the chairman of Recrion] represented the big investors, and there was tremendous pressure on him to sell out and make a killing.

"Even after Al Sachs took over as president of the Stardust, the pressure to sell the company continued. And right around this time, Allen Glick came along."

Allen Glick was tougher than he looked. In 1974, when the thirty-one-year-old San Diego real estate developer suddenly became the second-biggest casino operator in Las Vegas history, many of the state's gaming regulators and casino owners were astounded. Glick's impact on the town until then had been minimal. He had arrived in Las Vegas only a year earlier, when he and three partners obtained a $3 million loan to develop a parking lot for recreational vans on the site of the bankrupt Hacienda Hotel casino at the low-rent southern end of the Strip.

Glick's look and style—he was short, balding, and owlish—belied his tenacity. Few around him knew that the youthful, studiously mild-mannered Glick—who spoke so softly that he was sometimes barely audible—had spent two years hanging out of a Huey helicopter in Vietnam, where he won a Bronze Star.

"Vietnam taught me that life was short," said Glick. "I remember writing to my brother-in-law that I didn't think I was coming back. So when I did get back, I decided I didn't want to do what I didn't want to do. First, I really didn't want to be a lawyer. I had a bachelor's from Ohio State and a law degree from Case Western Reserve, but the thing I knew was that I didn't want to practice law. Second, I wanted to live in San Diego instead of Pittsburgh, where I was raised. A friend of my sister's got me a job doing some legal work for American Housing, the largest multifamily builder in San Diego, and Kathy and the kids and I drove out there. That started my education in real estate.

"By February of 1971, after about a year at American Housing, I teamed up with Denny Wittman, a nice, wild guy, in a real estate development that involved large tracts of land and commercial building.

"I was first introduced to Las Vegas in 1972. Denny Wittman had heard there was a sixty-acre site at the southern end of the Strip that could make a great mobile home park. The only problem with the property was that the bankrupt Hacienda Hotel was sitting on it and the casino had three IRS tax liens against it. I don't know why, but I just had an idea that instead of tearing everything down for a parking lot, maybe we could raise the money and revive the hotel and casino. But Denny Wittman didn't want to invest in a casino. He was a religious guy. He had a problem with it, so he begged out.

"At the time I personally had twenty-one thousand dollars to my name, but with smoke and mirrors and Denny helping us inflate the value of everything our little development corporation owned, we were able to raise the three million dollars from the First American Bank of Tennessee, where we had been doing business before and had friends.

"I had to get a Nevada Gaming Commission license as the owner of a Las Vegas casino, and there I was, at twenty-nine or thirty, chairman of a Las Vegas casino. Within a day, everyone in town had a deal for me.

"About five months later, Chris Caramanis, who ran an air charter service the hotels used, said that the King's Castle in Lake Tahoe was also in bankruptcy, having been foreclosed by the Teamster pension fund, and he suggested we raise the money and take over King's Castle the way we did the Hacienda.

"That was how I met Al Baron, the assets manager for the Central States Teamster Pension Fund. Chris introduced me to him. I thought I was going to meet a banker type in charge of the assets of a multi-billion-dollar pension fund. Instead, I meet this gruff, cigar-chomping guy who looks at me and says, 'What the fuck are you doing here?' Al was very annoyed at the time because a deal that had been put in place to take the bankrupt King's Castle off the Teamsters' hands had just fallen apart.

"When he was told that I had raised the cash to buy the Hacienda, he asked, 'Do you have any money?'

"I said, 'No, but I might be able to borrow it.'

"Baron was so anxious to get the bankrupt King's Castle off the Teamsters' books that he said he would be back through Las Vegas in two weeks and I should submit a proposal.

"When he came back, I gave him the proposal and he got angry. 'I've got no time to read this,' he said. All he wanted was for me to raise the money for a mortgage and get the Teamsters out.

"Anyway, the deal never went through, but shortly after, I got involved in developing a large government office complex in Austin, Texas, that would house Internal Revenue, congressional offices, and various government agencies. This was a larger deal than we could finance with our usual bank loans, so I thought, let me call Al Baron. I called him three times, left messages, and he never called me back. Finally, after four days, his secretary said that I shouldn't bother calling him again.

"I said fine, but I wanted him to know that the government had contacted me and I needed to talk to him. He called back in three seconds. When I told him that I had been contacted by the government about developing a huge government building complex, he started cursing me up and down. He used every foul word and image you could imagine.

"But in between his cursing I must have gotten across that this was a federal government project and a great opportunity, because he finally said, 'Okay, you sonofabitch, fuck, submit the loan package.'

"Baron and the Teamsters loved this government deal I had brought them because it was totally legitimate and because Denny Wittman, our Austin partners, and I did all the work, and the Teamsters were the government's landlords.

"Then came the Recrion deal. I had heard that Recrion was for sale and that Morris Shenker, the owner of the Dunes, was in negotiation to buy the company from Del Coleman. It turned out that Shenker was offering Coleman only forty-two dollars a share. My accountants had gone through the numbers and realized that you could borrow whatever you needed to buy the Stardust and the Fremont and still have money left over to cover your costs.

"It was the deal of a lifetime. I immediately called Del Coleman in New York to set up a meeting. I grabbed the red-eye and met him in his town house on East Seventy-seventh Street first thing on a Friday morning. Del Coleman was a very sophisticated man, and I believe he was married or engaged to a famous model at the time.

"I told him I wanted to buy him out. I told him I already owned the Hacienda Hotel and casino and that my development company supported me in an offer which I knew was at least two dollars a share higher than Shenker had offered him. I said I needed some time to raise the money, but I was certain I would have no trouble doing so.

"Coleman said up front that he was already in negotiation with Morris Shenker. Actually, attorneys were typing up the papers at that very moment, but I didn't know that. He said if I had money to put up he would be obligated to tell the shareholders, which meant I would be in a position to make a public offer.

"He said if I was serious I could have until noon Monday to come in with two million dollars in a nonrefundable cash payment, and he would give me a hundred and twenty days to raise the rest of the money. I agreed to the deal, but I gulped. I had to give Coleman two million dollars cash by noon Monday, and even if I could raise it, here it was Friday afternoon and the banks were closed over the weekend. I called Denny Wittman. I said I had to borrow two million dollars. He knew what was involved and he offered to let me use two five-hundred-thousand-dollar CDs our company had in the First American Bank in Nashville, Tennessee. He then said maybe I could get a million-dollar letter of credit from the same bank, where we had a very good relationship.

"I called Steven Neely, the bank president, and told him what I needed. 'You're crazy,' he said. I told him it was the deal of a lifetime.

"'If you're serious, you gotta get down here tonight,' Neely said. I hung up and called the airlines and found that there were no more flights heading anywhere near Nashville that would get me there in time.

"I took a car to Teterboro airport in New Jersey and chartered a Learjet to get me there. I had no money, but I gave the charter service a credit card, and thank God I had enough credit to cover the trip.

"When I landed in Nashville, Neely saw me get off the Lear and asked me where I got the plane, and I said a friend lent it to me. I didn't want to say I had just melted my credit card. We went to his house and worked all night setting up the holdings and collateral for the letter of credit.

"Wittman flew in the next day. He pledged everything I needed, and the bank gave me the letter of credit, and it was all completed by Sunday morning. I flew back to New York.

"I called Coleman from the airport. 'Del, I've got your money now and I don't want to wait until Monday morning.'

"'You've got two million dollars?' he said.

"'It's in my briefcase.' I said.

"I went over, we filed the escrow papers for the money, and Coleman said on Monday morning he would notify the SEC and stop trading in Recrion stock.

"I flew back to San Diego on Monday morning, got there before dawn, and began putting together lists of possible investors. I called Al Baron, because the Teamsters held the mortgages on the Stardust and Fremont, plus I knew they had liked the government office development I had brought them. I thought they might want to get involved in the package.

"When I told Al Baron what I had done and that I was now going to bid on the Recrion stock, he said, 'Listen to me, I'm giving you the best advice you've ever had—walk away from this thing. Call the deal off. You have no idea what you're doing. You don't know what you're getting yourself into.' He said there was no way he was going to get involved in the mess I was creating. Looking back, I realize he gave me all the red flags he could.

"Since the Teamsters looked bad, I had investment people try and find me other sources of money. One of the L.A. people came up with a guy named J. R. Simplot, an Idaho investor, who was interested. I went to meet him. He was very low key. He was wearing a two-hundred-dollar suit. He said he had some hotel interests and he would give me the money, except he wanted fifty-one percent of the deal.

"I had no idea who he was. When I got back to the office I called Kenny Solomon at the Valley Bank and asked him to check out somebody named Simplot. He said he didn't have to check him out. He said Mr. Simplot could give me the sixty-two-point-seven million dollars just by writing a check on his personal account. Simplot was the largest potato grower in the United States, and there probably wasn't a McDonald's french fry that didn't come through him.

"But I wasn't interested in giving up control of the company. So I called Al Baron back and said that in the morning he was going to hear that I was a partner with J. R. Simplot and that we were going to buy out Recrion and take over the Teamsters' interest in the Stardust and the Fremont.

"Baron said, 'Don't do anything until I call you back.' He calls me back. He says, 'Come to Chicago for a meeting.'

"'Why should I?' I said. 'Are you going to give me the loan?' He said he still didn't know.

"The next day I flew to Chicago to the pension fund office, where I met Al Baron. 'Now that you're in the ball game,' he said, 'you've got to come up to bat.' He then explained how the system worked.

"He said you had to know a pension fund trustee, because only trustees could make loan proposals. He said the trustees then turned the proposals over to the asset manager for due diligence, and then the applications went to an executive committee, which might or might not recommend, and then the proposal went to a vote of the full board.

"Baron then took me on a tour of the building and introduced me to Frank Ranney, who was coming back from lunch with Frank Balistrieri. Baron told me that Ranney was the Teamster trustee from Milwaukee and a member of the three-man executive committee that oversaw all loans west of the Mississippi, which meant Las Vegas.

"Baron said that Balistrieri could be my link to Frank Ranney. Balistrieri was a very quiet, very dapper man. He said he would be happy to help and the next time he was in Las Vegas we would meet.

"The next time I met Balistrieri he came into the Hacienda. We discussed the loan and the application package and he said he would help me. He told me that after I submitted the loan package in Chicago, I should drive over to Milwaukee, where I could meet his sons. I didn't exactly know how or where Balistrieri fit in, but the things I didn't want to think about I didn't want to think about, and Baron had said Balistrieri was my primary link to Frank Ranney, the trustee and member of the executive committee pushing my loan.

"After I submitted the package I went to Milwaukee, where I met his two sons, John and Joseph. They were both attorneys. Balistrieri said that he would like his sons involved in the operation in some way. He said Joseph had helped him run dinner theaters and was very knowledgeable about entertainment and might serve that kind of function at the Stardust. I didn't commit myself. I always said we could discuss it once I closed the deal on the place.

"When I got home I called Jerry Soloway. He's an attorney with Jenner and Block, a firm I had used. I asked him to check on a guy named Frank Balistrieri. I told him what I knew and hung up. I was due at the offices of the Gaming Control Board. Shannon Bybee, one of the board members, had said he had a 'funny feeling' about my buying one of the largest companies in the state after having been there only one year, and asked if I would do him the favor of taking a lie detector test. My lawyer said it was uncalled for and unnecessary, and Bybee agreed, but he said he would sleep better if he knew I was totally clean. I knew I was clean, so I wound up taking the kind of two-hour test they use on capital crime cases, and I passed like a breeze. That's what convinced Bybee and got me the gaming license I needed to be able to buy the place.

"A couple of days after taking the lie detector I get an emergency call from Jerry Soloway. He sounded hysterical. He wanted to make sure Frank Balistrieri was the right name. I said yes. He said, 'What are you doing with him?'

"I told Jerry I had been out to dinner with him. That he had been to see me at the Hacienda. That I had been in restaurants with him. That I had been to his home, met his sons, been to their law firm.

"Soloway went crazy. He said I couldn't be seen with Balistrieri. He said Frank Balistrieri was identified by the FBI as the Mafia boss of Milwaukee. He said my gaming license could be jeopardized with my just being seen talking to such a notorious organized-crime figure.

"I told Jerry he had to be wrong. I had met Balistrieri in the Teamster pension fund offices. He had just come back from lunch with Frank Ranney, one of the pension fund's trustees.

"He said he didn't care where I'd met Balistrieri, the man was the organized-crime boss of Milwaukee.

"I didn't sleep very well that night. The first thing I thought was, what would have happened had Jerry told me this before I took the lie detector test? Then I remembered I had been talking to Balistrieri just about every day on the phone discussing the progress of the loan arrangements. I had also been seen with him all over the place.

"On the other hand, I didn't feel there was anything I could do. What was I going to tell him? I know you're the head of the Mafia in Milwaukee, so don't help me get the loan? I was now very, very wary, but I felt I could maneuver it.

"The next time he called me, he was happy. He said we had gotten the approval of the executive committee for the sixty-two-point-seven-million-dollar purchasing loan, but Ranney had said there was a debate about the second part of the loan for sixty-five million dollars. Bill Presser, the Cleveland trustee, was resisting the second part of the loan. We needed the additional money to renovate and expand the Stardust.

"Balistrieri said he wanted to meet me in Chicago about the second part of the loan. I was terrified of being seen with him. But I wanted the loan application to go through. He said he wanted to meet me at the Hyatt Hotel near O'Hare Airport. I went. When I got to his room he said that the executive committee was now considering the second part of my loan—the first twenty-million-dollar installment to begin the renovations. The rest would come a little later, and that would be used to expand the Stardust and build a luxury guest tower. This had all been worked out and agreed to in principle, since the properties needed extensive work to stay competitive with the market.

"Bill Presser was still opposed, Balistrieri said, and there were only two weeks left to pass the entire loan package. I see now that he was building up the pressure.

"Then he reminded me about the promise I had made about his

sons getting jobs with the new corporation, and I said that we'd work it out as soon as the deal went through. Balistrieri then asked me to go with him to Milwaukee and see his sons.

"I agreed. The next day we met in his sons' law offices, and Balistrieri said he would like to have something formalized. Balistrieri then left the room and his sons, Joe and John, discussed an agreement, actually an option agreement, in which for twenty-five or thirty thousand dollars, I don't even remember, they would have the right to buy fifty percent of the new company if and when I decided to sell.

"'Without this,' one of the sons said, 'you're gonna get turned down tomorrow.'

"I asked if we could talk about it later, after the deal.

"They said no.

"I'd already sworn to the Gaming Control Board that I had no partners. I knew the Balistrieris would never get licensed.

"I said I'd like to do it, but I'd signed with the state that I had no partners. They suggested I postdate the option.

"I asked if they thought they could get licensed, and they said they both felt licensing would be no problem for them. I began to sense these people were living in a fantasy. They didn't seem to know who they were or what baggage they carried. Or they didn't know that I knew and were simply carrying off a charade. Whatever it was, I felt like Alice in Wonderland.

"I said that I would sign it, but they had to promise they wouldn't do anything with the option. They agreed.

"That night I changed my mind. I called Joe and said I can't go through with the option agreement. If the control board comes back and finds out about it, everything will be jeopardized. I'll lose it all.

"I said if the deal was contingent on the option, as much as I would hate to, I would have to step away from the deal. I said I respected his dad and was grateful for what he had done, but I couldn't jeopardize everything I had, including the Hacienda. I said I didn't have a problem with retaining them as lawyers—I eventually retained them as counsels for fifty thousand dollars a year—but that option could destroy everything.

"A few minutes later, he calls me back. He says, 'My dad is going to call you and say he's "Uncle John." He wants to talk to you.' Uncle John! He had never used code names before. Why? I didn't know and I couldn't even act surprised, because I didn't want them to know I knew who they were.

"Balistrieri called, identified himself as Uncle John, and said, 'You can't back out.'

"I said, 'I can't do it the way it is.'

"'Are you sure?' he asks.

"I said, 'Yes, and I'll just have to take the consequences.'

"'You disappoint me,' Balistrieri said. He sounded very sad.

"His son Joe then calls back and says they'll rip up the option and we'll work something out after the deal goes through.

"I told him not to rip it up, but to send it back to me. I had already shredded my copy and I didn't want another copy floating around and finding its way to the control board.

"'You don't trust me?' Joe said, almost hurt.

"I told him it wasn't a matter of trust. It was business. He said he would send me the copy, but of course he never did.

"A week later or so the loan went through. It got a full-board approval. The board's discussion of my loan took no more than two minutes. At the end, Bill Presser, the Teamster boss from Chicago, who had been the most reluctant of the trustees, said, 'Good luck,' and that was that.

"I had gotten the sixty-two-point-seven-million-dollar Teamster loan in sixty-seven days."

On August 25, 1974, over 80 percent of the Recrion shareholders tendered their stock to Allen Glick's company, Argent. The company name was an acronym for Allen R. Glick Enterprises and, of course, meant "money" in French, a language in which no one connected with the deal was fluent.

"I was euphoric," Glick recalled. "Joe Balistrieri called and said his father was coming into Chicago and wanted to have a celebration dinner.

"I said I didn't think it would be a good idea, but Joe insisted. He said, 'You can't tell my father no.'

"I didn't even want to be seen in an out-of-the-way restaurant with him, but we wound up in the Pump Room at the Ambassador Hotel in Chicago. He was well known in the place. Waiters, captains, they all came over. He was ordering Dom Pérignon. All through dinner I'm thinking, if the FBI was tailing him tonight, my life in Las Vegas is over.

"Toward the end of the dinner he said if I had any questions concerning the loan—especially the additional sixty-five million dollars for renovations and expansion—I should talk to him and only to him. I shouldn't try and discuss anything about what we had done with other trustees or union officials. He said the two of us had established a successful pattern that's the pattern that should remain established.

"Then, as we were leaving, Frank said to me, 'You've got to do me a favor, Allen. There's a guy living in Las Vegas; he's working for you now. It would be helpful if you give him more recognition. He can help you.'

"'Who?' I said.

"'I can't tell you now,' he said.

That was the end of the evening.

"One week later I got a call from Uncle John. He said he wanted me to meet the guy he had mentioned to me. I was in La Jolla, and Balistrieri said, 'He'll come to see you there. I want you to give him a promotion. More money. Okay?'

"I asked, 'Who is it?'

"He says, 'His name is Frank Rosenthal. If you don't like him, you can call me up and I'll straighten him out.' He said there were people on the fund who would look very favorably on the rest of my loan application if I were to promote Rosenthal. When I hesitated just a little, I could hear the tone of his voice change. He sounded annoyed. After I agreed, he asked me to meet with Rosenthal as soon as I could.

"I phoned Rosenthal right after I talked with Balistrieri. He said that he was expecting the call.

"Rosenthal came to La Jolla. He came to my home. He told me that Al Sachs was a moron. He told me that there was a lot of potential in the company. He was very good. Plus, he was very smart. He may be the devil—which I personally think he is—but he's very smart.

"I told him I knew about his expertise in gaming and that I would appoint him as my assistant or as an advisor. At first he was very conciliatory. He said he understood and he would do as I said and that he appreciated the promotion and that he would do his very best.

"He asked me to acknowledge his promotion through a memo, and asked me for a raise. I gave him the memo and the raise.

"The next day I checked with the chairman of the Gaming Commission. I learned that Rosenthal was a genius with numbers, a master handicapper. He knew all the casino games. I also learned he would probably never get a license."

Frank Rosenthal returned to Las Vegas with a new job description and a raise from $75,000 to $150,000 a year. He immediately began to make changes in the operations of the casino. "Almost all of the executives viewed him as the man with all the authority," Glick said. "He was supposed to clear everything with me, but he didn't. At the outset, when I questioned him about these things, he wasn't disrespectful. But every day I would hear that he had taken a little more power. I heard that when he walked through the casino, dealers used to jump to attention. He would fire a dealer for not standing with his hands folded before him, even at an empty table. He hired whoever he wished. He changed certain purveyors. Without clearing it, he changed the car rental company, the advertising company, and he tried to bring in his own ticketing agency for the Lido Show.

"When these things were brought to my attention I would either stop them or rescind them, but he was hard to stay ahead of. While I was unraveling one thing he did, he'd be in the kitchen telling the chefs how to cook.

"I was commuting between my home in San Diego and Las Vegas, and whenever I would get to town I would hear all the stories about what he did while I was away. Then, for a few days, I would have almost daily confrontations with him. I saw him in operation. He was the kind of man who held out his cigarette and expected it to be lit. He could be withering with people. He did not curse. He did not raise his voice. But you'd rather get hit in the mouth than have him harangue you.

"He designed himself an office that Mussolini would envy. It was four times larger than any office in the place. He didn't like the wood paneling he had ordered and had it all ripped out and replaced. It was all ego. He wasn't satisfied being a boss behind the scenes; he had to let everyone know it.

"Finally, in October 1974, I called him into my office. I had just arrived from California. It was a Monday. Again, I'd learned that certain things had gone on in the casinos over that weekend, and I felt that this was the time to terminate his position.

"I met him in the coffee shop of the Stardust, which was called the Palm Room.

"I said, 'Let's go to the back of the coffee shop. I want to explain a couple of things to you.'

"I told him what I had told him on repeated occasions—that he had to control his activities and that he was supposed to work within the parameters of what I had outlined to him in our meeting in September in California.

"I said that on repeated occasions he had lied to me, that there was subterfuge, and I learned that he had even instructed my secretary to tell him on a daily basis what my movements were, where I was going and what I was going to do. I said that I found that intolerable.

"He looked surprised. He asked if my secretary had told me that. I said yes. And instead of apologizing for spying on me, he said that he was going to fire her.

"That's when I realized I wasn't dealing with a normal man. We were in the back of the coffee shop. It was a closed section. He hesitated for a second and then he got up and he walked away from the table. Then he came back to the table. I could see his blood pressure rising.

"He said, 'I think it is about time that we have a discussion, Glick.' He referred to me by my last name. He had always called me Allen. But he called me by my last name as in setting the stage.

"He said, 'It is about time you become informed of what is going on here and where I am coming from and where you should be. I was placed in this position not for your benefit, but for the benefit of others, and I have been instructed not to tolerate any nonsense from you, nor do I have to listen to what you say, because you are not my boss.'

"I began to argue with him and he said, 'Let me just cut you off right here.' He said, 'When I say you don't have a choice, I am just not talking of an administrative basis, but I am talking about one involving health.

"'If you interfere with any of the casino operations or try to undermine anything I want to do here, I represent to you that you will never leave this corporation alive.'

"I felt like someone had just arrived from an alien planet. I was a businessman and everything I had conducted was in a businesslike manner, and this was almost totally a different subculture. I didn't know what to make of it. In respect to the conversation that I had had with Jerry Soloway in regard to Frank Balistrieri, I realized that I just entered into a trap.

"I told him I wanted him out of the hotel. He said, 'I hear what you are saying, but I want you to listen to me carefully again. When I said you will not leave this corporation alive, I meant the people that I represent have the power to do that, and much more. You should take me very serious. You are an intelligent individual, but don't test me.'

"After I recovered, I was in somewhat of a state of shock. I called Frank Balistrieri and I said, 'You got me into something I did not bargain for, or I would not have accepted anything like this.' I said, 'I felt that the appointment of your sons as corporate counsel was done in a businesslike manner, and I have no problems with that, but I do have problems with this.'

"I related to him the conversation I had with Rosenthal and he was very conciliatory. He said he would get back to me. But just remember, he said, the only one I was to talk to about this matter was him. Frank Balistrieri. If anyone else approached me and I talked to them, I would be doing it irrespective of his wishes. He was very firm. I did not pursue it with him.

"Within a few days Balistrieri called back. He explained to me on the phone that he understood the situation, but at this time there was nothing he could do about it and that I should heed Mr. Rosenthal's advice and keep him in that position.

"I discussed Rosenthal's mention of 'partners,' and I said that I bought this corporation through my own efforts, acknowledging that he helped me get the pension fund loan, but there were no partners.

"But Balistrieri said, 'What Mr. Rosenthal told you is accurate.'"

For several months, Glick fenced with Rosenthal. He was afraid to confront him, so he tried to limit his activities. He excluded him from meetings. He tried to keep him out of the loop. He countermanded his orders. He rejected his suggestions. And finally, one night in March 1975, Allen Glick's wildest nightmare came true. He was having dinner in the Palace Court Restaurant in the Stardust when Rosenthal called. "He said there was an emergency. I had to join him at a meeting. I asked what emergency. He said he couldn't tell me over the phone, but I had to meet him. I said I'd rather not. I said we could deal with whatever it was in the morning.

"Then he said, 'It's an emergency and you don't have a choice.'

"I said, 'Okay, where is it?'

"He said, 'Kansas City.'

"I thought that was ridiculous. I told him I couldn't get there before three or four in the morning. He said, 'We are going to come and get you, or you are going to come voluntarily.' He said he would meet me at the airport. The corporation had a couple of Lears at the tune, and by two thirty or three in the morning I landed in Kansas City.

"Rosenthal was waiting for me with a car at the airport and introduced me to the driver, Carl DeLuna, a really gruff, vulgar man. Rosenthal referred to him by his nickname, 'Toughy.'

"We then took a circuitous route to wherever we were going, because I noticed that we were passing the same places time and again. It took about twenty minutes. Round and around, and no one is saying anything. Finally we got to a hotel. We go up to the third floor. It's a suite with a connecting door that is only partially open to a connecting room.

"The suite was pretty dark. As I walked in I was introduced to a white-haired older man named Nick Civella. I had no idea who Nick Civella was. He turned out to be the Mafia boss of Kansas City. I put out my hand to shake and he said, 'I don't want to shake your hand.'

"There was a chair and an end table with a light on it. He told me to sit down. I saw Rosenthal leave the room. I was in there with DeLuna and Civella, except I could hear people moving in and out of the room through the interconnecting door of the suite, but that was to my back.

"Civella called me every name under the sun and then he says, 'You don't know me, but if it was my choice you'd never leave this room alive. However, due to the circumstances, if you listen, you may.'

"When I said the light was bothering my eyes, he said he could accommodate me by pulling my eyes out. Then he said, 'You reneged on our deal. You owe us one-point-two million dollars, and you're gonna let Lefty do what he wants.'

"I was amazed. I said I didn't know what he was talking about. I meant it.

"He looks at me and says, laying a gun on the table, 'You're going to start telling me the truth right now or you're not leaving this room alive.'

"He asked about my agreement with Balistrieri, and when I said I didn't have an agreement with Balistrieri, he said, 'What?' Kind of surprised. He said he wanted to know about the agreement he had been told I had with Balistrieri.

"I said the only agreement I had with Balistrieri was about hiring his sons, and I told him about the option, but I explained that the option was voided and we were going to work something out now that the deal had gone through.

"Later, I found out that Civella did not know about my deals with Balistrieri—about hiring his kids and their fifty percent option. He thought Balistrieri had been given a one-point-two-million-dollar cash commission for getting me the loan. Since Civella felt he had also helped get me the loan through his trustee—Roy Williams, the Teamster boss of Kansas City and the next president of the entire union—he too was entitled to one-point-two million dollars.

"Balistrieri had told me never to talk to anyone else about our arrangement, but I felt under these circumstances I had no choice. I also began to see why Balistrieri insisted I never talk to anyone else.

"Civella was a tough guy but a smart man. When he asked me questions I could see that he was putting things together. All of a sudden, something rang a bell and he got up. He said I still had a commitment to him and he wanted the money paid.

"When I said that I didn't know how the corporation could pay him this money, he said, 'Let Lefty handle that.'

"He said that because he did not like me, he was going to personally see to it that I did not get the additional Teamster loans for renovation and expansion.

"Then he said, 'Get him outta here,' and told DeLuna to take Lefty and me back to the airport and 'drive down to Milwaukee and yank that fancy-pants sonofabitch out of bed and bring him here.'

"This time it only took us five minutes to get back to the airport from the hotel, and all the while DeLuna was griping about how he had to drive all the way to Milwaukee to pick up Balistrieri, as though Balistrieri were a sack of laundry.

"When I met Rosenthal the next morning I told him that I could not accept Civella's conditions about paying him money and having partners, and Rosenthal said that I was really no longer in a position of authority. He said I could no longer determine my destiny.

"When I told Balistrieri about my meeting with Civella and told him about the threat to cut off our additional loans, Balistrieri said there was nothing he could any longer do to help me. He said the pension fund matters were now out of his hands."

from Mafia Cop
by Lou Eppolito
and Bob Drury

Lou Eppolito (born 1948), the son of a mafia capo, grew up to be a New York City policeman. He was accused of selling secrets to the Mob, but acquitted after a well-publicized 1978 trial. Eppolito later teamed up with writer Bob Drury to write Mafia Cop, *which includes this soliloquy by Lou's long-suffering mother. She describes the ups and downs of her courtship and marriage to the future cop's mobbed-up Dad.*

Tess Eppolito: "When I married into the Eppolito clan I can honestly say I didn't know what the hell I was getting into. I was Italian, but I was fourth-generation Italian, as American as a Roosevelt or a Whitney. My mother's side, the Fenimores, were descended from the writer James Fenimore Cooper. And even though my paternal grandfather's people, the Mandelinos, had come from Italy, I didn't know a cannoli from a can of beans.

"Well, the first thing I notice about Ralph's people is this heavy emphasis on *honor* and *respect*. I mean, we were brought up to show respect to our elders, don't get me wrong. But not to the point where it was sickening. It was shocking to me in the beginning. I mean, my father walked into a room, it was 'Hi, Pa.' Nobody got up and kissed him.

"But with the Eppolitos, Christ, old man Louis would enter a room and stand there waiting for his kisses. Sons and daughters rose as one and formed a line. You'd think the Pope had just breezed in. Once, I asked my sister-in-law, Louise, 'What happens if you don't get up and kiss him?' A solemn look spread over her face. 'Very disrespectful,' she whispered. It was like a bad movie.

"When I told Ralph I thought this whole honor thing was a little silly—I mean, we'd go to a family gathering and it took a half an hour to say hello and a goddamn hour to say goodbye—he said I didn't understand because I wasn't brought up with respect. 'This kissing is respect?' I asked him. 'Half the time it's the goddamn kiss of death. You kiss these guys before you blow their brains out. Killing is respect?' He was steamed, but he didn't have an answer.

"At any rate, I didn't figure out this whole honor thing until much later on. I was seventeen when I met Ralph. He was an older man, going on twenty-six, and my parents weren't thrilled about me seeing a man eight years my senior. I used to love to go dancing, but Ralph couldn't dance a step. Yet he'd bring me to the clubs and watch as I danced with everyone else. We'd go to the Ansonia Ballroom and the Roseland in Manhattan, and there were two or three dance clubs alone along Brooklyn's Dekalb Avenue that we'd hit all the time.

"Before I met Ralph, all the girls would meet and head down to the cellar clubs in Brownsville. We danced with guys from Murder Incorporated. I remember Abie Reles* in particular. He could trip the light fantastic. But with these guys there was never a problem. We were young, we were carefree, and my group wouldn't have known a Mafia man from a matador. If the guy was dressed up, had a decent haircut, and sprung for a hot dog and a Coke afterward, we honestly weren't all that inquisitive. I danced with Sonny Francese** almost every Sat-

---

*Abe "Kid Twist" Reles was one of Murder Incorporated's most proficient practitioners. Known as the best "shiv man" in the business, he perfected the art of approaching a victim on the street with his knife folded into the *Daily News*. After accidentally "bumping" his target with the tabloid and shivving him through the heart, Reles would be around the corner before the unfortunate hit the sidewalk. He was arrested in 1940 and provided investigators with information that led to convictions in numerous previously unsolved gangland slayings. He died on November 12, 1941, following a mysterious plunge from the sixth floor of the Half Moon Hotel in Coney Island while under the protective custody of half a dozen police officers. "Abie tried to go out a six-story window with a six-foot sheet," was how Tess remembered the incident.

** John "Sonny" Francese rose from soldier in the then-named Profaci Organized Crime Family to head that organization in 1978. By that time the Family was named after one of Profaci's successors, Joe Colombo. Francese ruled the Colombo Family for two years before giving way to Carmine Persico in 1980, when Persico was released from jail.

urday night in Big Ralph's Cabaret, a supper club between Myrtle and Broadway, and I never had any idea what he did for a living.

"I was working part-time as a waitress in a pizzeria on Utica Avenue where Ralph used to come in and order a pie. He was usually with his brothers, and sometimes his father—they called him Luigi the Nablidan. I'd see one of the Eppolitos at least once or twice a week. One night we closed late, and Ralph offered to take me home. He was from Greenwich Village, and I was just a farm girl from Pigtown, but to be quite honest, at first I wasn't all that interested.

"I was a hellion, a gypsy, and he was so quiet. I thought of Ralph as the old reliable. He wasn't a big man, in fact he was small and wiry. And he was involved with the numbers when I met him, although I wasn't sure specifically what he did. He would mention names like Vito Genovese and Joe Profaci, but, to me, they might as well have been men in the moon. I never gave his job a second thought, except to notice that sometimes the money wasn't so steady. At that time there were certain things a girl just didn't ask about.

"We dated on and off for four years, one thing led to another, and eventually he proposed. He didn't sweep me off my feet or anything like that. But he was a good man, and with the war on, good men were getting scarce. We were married on October 23, 1943. The night we wed he took me to Ernie's Three Ring Circus, a club in the Village owned by one of his cousins. I think his brother Freddy may have had a piece of it, too. Vito Genovese was at the bar, and when he found out that we had just been married, he closed the bar and ordered champagne drinks for everybody. We had an all-night party.

"I had no idea who Vito Genovese was personally, but I certainly got the impression that he was some kind of important guy. Don't misunderstand me—I wasn't naive. But also don't forget, this was in the 1940s, when the Mafia wasn't as well known as it is today. New York wasn't like Chicago, with Al Capone's gang driving down the street with machine guns blazing. There were murders and such, but they were more hush-hush.

"Later on, when Vito Genovese's name began appearing in the

papers and I realized he was wanted for ordering murders and dealing drugs, for being a Mafia don, it was very hard to make the connection that this was the same man who threw us the party on my wedding night.

"After we were married, Ralph tried working a straight job, as a long-shoreman. But he couldn't take the labor because of his bad lungs. See, he was a four-pack-a-day smoker. The whole family smoked heavy, the mother, the father, all the brothers. Ralph's mother died at forty-six, before I met him. She had complications from diabetes. The only other legit work he ever did after that was on and off, mostly off, as a bar-tender at a place my family owned in Pigtown, or sometimes over at his brother Freddy's Bed-Stuy place, The Grand Mark.

"As for my father-in-law, I knew him as a jeweler, always with the watches. He didn't display anything, but if some mob big's daughter was getting married, he'd say, 'Send the bride down to such and such an address.' By this time he had closed his shop in the Village, remar-ried, and moved to Brooklyn. He was operating out of his home. But he still had connections. Watches in one place, rings in another, bracelets in yet another. He'd get you a good deal. He knew stones, and he knew jewelry. Even my sisters went to him for their rings. He had a nice business going until the day he died.

"My father-in-law adored his grandchildren, although I must admit that Louie got on his nerves a little bit as a boy. Every time Grandpa Louis gave Louie a watch it would be broken within the week. One day he took a broken watch and threw it out the window and told Louie, 'No more watches. All you do is break them.'

"It dawned on me early in my marriage that my father-in-law was somehow involved with the rackets, most probably the numbers, and that his kids were looking to inherit the family trade. Every Sunday Louis had to go pick something up, and my husband would always drive him. I knew that what they were doing wasn't kosher, because they treated it like some military secret. But I never understood the big mystery. Everybody played the numbers.

"Ralph never accounted to me for his whereabouts. And I never asked. There were times he didn't come home all night, and if he said anything at all by way of explanation it usually involved dice or cards. God knows where he was. But he always gave me his 'winnings,' and when he'd throw seven hundred dollars, eight hundred dollars down on the bed, who was I to argue? As time went on, I realized what business he was in. But by then it was too late. I had the kids, Pauline and Louie. What was I going to do, walk out?

"Ralph and his brother Jimmy were sedate, just like their father. Always immaculately dressed, always very presentable, never talked out of turn. People thought that Jimmy looked a little bit like Tyrone Power, but Freddy was the flashy one. He was handsome, taller than his bothers, about six-one, with jet-black hair and pale-blue Paul Newman eyes. Eyes to die for. More than a few did, I think, in both senses of the word. Freddy was a real lady-killer, with a devil-may-care, I-don't-give-a-shit attitude. It was always wine, women, and song with Freddy.

"Our household did not lead what you would call a normal lifestyle. There were the phone calls in the middle of the night, for one thing. Then the word would be passed: 'Somebody got hung in the Sahara Club,' and my living room would turn into Grand Central Station. My brothers-in-law would come over, the phone would be ringing off the hook, then the next day, sure enough, you'd pick up the paper and read about a murder in the Sahara Club. It still boggles my mind.

"In my house, when the phone started ringing at two or three in the morning, I could almost guarantee you that somebody had been dropped. When my husband would get up and get dressed in the middle of the night and go out with his gun, I knew there was real trouble.

"Freddy was getting bigger in the Mafia, and he was dragging Jimmy and Ralph along with him. They started a shylocking business to go along with their numbers operation. And they all did a little book-making on the side. But Freddy was always the point man. Neither Ralph nor Jimmy were the type of men to cabaret at night, to run with the uptown crowd. Freddy was the big wheel.

"It really began after the war, when Freddy and Jimmy returned from the service. The Army had rejected Ralph because of his lungs. The older brother, Joey, was never involved in any of this stuff. Nobody ever talked about him. It was like he was a black sheep because he'd gotten an honest job as a longshoreman. When Freddy returned from overseas, he said he was working as a bartender. But you had to figure that with the women, and the flashy clothes, and the fancy cars, he wasn't working for tips serving Seven and Sevens.

"Freddy got the big car first, he got the big house first, he was always the first in the family to get the goodies. And he was involved in an awful lot of trouble. If there was a murder, they'd pick Freddy up, then they'd pick Jimmy up, and Ralph would be the last man on the totem pole.

"Freddy got in trouble a couple of times. He'd go out and be missing for a week. Maybe he was shacked up. Maybe he killed somebody. Who knew? Then he was caught that time at that big upstate meeting, in Apalachin.* God, did the phone calls start after that. Jimmy had to go up and get him. 'What the hell is he doing up there?' I asked my husband. 'There's all gangsters up there.' Ralph's answer: 'Well, Tessie, you know Freddy, he goes all over.' You had to be really stupid not to know what these brothers were into, but Ralph would never admit it.

"One night there was a family meeting at our house—it was like these guys had radar—and the next day I read that some mug took five bullets in the Joy Lounge over in Flatbush. Freddy disappeared for six or eight months after that. Ralph said he was 'on vacation.' Three weeks after he returned, the phone rang again, and again Freddy couldn't be found. There was always a 'dropout' when somebody got killed. And it was always Freddy doing the dropping out. I'd

---

*In November of 1957, near the bucolic upstate New York hamlet of Apalachin, an unprecedented nationwide convocation of the Cosa Nostra leadership was called. Its agenda, in part, was to confirm Carlo Gambino's ascension to the throne of the Family previously headed by the late Albert Anastasia, who had succeeded the Mangano brothers. Three weeks earlier, Anastasia had been the victim of a hostile corporate takeover, engineered by Gambino and Vito Genovese and carried out in the barbershop of New York City's Park Sheraton Hotel. The number of delegates, henchmen, and drivers arrested during a police raid of the meeting totaled sixty. Among them was Alfred Eppolito.

hear Ralph on the phone saying, 'That crazy bastard is at it again.' And the next day, sure enough, there'd be a story in the papers about a murder.

"Except for when they killed Johnny Roberts,* then it was Jimmy who had to drop out. Ralph never told me in so many words, but it was Jimmy and Ralph who did Johnny Roberts. I think Ralph went along just to make sure his kid brother would be safe. And that's what got him his button. You might even say Ralph became a made man by accident, looking out for his little brother. They said Johnny Roberts was a rat, and if there was anything Ralph couldn't stand, it was a rat. They were all that way. I guess to them, that made murder okay.

"The cops eventually picked up Jimmy for the Johnny Roberts killing. The story went that Jimmy and Johnny Roberts were having a drink in one of Johnny's clubs, when Jimmy invited him for a ride. They left the club together, and five minutes later Jimmy came running back in, shouting that someone had shot Johnny Roberts. No one ever knew who shot him.

"My most vivid memory of Johnny Roberts is of him walking through the Italian feast, handing out dollars to the kids flocking around him. It was hard to believe that someone put five in his head. It was even harder to believe that my Ralph had been part of it.

"After the killing the newspapers ran a picture of Jimmy, called him 'the Sleeper' because he snored through his entire arraignment.

"But to his friends Jimmy was known as 'the Clam.' Christ, they all had to have nicknames. There was 'the Blood,' and 'the Bug,' and more goddamn 'Sheiks' than you'd find in a harem. Every guy who knew how to comb his hair and brush his teeth was a 'Sheik.' Every neighborhood had a 'Sheik,' sometimes two. I think Freddy may have been

---

*John "Johnny Roberts" Robilotto, a flashy restaurateur with nightclubs in both Brooklyn and Manhattan, was a made man in the Gambino Organized Crime Family. He was shot to death on September 7, 1958, after being lured out of Sam Shell's, a Canarsie nightclub and notorious Mafia hangout. Joe Valachi told author Peter Maas in 1968 that Robilotto had been killed because, as an Anastasia loyalist, he was plotting a counter-coup against Gambino. That may have been true, but subsequent intelligence sources have confirmed that Robilotto was also supplying information to federal agents. His assassins were never found, and the Robilotto murder remains an open file in the New York City Police Department.

a 'Sheik.' Even Ralph had a nickname, though he never told me about it. I found out accidentally from one of his pals.

"Once, at a wedding, some crum-bum from Greenwich Village came up to me and asked about 'Fat the Gangster.' I asked him what the hell he was talking about, and he said, 'Well, aren't you married to Ralph Eppolito?' When I nodded yes, he exclaimed, 'That's Fat the Gangster.' I almost doubled over laughing. Imagine me, Mrs. Fat the Gangster. Ralph must have picked up the name before he lost all his teeth, which I guess cut down on his appetite.

"Except for the pyorrhea, Ralph was a fairly healthy man when I met him. It wasn't until about five years after we were married that his health really began going downhill. The lungs went first. He had such trouble breathing that he couldn't lie down at night, and he took to sleeping in a chair, choking until dawn. Finally, while I was pregnant with Pauline, he had the left lung removed. They wouldn't let him smoke in the hospital, so five days after the operation he walked home in the snow just so he could have a cigarette.

"Then there was the heart attack, when Louie was recovering from the rheumatic fever. That was followed by more lung problems, but they couldn't do surgery because of his heart condition. And, of course, the man refused to stop smoking. Oh, he was a terribly stubborn bastard. I said to him once, 'Do me a favor and just drop dead now and stop putting me through this anxiety.' But each time he got sick, it wasn't more than a few weeks before he was back to work with his brothers.

"I guess they picked Jimmy up for a couple of murders, but they could never pin anything on him. You'd read about one of these killings, and it would just make you feel unreal. I never knew Ralph to kill anybody personally, to actually pull the trigger. But he may, like in the Johnny Roberts thing, have been along for the ride. Word would get around of a murder, and I'd say to myself, 'It couldn't be my Ralph involved. He was here all afternoon. And so was his brother Jimmy.' But then you'd realize that these guys were night crawlers, and who knows what was going on while the kids and I were asleep. I sure as hell didn't want to know.

"I'm telling you, I met some of the supposedly meanest, cruelest guys, men who would end up doing life in prison, but to us they were always nice people. Take Joe Profaci. He was a real gentleman. He'd stop over the house, always polite, respectable. Maybe he'd bring a little present for the kids. He'd have his black coffee, talk to Ralph in the kitchen, and then leave. Carlo Gambino used to like to dip his goddamn Graham crackers in milk, for chrissake.

"I can't say it didn't bother me that my husband might be involved in some of these killings. I mean, the guy who got killed might have a wife, a couple of kids. Okay, I know the code: 'Nobody never gets killed for no reason.' But nobody has a right to take a life. I'd mention that to Ralph. He'd just shrug me off, or say it was a 'matter of honor.'

"But all this big talk about respect and honor just boiled down to one thing. Easy money. These guys were always on the lookout for the quick scam, and if you threw five dollars on the sidewalk you could watch that honor go south real quick. I knew some of these big, macho Mafia guys who would drive to the factories in Secaucus, New Jersey, or to Orchard Street on the Lower East Side, and fill up the trunk of their cars with wholesale shirts, belts, scarves, whatever.

"Then they'd come back to Flatbush with this load of shit, spread the word that it's hot stuff, swag, and the neighborhood would go crazy for it. Maybe they'd make a buck or two on each item. This is the big Cosa Nostra Code of Honor? Give me a break. I'd call them glorified peddlers. And half the take would eventually wind up as kickbacks to the cops.

"The cops were crumbs, and that's why Ralph detested them so. I don't know who he hated more, cops or rats. Cops were always looking for a payoff, yet their take was so minute it was laughable. I mean, if they caught one of Ralph's numbers runners, two dollars was all it took to make them look the other way.

"My major concern was raising my kids in this kind of atmosphere.

After a while, it became embarrassing to read your name in the paper every time you went to the corner market. It was Eppolito this and Eppolito that. Freddy, Jimmy, Ralph, whoever, one of them was always getting locked up, although the most they ever got Ralph for was book-making. I wondered what kind of an effect it would have on the little ones when they were old enough to understand.

"Plus, there was the general annoyance of a working stiff—namely, me—trying to make an honest buck while being part of a family that was getting a reputation as the second coming of the James gang.

"I was embarrassed for my kids, too, and not just because of the mob stuff. The Eppolitos were known throughout the neighborhood as wild men, although I must admit that I think my son Louie loved that. There was that incident with that priest, for example. Father Pulio was his name. Christ, I could have died. But by that time I was used to Ralph's moods.

"Once, just after Pauline was born, I was out in the neighborhood walking her in the baby carriage. One of the neighborhood drunks accosted me, an older guy named Sal D'Antoni, who had bothered me since I was a kid. He came up to me and said the nastiest thing a man could say. He said that since the baby had been born I was looking pretty good again, and maybe it was about time I got laid. He said he was willing to do the job.

"I saw black. I turned the baby carriage around, ran home, and woke Ralph up. It was about one in the afternoon. Well, after I hysterically blurted out Sal D'Antoni's insult, Ralph was so calm you'd think he was going to church. 'Don't get excited, Tessie,' he said. 'I'll take care of it.' Then he took his time showering and shaving. He even asked me to make him some breakfast.

"By now I'm boiling, both at Sal and at my husband, who doesn't appear all that interested in rushing out to defend my honor. I was insulted that he wasn't going crazy. Eventually he puts on his suit and tie and walks out the door without saying a word.

"Ralph found Sal D'Antoni stone drunk asleep, his head resting on the bar of my aunt's joint down the street. He walked into the bar, picked Sal's head up, and hit him in the face so hard he knocked him across the room. Sal was out cold. Just as Ralph hit Sal, another neighborhood guy, Louie LaBaun, entered the bar. Louie made the mistake of asking Ralph what the hell he was doing beating up a drunk. So Ralph hauled off and smashed LaBaun's face. Louie was tough, nobody in the neighborhood messed with Louie LaBaun, but when Ralph got lathered up into that rage of his—although it may have taken a while—there was no holding him back.

"Anyway, Louie LaBaun wore false teeth, and after Ralph's punch, his teeth went sailing out the door, into the hedges that surrounded the bar. Word flew around the neighborhood that Ralph Eppolito had knocked Louie LaBaun's teeth out of his mouth. Within twenty minutes there was a crowd at the bar, and it continued to grow as the afternoon wore on.

"Freddy gets the word. Jimmy gets the word. And that night there must have been fifty guys, all mafiosi, milling around the neighborhood looking for Sal D'Antoni and Louie LaBaun. 'My God, what have I done?' I thought, 'this is going to turn into a catastrophe.' Anyway, LaBaun made himself scarce, and someone hid out Sal D'Antoni until a sit-down could be called and tempers cooled down. It was explained to Sal that he had done a very bad thing, and that it wouldn't be tolerated again. It was also taken into consideration that he was a hopeless drunk. From that day on it was 'Why, hello there, Tess, are you having a nice day?' whenever I ran into Sal D'Antoni. Louie LaBaun wasn't given so much as an apology. I think he felt he was lucky to be alive.

"That episode taught me a lesson. Ralph Eppolito didn't handle slights and insults like ninety-nine percent of the world. He had to avenge his *honor*. And his brothers were no different, no matter the opposition.

"Freddy once had a beef over a girl with a neighborhood guy named Sonny 'Scans' Scandiffia. Now all five Scandiffia brothers were about six-foot-five and three hundred pounds, and they took the jobs even the Polacks would sniff at. Loading cement trucks, hauling beef, anything that required sheer strength from gigantic people. Sonny had once thrown a punch at a guy, who held up one of those old-time wooden milk cartons to block it, and the punch had shattered the box.

"Freddy had terrible ulcers, and at the time of this insult—Sonny Scans threw a drink in his face—he had just gotten out of the hospital and had a drain attached to his belly.

"Freddy left the bar telling Sonny he couldn't fight him, because one punch in the stomach would kill him. Then he returned an hour later attempting to smooth things over. 'Let's go for coffee,' he said to Sonny Scans, and the two of them drove off in Freddy's car. On Troy Avenue, a dead-end street down by the Boys High athletic field, Freddy pulled over and said, 'Gee, Sonny, I think I got a flat and I'm not going to be able to change it myself.' When Sonny bent over the wheel, Freddy caved in the back of his skull with a lug wrench. Then he hit him again. And again. He just massacred the guy's face. Beat him to a bloody pulp.

"Freddy left Sonny Scans for dead. But like I said, none of the Scandiffia brothers went out that easily, and Sonny managed to crawl down the sidewalk. After a block of crawling he was right in front of our house. I hadn't any idea what had happened. All I knew was that Sonny Scans's brains were leaking out all over our front porch.

"Ralph was home, but he wanted nothing to do with this situation. 'Let the fucker bleed to death,' was his advice. Thank God he didn't know his brother was involved or he would have finished him off. So I called a neighbor to bring a car around, and together we got Sonny to Kings County Hospital.

"Sonny lived, and I ended up mediating the proposed war between the Scandiffias and Eppolitos. It was all settled when Ralph, Jimmy, and Freddy agreed to fork over fifteen hundred dollars for Sonny's plastic surgery. But I continued to be amazed at the mere fact that someone throwing a drink in someone else's face could constitute an insult that called for this kind of retaliation. After that there was a saying around the neighborhood: 'Be careful or you'll be asked to go for coffee with an Eppolito.' Some honor, huh?

"Now all this stuff might have been easier to take if we were living the life of Riley in a twelve-room mansion with servants and chauffeur.

But we weren't. Sure, there were weeks when Ralph would saunter in with a score, maybe twenty-five hundred dollars or so, and that was damn good money in the 1950s. But there were also long stretches when we were living off my paycheck because too many numbers came in, or a loan went south, or the dice rolled the wrong way. People think being married to a Mafia guy is all hot cash and swag. It ain't always so. And I had kids to raise.

"From the time he recovered from his heart murmur, we knew Louie was going to be a smart kid. Personally, I think he would have made a terrific member of the Mafia. He was fearless, and he loved to fight. If his brain had been challenged in the other direction, he would have made his Uncle Freddy look like a Christian Brother.

"Even though I would never hit my children, I must admit that most of the time when Ralph would smack Louie, the kid deserved it. Let me tell you, he was no bargain to raise. I loved him dearly, but sometimes I'd just have to sit in the kitchen and shake my head when he'd purposely go out of his way to piss Ralph off. Louie would go into the refrigerator and break six eggs looking for just the right one to fry sunny-side up. 'I was looking for the perfect egg,' he would explain with this shit-eating grin on his face. Little things like that would agitate Ralph. Pauline you could put on a pedestal right now. The girl was a saint.

"But sometimes Ralph would hit Louie and it would make me furious. I wish I had a penny for every time I almost chopped his head off. But he'd just turn to me and say, 'Don't worry, Tessie, I know what I'm doing.' He wasn't a mean man, but he had what I thought was an odd way of showing his affection. Yet that kind of upbringing may have worked, for even as a child Louie always stood straight and tall, and never whimpered when Ralph would knock the crap out of him.

"From the day Louie learned to comprehend English, Ralph tried to impress upon him this need to have respect. It must have been something in the Eppolito genes. As a youngster, Louie was a defiant sort of kid, always getting in some kind of trouble, usually fights. He was fearless, and had this tendency to think he was the toughest guy in the world. He had this I-don't-take-shit-from-anybody attitude. And the irony was, I think his father molded that into him.

"But I know my husband never wanted Louie to follow him in his line of business. Christ, he cried like a baby when Louie graduated high school. And from the looks of things early on, Ralph got his wish. You see, Ralph was the fussiest dresser in the world. He wouldn't leave the house to go down to the corner for a newspaper without his white shirt, suit, and tie. It could be one hundred and fifty degrees out and Ralph would be buttoned up like Lord Astor. Now that I think of it, I'm surprised he wasn't a 'Sheik.' One to a family, I guess, since Freddy already had the nickname nailed down.

"Anyway, Louie was the sloppiest kid God ever put on earth. And that aggravated his father no end. He'd throw his jacket on the chair, and his shoes were always in the middle of the floor. Once, his Grandfather Louis even made him a shoeshine box. It was a hint, I think. But it never came out of his closet. So I figured, if they were so different in their attitude toward outward appearances, maybe there was hope for Louie.

"As Louie got older his father drilled the same lecture into him over and over. 'Respect everyone's rights,' he would say. 'No matter what color they are, no matter what religion they are. But be a man at all times, and stand up for *your* rights at all times. Don't take shit from no one.' Then one day, I guess Louie was about twelve, they walked out the door together. I was heartsick. Like every other father, Ralph was taking his kid to the office.

Defending the Mafia

by Fredric Dannen

Mobsters often carry themselves like movie stars, and their allure can be intoxicating. Fredric Dannen (born 1955) recounts the cautionary tale of Gerald Shargel, a Mafia lawyer of surpassing skill and intelligence, who somehow allowed the intoxication to go to his head...and almost ended up being prosecuted himself, as "house counsel" to the Mob.

On April 3, 1991, Gerald Shargel, a criminal lawyer considered quite possibly the finest of his generation, a man of elegance in the courtroom, who has said he models his oratory on Martin Luther King, Jr., awoke to bad publicity. The front page of the *News* reported that he had run into trouble with the mafioso John Gotti. In brief, Gotti had threatened to kill him. The headline blared, "SHADDUP." An F.B.I. microphone hidden at the Ravenite Social Club, in Little Italy, a year and a half earlier had discovered Gotti raging against Shargel for talking too much to a *News* reporter. A tape of Gotti's tirade was kept under seal, and the *News* had just caught wind of its contents. Shargel represented several members of the Gambino crime family, and Gotti, the boss of the family, had noticed that Shargel's clients appeared to be getting favorable treatment in the *News*, while "everybody else is bad." One day, Gotti said, "I'm gonna show him a better way than the elevator out of his office!"

Once again, colleagues of Jerry Shargel shook their heads and wondered why so outstanding an attorney, who, as one of them put it, could have been a venerable corporate lawyer—"the Arthur Liman of his generation"—had instead chosen so different a career path. Time and again, his penchant for Mafia clientele had placed him in jeopardy, less so from the mobsters themselves (Gotti has an operatic way of expressing anger, and it was unlikely that he truly considered tossing Shargel out of his thirty-second-floor window) than from the government. For the real danger lurking in Gotti's tantrum was that it played perfectly into a prosecution theory about Shargel—that he was not permitted to put the interests of his individual clients ahead of those of the crime family as a whole.

Shargel's fellow-lawyers were equally astonished to learn that he had visited the Ravenite club several times, where he had been picked up on F.B.I. bugs talking legal strategy with Gotti. It seemed a terrible error in judgment for a lawyer to appear at a Mafia headquarters; it fostered an image of subservience. The day after Gotti lashed out against Shargel, for instance, Shargel went down to the club and made amends. The conversation was not recorded, but Gotti was overheard talking about it the following day: "Jerry said, 'Listen, John. You know I got one love—you.'"

Shargel does not convey even the outward appearance of a Mafia lawyer. He is over six feet tall, bald on top, with black hair around his ears and a trim black beard. In court, where he wears chalk-striped Polo suits with pocket squares, he is soft-spoken and deferential. Out of court, he is youthful and full of fun. The son of the proprietor of a paint-and-wallpaper store in small-town New Jersey, Shargel has been married to his college sweetheart for three decades. They sent their daughter and son to the Dalton School, live off Park Avenue, and rent a summer home in East Hampton. Shargel used to teach law at New York University, and on high holy days he is an usher at the Park Avenue Synagogue.

Bruce Cutler, who is Gotti's personal attorney (he was also tape-recorded at the Ravenite club), has always made more sense as a Mafia lawyer; he has nowhere near the range of Shargel. This became apparent even to Gotti when in early 1990 he stood trial in New York state court with one of his Gambino soldiers, Anthony (Tony Lee) Guerrieri, on a charge of ordering the shooting assault of a union official. Cutler's bullying of witnesses—an approach that was dubbed "Brucification"—was not working and was exasperating the judge. ("The record shall reflect that Mr. Cutler threw Exhibit W," he noted.) By the second week of trial, Gotti had demoted Cutler, leaving Shargel, who officially represented Guerrieri, in charge of the case. The prosecutor, Michael Cherkasky, says that he was unprepared for Shargel's "brilliance," which he believes had a lot to do with Gotti's surprise acquittal.

The acquittal made Gotti's earlier tirade about Shargel savor of ingratitude, but there was much worse to come when the contents of several other Ravenite tapes were made public. It seemed that whenever Gotti was not discussing murder or labor racketeering he was complaining about his attorneys. Shargel and Cutler were "Muck and Fuck," his "high-priced errand boys," whom he paid "under the table," and paid too much (three hundred thousand dollars to Shargel in one year to defend other family members, he said). "Was it you that put me on this earth to rob and make you rich and me poor?" he complained. "Gambino crime family? This is the Shargel, Cutler & Whattaya-call-it crime family!"

To a certain federal prosecutor, these pronouncements were no joke. John Gleeson was chief of the criminal division of the Brooklyn United States Attorney's Office, and, apart from an inconclusive investigation of David Dinkins for alleged stock fraud, most of his work has been in the field of organized crime. John Gotti, who lost his most recent case to Gleeson in 1992, called him a "bum" and a "rat motherfucker" and a "fucking Irish faggot" and—equally inaptly, because Gleeson is a dull dresser—"Lord Fauntleroy." Gleeson was considered an excellent lawyer but something of a zealot. He is tall and trim, and looks like an angry Clark Kent. Gleeson took Gotti at his word—that he did pay the legal bills for the members of his crime syndicate, because the lawyers were actually working for the syndicate. "The reality," Gleeson has written, "is that attorneys are as integral a part of the Gambino Family as any of its other members."

The term that Gleeson uses to describe Shargel and Cutler, and other men he perceives as enterprise lawyers, is "house counsel." (Not consigliere—Italian for "counsellor"—a position in the administration of a Mafia family for which a law degree is scarcely a requirement. The misperception about the meaning of "consigliere" probably stems from the character of Tom Hagen, the family lawyer in "The Godfather.") "House counsel" is a label that Shargel says he resents, but it did not originate with John Gleeson. In 1984, Shargel was accused of having accepted a paper bag containing a hundred and fifty thousand dollars in cash from the Gambino captain Roy DeMeo to defend two of DeMeo's associates. Shargel was summoned before a grand jury, where he testified that the bag had contained only two thousand dollars, and that the money was to defend DeMeo. Shargel was unable to substantiate this claim, because he kept very few financial records— deliberately, he said, in order to protect his clients. No charges were brought against Shargel, but Judge Abraham Sofaer, in a vitriolic opinion, disqualified him from representing one of DeMeo's crewmen and questioned the propriety of his recordkeeping practices.

Shortly after Gotti was indicted in December, 1990, John Gleeson wove several Ravenite conversations in which Shargel and Cutler and a third attorney were mentioned, or were actually present, into an eighty-nine-page brief requesting that they be barred from representing Gotti and his co-defendants at trial. They should not be allowed to sit in the courtroom as defense attorneys, he argued, because the government was planning to portray them to the jury as participants in the enterprise.

Judge I. Leo Glasser granted Gleeson's motion. It was the second time a federal judge had disqualified Shargel from a trial on the house-counsel theory, and, to make it worse, Glasser was Shargel's former law professor.

Soon after the disqualification of Shargel and Cutler from the Gotti case, Gleeson threatened to bring criminal charges against the two lawyers, for obstruction of justice or tax fraud. He seemed to believe, for instance, that Gotti meant it literally when he said he paid his lawyers under the table. An investigative grand jury conducted by Gleeson demanded that Shargel and Cutler produce financial records. Even more ominiously, Salvatore (Sammy Bull) Gravano, Gotti's underboss and one of Shargel's former clients, had become a most cooperative snitch, and was providing information to Gleeson.

In 1994, Cutler was sentenced to six months of house arrest for making statements to the press in violation of a judicial order—a matter unrelated to Gleeson's investigation. Soon afterward, Gleeson was named a federal judge, and the obstruction and tax case against Shargel and Cutler came to an abrupt end. Though Shargel eluded disbarment and prison, he would never be able to shake off the stigma of having two federal judges brand him a house counsel. How had so talented and intelligent a lawyer allowed himself to get so close to a Mafia family—so close that John Gotti saw him as an errand boy and John Gleeson as a conspirator? Didn't he know there would be consequences?

Shargel is a man of immense charm. He has a soft chuckle and the soothing voice of a bartender—a job he once had in college. In interview sessions, Shargel stretches out his long legs, which are occasionally clad in cowboy boots, puffs on a cigar (defense attorneys are great consumers of cigars), and seems the picture of contentment. He smiles a lot. Despite the beard and the bald top, he has a boy's demeanor. His conversation is sprinkled with "cool" and "neat" and "sucks." Jeffrey Lichtman, an associate, recalls Shargel once running up to show off a pair of hard-to-get Knicks tickets, declaring, "Aren't these neat?" Lichtman says, "Under the surface, Jerry is a twelve-year-old. He's such a sweet, funny, self-deprecating guy. You can tease him. It's amazing his ego is not bigger."

Shargel is proud of his equanimity. Many attorneys, he suggests, would have "crumbled" under the pressure of Gleeson's investigation. Even while the investigation was pending, he had seldom been busier,

despite the fact that many of his clients had to sign waivers acknowledging their awareness of the investigation. He possesses a trait that is
enormously useful in a criminal lawyer: the ability to banish
unpleasant thoughts.

Relaxed and happy as he seems, Shargel is a perfectionist who works
seven days a week and suffers from insomnia, especially when he is
trying a case. Sometimes he gets up in the middle of the night and, not
wishing to disturb his wife, Terry, scribbles furiously in the dark. The
only time he appears to be in torment is when he believes he has made
a mistake. One time, in his summation in a rather routine assault case
(the son of a former client had gashed a man's forehead with a beer
mug at a pool bar), he forgot to mention a seemingly minor detail
about the victim's bruise. He went out for a drink while awaiting the
verdict—an acquittal, on self-defense grounds, it turned out after some
four hours—and spent the whole time brooding and making himself
miserable. It caused him to relive a low moment in the Gotti assault
trial of 1990, when he had two slightly different transcripts of the same
tape read into the record, to demonstrate that transcripts can be unreliable. It turned out to have been a brilliant ploy, but at the time he
believed he had made a tragic error, since both transcripts were
damning. "Give me your gun," Shargel recalled telling Gotti. "I'm
gonna shoot myself."

Shargel is so disarming that one must remember to be wary of his
shrewdness. The pool-bar-assault trial provided an illustration. The
prosecutor, a twenty-seven-year-old woman in the Manhattan D.A.'s
office, was so outmatched by Shargel that Shargel feared the jury would
sympathize with her, and he took every opportunity to belittle himself.
At one point, he asked the judge's permission to read from a document
labelled Exhibit F. The judge was puzzled. Was Shargel sure it said
Exhibit F? "It might say something different if I put on my glasses,"
Shargel said. "Ah! Exhibit B." The jurors laughed, visibly charmed. But
Shargel's weak eyesight was an act—and one he had used before.

"You have to be careful with Jerry," says Michael Cherkasky, the
prosecutor in the Gotti assault trial, who is friendly with Shargel. (The

two were spotted some time after the trial having lunch at Forlini's, an Italian restaurant near the Manhattan D.A.'s office.) "I like him enormously, he's very endearing. But he's so smart and manipulative that you always wonder if he's calculating the next move. Is his sensitivity real or is he trying to get an edge?"

At times, one suspects that Shargel is elusive even to himself. To defend a public enemy and delight in getting him acquitted, a criminal lawyer must bond in some way with the criminal. Defense attorneys can seldom account for this quirk of personality, and Shargel is no exception; when he is pressed, he speaks lamely of "anti-establishment" leanings. Shargel is the kind of guy who considers it hip to quote Bob Dylan, Bruce Springsteen, or the Rolling Stones at every opportunity. (After winning a bribery case on Long Island, he turned to a reporter, tossed off some Dylan lines—"I'm going back to New York City/ I do believe I've had enough"—and then sped away in his Jaguar sedan.) "You can't do what I do and be an establishment person," he said one afternoon in his office. "You have to be the kind of person who wants to defy convention." As he spoke, he was dressed in his trademark navy chalk-striped suit, with a white pocket square, and he gestured with his cigar.

Shargel would be easier to figure if he *were* more outwardly unconventional, a William Kunstler or a Bruce Cutler. He does have an irreverent sense of humor, and it shows in the trappings of his office. There are a pair of shoes in cement, and there is a piece of folk-art sculpture of an angel in a tug-of-war with the Devil, whose tail is wrapped around a tree stump. The walls are covered with Second World War posters cautioning secrecy. One shows a German officer reading a book embellished with a Union Jack, and it says "DON'T KEEP A DIARY— IT MIGHT GET INTO THE ENEMY'S HANDS." Shargel added that one to his collection after destroying *his* diaries, to avoid the threat of having them subpoenaed by the government.

Around the time this account was first published, Shargel relocated his office to a suite occupied by a civil-litigation firm, all the while ridiculing the notion that he was trying to clean up his image. He was merely trying to reduce his overhead, he said, and had no intention of cutting down on his Mafia work or, heaven forbid, trying a civil case. White-collar crime, however, has always constituted a large part of his practice; over the years, he has defended people such as the Bronx Democratic boss Stanley Friedman and the real-estate tycoon Norman Dansker.

In recent years, Shargel has been in court defending mafiosi, and numerous non-Mafia clients, on charges as diverse as heroin smuggling, assault with a deadly weapon, murder, vehicular homicide, money laundering, real-estate fraud, insurance fraud, and tax fraud. The reason he is so much in demand, despite all the controversy, is that in the upper echelons of the criminal bar there are trial lawyers and there are "law persons," but Shargel is among a very few lawyers who excel as both. The trial lawyers are the born actors, expert at demolishing witnesses and captivating juries but, as a class, often barely capable of writing briefs and arguing motions. The law persons, their brainier but less theatrical counterparts, handle those chores and, increasingly often, sit at the defense table throughout the trial as intellectual support. Shargel began as an appellate expert, and his knowledge of case law is encyclopedic. The most scholarly judges treat him as an equal. For five years, he taught criminal appellate practice at New York University Law School. He studies every slip opinion issued in a criminal case by the Second Circuit Court of Appeals.

He is also one of the best pure trial lawyers in town, known for the exceptional skill of his cross-examinations and for his physicality. Though he is far less flamboyant in private than many of his colleagues, something happens to him when he is in a courtroom. Tall and graceful, he acts with his entire body, and makes a point of always moving around the floor. It sends a message that "the courtroom is yours," he says, and forces the jury to watch him. "It's like acting, and the more crowded the courtroom is, the more I let loose. I love to use my body. I forget everything except the role I'm in. In a summation, I'll talk about what a witness said, and I'll jump up and I'll sit in the witness box: 'You remember, he sat right *here!*'" When Shargel addresses a jury, his voice quakes with passion, and there is an iterative rhythm to his words which he has picked up from listening to tapes of Martin Luther King's sermons. After Shargel won an acquittal for Bill Banks, a former campaign aide to David Dinkins, on charges of grand larceny, a black juror said of him, "He must have gone to a Baptist church, because he sure can preach."

Shargel exudes so much happiness in private that it always comes as a surprise to observe his angry, aggressive alter ego in the courtroom. Like most good trial lawyers, he can manufacture hatred for government witnesses. The moment the prosecutor finishes his direct examination, Shargel leaps up from the defense table and projects his first question before reaching the lectern (to convey to the witness, he says, "Fuck you, you can't hurt *me*"). There is, he points out, an "elegant wrapping" to his attack, but cross-examination is invariably a cruel science. "You've got to smell the weakness," Shargel says. "Where is this person vulnerable?" He is masterly at what trial lawyers call "control"—damaging a witness's credibility while simultaneously confining him to short answers, so that he cannot make harmful speeches about the defendant. Shargel rarely raises his voice; his weapons are wit and sarcasm. ("You sold drugs, right? . . . You *did* drugs, right? . . . You worked in gambling parlors, right? . . . Would you lie to get out of jail? . . . Never? . . . Because you wouldn't stoop to something like *that*, would you?")

One of Shargel's proudest achievements was a merciless two-day cross-examination, in February, 1992, of Ronald Rivera, the key witness in People v. Gambino. On behalf of the Manhattan District Attorney's Office, Rivera, a state trooper working undercover, ran Chrystie Fashions, a garment factory in a loft on the edge of Chinatown. While his "employees" sewed children's jeans, elastic pants, pleated skirts, and other garments for various clothing manufacturers, Rivera gathered evidence that the sons of the late Carlo Gambino, Thomas and Joseph, had taken extortionate control of trucking in the New York garment industry. Shargel, who represented Joe Gambino, committed Rivera's daily reports to memory, and he made a fool of Rivera by continually correcting his testimony: "Look at your report of September 7, 1988. . . . Does that refresh your recollection? . . . Look at September 30th. . . . One p.m., if you can't find it, Trooper Rivera." By the end of his cross, Shargel had thoroughly humiliated the state's star witness. ("How can I be accurate?" Rivera finally pleaded. "There's too many details.") Less than two weeks later, the District Attorney's Office agreed to an unusual disposition: Tommy and Joe would plead guilty to antitrust charges, pay several million dollars in fines, and agree to sell part of the Gambino trucking fleet and, in return, they would face no jail or probation. Shargel is still gleeful about his mauling of the trooper, but today he does not even remember the trooper's name. "I don't have any feeling one way or another toward that cop," he says. "He had a job to do, and I had a job to do, and I just did it better." He laughs.

The Gambino deal is one of the coups for which Shargel is best known, along with the Gotti acquittal, but he has won other surprising victories. In his 1992 defense of the real-estate developer William Romano, he played on the distrust that jurors often feel toward law officers. Romano had been arrested at Kennedy Airport by a customs inspector, after the inspector and another customs officer claimed they had discovered more than three pounds of heroin strapped to his body. The first witness was the arresting officer. ("He was sweating a lot. . . . I removed the bulge from his back. It was a package in brown tape.") The other officer corroborated his testimony. The heroin was shown to the jury. Shargel argued that his client had been framed. He pounded on the fact that no photograph was taken of Romano wearing the heroin. He portrayed the arresting officer as greedy for a promotion. He called nine character witnesses for Romano, including a pastor. "Only if you accept with blind faith . . . that cops will never lie" could there be a conviction, he told the jury. Romano walked.

Shargel does not like to settle cases, although his reputation as a trial lawyer often enables him to strike good deals, even in the face of overwhelming evidence. One of his clients, the real-estate executive Robert Goldberg, tried to have his wife murdered so that he could run off with a Korean prostitute. On October 1, 1992, at the main branch of the

New York Public Library, Goldberg met with Thomas Beltraz, a private detective who said that he would arrange the hit in exchange for eleven thousand dollars; Beltraz in fact was working undercover for the police. During the meeting, Goldberg gave Beltraz a down payment of twenty-five hundred dollars, and suggested that the hit man stalk his wife and her best friend at the shopping mall, and kill them both, to make it look like a robbery. He asked that the assassin wait a week, until after the Jewish holidays—because "there's gonna be a lot of friends and family around"—and said of his wife, "Look, the last thing I want is for her to be in pain. . . . I might hate her guts, but it's a human being." The entire meeting was captured on videotape and audiotape. Shargel was eager to try the case; he formulated what he called his "nerd defense"—that Goldberg was too pathetic to be a calculating killer. Last summer, however, Goldberg decided to plead guilty, and Shargel negotiated a sentence that could have him out of prison in three years.

Shargel often takes unwinnable cases, and, not surprisingly, does not win them; even the best defense attorneys lose a lot of the time. His defense, in 1987 and 1988, of Jimmy Coonan, the leader of the Westies, the Irish mob that operated in Hell's Kitchen, ended in conviction and a seventy-five-year sentence for Coonan, although Shargel still counts it as one of his best efforts. Coonan's motto was "No corpus delicti, no investigation," and it was his practice to dismember the bodies of his murder victims and dispose of the parts in plastic garbage bags. By the time his case came to trial, a number of Westies had turned informant. One, Billy Beattie, described how Coonan took a serrated kitchen knife to the corpse of a loan shark and "whacked his head off." Another, Tony Lucich, testified that Coonan gave him a plastic bag containing the severed hands of a rubout victim, to store in the freezer, so that the fingerprints could be planted on a murder weapon. The star witness was Coonan's former No. 2 man, Mickey Featherstone, a paranoid schizophrenic who once tried to strangle his wife while hallucinating that she was a Vietcong agent. Featherstone said he had committed murders on Coonan's behalf.

"One of the best summations I ever gave was for Jimmy Coonan,"

Shargel says. "It had a great ending. I thought of it in the shower as I was getting ready to go to court. The idea came to me from listening to Martin Luther King's kitchen-epiphany sermon. You know, King is despondent, and he's sitting in his kitchen late at night, and he hears the voice of Jesus: 'He promised never to leave me, never to leave me alone, no, never alone.' In the Westies trial, there was such a focus on Mickey Featherstone, and his craziness, and how he kept hearing voices. So I said, right at the very end of the summation, 'Let me share something with you. Mickey Featherstone hears voices calling him back to Vietnam. Jimmy Coonan hears voices, too.' Everybody went silent. *What?*"

>Jimmy Coonan hears voices, too.
>
>He hears the voice of a Bill Beattie, saying, "I don't want to go to jail for life." Those are the voices that he hears. . . .
>
>And he hears the voice of a Tony Lucich, who says, "You left me here on Tenth Avenue. I got problems with a drug case that has nothing to do with you. . . . You left me behind. You promised never to leave me. . . .
>
>He hears those voices. . . .
>
>And he hears the voice of a Mickey Featherstone, saying, "I loved you once but now I hate you. . . . " He says, "Jimmy, I'm drowning. I'm drowning. My life is going before me. . . . I need you because you are my ticket out of here. I loved you once and now I hate you. And you promised never to leave me!"
>
>These witnesses are reaching out from their prison cells, their cesspools of perjury . . . and they are trying to drag Jimmy Coonan down. They won't let him live.
>
>And I am asking you to let him live.

"I had jurors crying," Shargel recalls. "I had tears in my own eyes. I loved it. Didn't work, though."

Attorneys are not an admired species: in opinion polls, they rank somewhere below journalists. Even people who believe firmly in the right to counsel often begrudge lawyers like Shargel what they do for a living. It seems far too cynical. A criminal trial is a search for truth, yet the defense attorney does his best to confound that search even when he *knows* that his client is guilty. He takes the prosecutor's nice, orderly story about the defendant and attempts to obfuscate it with doubt and reduce it to chaos. He tries to make a witness who is telling the truth appear to be a liar. If he does his work well enough, the guilty party goes free.

Critics tend to forget that in our adversarial system it is defense counsel's prescribed role to be disingenuous if it will help win an acquittal for his client. Supreme Court Justice Byron White wrote, in United States v. Wade, "Our interest in not convicting the innocent permits counsel . . . to put the State's case in the worst possible light. . . . In this respect . . . we countenance or require conduct which in many instances has little, if any, relation to the search for truth." If the average person finds this precept hard to swallow, he can take solace in the fact that many prosecutors, and even many judges, cannot accept it, either.

Of the varieties of defense attorney, the Mafia lawyer presumably ranks among the very lowest in public esteem. By Shargel's estimate, there are, at most, fifteen lawyers in New York state who consistently defend major organized-crime figures. In attempting to account for his membership in this small corps, Shargel speaks exultingly of "the action." He is at a loss to understand why Jay Goldberg, another top trial lawyer, rarely takes on a mob case and has spent far more time handling civil litigation, for the likes of Donald Trump. "Jay made more money than any of us," Shargel says. "But he missed the action."

Not that Shargel doesn't make good money. He has a reputation for charging high fees. When he is paid on an hourly basis—a practice he discourages—he bills at what he calls a "normal" rate of around four hundred dollars an hour. For the most part, he commands flat fees of five or six figures, depending on the case. He will not give details. By the typical workingman's standards, Shargel is surely a rich man, but he is only occasionally ostentatious about his wealth. (A friend recalls,

"I once went over to Jerry's apartment for pizza, and he couldn't pay the pizza man, because all he had was hundred-dollar bills.")

But Shargel appears to be telling the truth when he says that the action, rather than the money, is what motivates him. One of his formative experiences occurred when he was sixteen. By lying about his age, he landed a job as a soda jerk and busboy at the Lido Hotel, in Lido Beach, Long Island. Up to then, his social life had revolved around a Jewish community center in New Jersey, but at the Lido he was exposed to gamblers, politicians, garment-center tycoons, and what his childhood friend Bernie Diamond, who worked with him at the Lido, calls "Damon Runyon characters." Diamond says, "Jerry seemed to have an addictive fascination for the seamy."

This fascination remains the best explanation of why Shargel has found himself at the Ravenite, and also at numerous private gatherings with mobsters—at the wedding of Nino Gaggi's daughter, at Tony Lee Guerrieri's wake, sipping cappuccino in Little Italy with Joseph (Joe Butch) Corrao. When the subject of Shargel's proximity to his clients was broached, he at first took a belligerent, I'm-not-in-business-to-satisfy-the-government attitude. "I could never be John Gleeson's ideal of a criminal-defense lawyer," he said. "The government's attitude is absurd—they're saying I should *distance* myself from my clients. I'm not interested in distancing myself. My wife always says I fall in love with my clients. It imbues me with some serum to go into court and fight for a guy and have passion in my voice. You don't get that by saying, 'I'll meet you, but only between nine and five in my office. I'll speak to you, but I won't come to your wedding. I'll defend you, but if a member of your family dies I won't come to the wake.' What kind of retainer is that?"

However, Shargel also admitted to a visceral thrill in being close to the powerful and dangerous. "Sure, there's a thrill involved," he said. "Don't you think Bernie Nussbaum is thrilled to be in the car with Bill Clinton? If you are a person's lawyer, you provide counsel at the highest level, whether the client is John Gotti or Mick Jagger. The guy who feels most important at a rock concert is the lawyer in the third row with the backstage pass clipped to his belt. People were critical of me for going to the Ravenite Social Club. 'You're a lawyer. Why'd you go down there?' I went to the Ravenite Social Club because I *loved* to go to the Ravenite Social Club. I loved the idea. I love the fact that when you represent someone you are automatically elevated to that person's level. So if John Gotti sits in the back at the round table at the Ravenite you can just walk in and walk past everybody and sit down at his table. You're elevated. If I was on Mulberry Street having dinner, I would want to go there; I'd look forward to going there; I was anxious to go there." He added, "Sometimes I would step back and imagine I was in a movie. Going to the Ravenite's cool because it's like a movie."

Terry Shargel does not share her husband's fascination. "I really had no interest in going to the Ravenite," she said one evening over dinner at the Shargels' apartment. She used to socialize with Jerry's Mob clients, and once attended a Mafia wedding ("I couldn't believe their names—Joe Butch and Danny Boy and Lucy Girl!"), but she stopped sometime in the mid-eighties. Terry is five feet four, auburn-haired, attractive, and tense. She deals in antique advertising posters, and the walls are covered with them. The apartment takes up an entire floor, but it is a moderate size for a couple with two children. Johanna was born in 1971, and David is five years younger. Shargel took his daughter's name from Dylan's "Visions of Johanna." She graduated summa cum laude from Yale, and was accepted to Yale Law School. David, the less scholarly sibling, studied for a pilot's license and, at sixteen, was already flying a Cessna, to his father's delight. The Shargels' cook, Bea, who served dinner, was one of their few extravagances. Besides renting the East Hampton summer home, they had two Mercedes-Benzes and a small boat called Defense Rests. "Jerry has always earned lots of money by my standard," Terry says. "We realized our dreams very young. Maybe our dreams weren't big enough."

The Shargels have a strong marriage. "They really love each other," Johanna says. "They still dream together, and move forward together. He makes her laugh. She supports him a hundred per cent." They are remarkably opposite in temperament, however. Terry says, "Jerry is friendly and sunny and outgoing, I make people uptight." Shargel, unlike his wife, is incapable of holding a grudge. His younger sister, Judy Shargel Greenberg, who operates a health-care agency, points out a quality in Jerry that is immediately discernible: he wants people to like him, and he will go to extraordinary lengths to repair a rift. One cannot help thinking that it must have been excruciating for Shargel to learn that Gotti was enraged at him. Yet when the subject of the "SHADDUP" incident came up at dinner Shargel was dismissive. "Was I nervous or upset when Gotti talked about throwing me out the, uh, not at all," he said. "I think I saw it for what it was—a momentary expression of anger. It wasn't something anyone would take seriously, except government agents without a sense of humor." And of Gotti's complaint that Shargel was overpaid he said, "It would only have bothered me if it pushed a button: the guy's right, I can't perform in a courtroom, and I charge too much money. But I heard that tape after I played a major role in winning a case for Gotti, so I certainly didn't feel it was right. In large measure, I found it amusing."

Terry said nothing then, but in a subsequent conversation, out of earshot of her husband, she made her feelings known. "I wasn't fearful—that was just nonsense," she said. "But I had to ask, 'Why are we in this picture? Why are you defending this man who has nothing nice to say to you? Isn't there anything better than "shaddup"?' It's so typical of John Gotti. Most of Jerry's clients adore him—they come up to me and hug and kiss me, because they've never had a lawyer who cared about them so much. I've met John Gotti, we've had coffee together, and he's very charming and witty and fast on his feet. But I'm not quite as fascinated as Jerry."

"SHADDUP" was not the only headline that the Shargels had to contend with. In the summer of 1991, segments of the Ravenite tapes were disclosed in court documents, and the tabloids had a field day. The *News* weighed in with "MY LAWYERS ARE 'RATS'" (one of Gotti's numerous put-downs) and, trumpeting Gleeson's investigation of Cutler and Shargel, "THE BOYS & THE HOOD." Terry's biggest concern was the effect of the publicity on David. "My son was a vulnerable age, thirteen or fourteen," she said. "He's a closed person and he doesn't discuss his emotions, so I really don't know even now how much he's affected, or if the kids in school are gossiping about his father." Shargel had taken his son to hear his opening statement in the Gotti assault trial, and Gotti had tried vainly to coax a reaction from him ("So, what did you think of your father? Was he great? Or was he a potato?"). But lately, Shargel says, David was beginning to question him. "He'll see a news story on TV, and ask me, 'Would you defend that person?' Not just once but over and over."

Johanna has found it difficult to be the daughter of a Mafia lawyer. Her problem, she says, is not so much with the clientele—to whom she has been exposed since the age of one, when her parents took her to an Italian restaurant in Brooklyn to have lunch with acting Colombo boss Joseph Brancato—as with "the negative publicity, and people regarding my father as doing something wrong, and looking down on him. I felt my own reputation was somehow damaged." At Yale, she says, the fact that her father had defended Gotti was "the first thing a lot of people knew about me, including my boyfriend." When the investigation of her father hit the newspapers during what she ruefully calls "the Gotti summer" of 1991, Shargel did not discuss it with her in any detail. "He'd just give me a five-sentence summary," she says. "He doesn't like to talk about unpleasant stuff."

Shargel admits this. He says he is most comfortable socializing with other defense counsel, so that he doesn't have to contend with the usual cocktail-party question about how he is able to defend bad people and keep from making judgments about them. "I know the question's coming, and I try to avoid it at almost any cost," he says. But after dinner, when the conversation continued in the living room, Shargel warmed up to the topic, as Terry listened in, with amusement.

"A lot of clients tell me they're innocent, because they think I'll work harder for them," he said. "That's not true. It's irrelevant. The question is: Can the State prove its case? The guy can be guilty as hell, but if I win an acquittal it means *a fortiori* that there was something infirm or wrong with the prosecution's case, and they weren't entitled to the conviction. I am intellectually satisfied and I am morally satisfied, because the system worked. I think I served society. On another level, I'm in it to win it. I was in a contest, and I won the contest. So, of course, I'm elated."

Did he ever feel compassion for the victim?

"No. I don't think about it. I'm detached. I've seen death of every kind and description, and it simply does not affect me. I once handled a murder case in Nassau County. They showed color photographs of a young woman who had been stabbed multiple times, and her body was found lying in a bathtub. That's as bad as it gets. I can look at those gruesome pictures with the cold eye of a surgeon. I just get to work. I have to be divorced from the underlying acts, because a man who's charged with not only killing someone but disembowelling the person or cutting the person up into little pieces—it's a horrendous, horrendous act. Would probably make some people of weak stomach vomit. But if my mind is influenced by that act then I can't be a formidable advocate for that person. I mean, I guess I've had dinner with people who are perfectly charming, and I don't think, Geez, this guy was out slaughtering people."

Was this a conscious decision?

"No, just the opposite. I think it's probably subconscious. If it were conscious, it would mean that I filter out the thought and push it aside. I don't do that. The thought never gets to that process."

Terry said, "It's like we can't sit around thinking about people starving in India, because if we did we'd all be dysfunctional."

"Don't you see?" Shargel said. "I would start thinking, If I get Client X acquitted, he's almost certain to go out and commit a violent act again, because of his history. What would that mean? I can't sleep at night, I can't eat because, Jesus, I'm fighting for this guy, and he's gonna get out. That would have to affect the way that I work, and my summation or cross-examination might not be that vigorous. Not only does that sell out my client but, on a broader scale, it sells out the system. And you know what really sucks? Probably many of the people who call themselves criminal-defense lawyers judge their clients. I go in and fight as hard as I possibly can, and I don't worry about what's going to happen next. Because if I do, I'll lose my effectiveness."

Shargel gets his happy disposition from his father, Leo, whose paint-and-wallpaper store was in Somerville, New Jersey, ten miles from New Brunswick. That is where Shargel was born, on October 5, 1944, and where he grew up, with his younger sister, Judy. Although Leo did not go to college—Shargel was the first in his family to do so—he loved books, and Shargel's friends considered Leo an intellectual because he read the *Times*. Shargel's mother, Lillian, was "the planner and organizer in the family," according to Judy. (Both parents are still living but declined to be interviewed for this account; Judy says they were badly shaken by the negative publicity in 1991.)

Shargel did not get good grades in school, and he says his parents never pushed him. Judy recalls that "he always knew he would be successful, and go places with his charm and personality." Shargel claims his tendency to defy authority began in school, where he was "a discipline problem" and "a wise-ass." When he reached the tenth grade, he was bused to Bound Brook High School, as one of perhaps a dozen Jewish kids in a class of two hundred and fifty. His best friend at the time, Ed Steckel, recalls the Italian boys as "working-class tough guys who drove big Mercurys and wore black leather jackets," and who picked on Shargel in the school bus and the locker room. "A number of years ago," Steckel says, "I said to Jerry, 'Isn't it goddam ironic? The very guys who used to fuck with you are now your clients.'"

In 1962, despite his poor grades, Shargel gained admission to Rutgers—just barely, because his mother worked there as a secretary. He majored in history, became the rush chairman of his fraternity, and drove a motor scooter. In his senior year, he got his job as a bartender—an experience as educational, he says, as anything he learned in class. By then, he was pinned to Terry Krapes, a speech-pathology major at Douglass College whom he had met at a school mixer. Reflecting fondly on the action at the Lido Hotel, Shargel saw himself becoming a maitre d', but Terry nixed the idea. "I tried to explain that it wouldn't work, me being the wife of a hotel manager," she recalls. "I was too artsy for that—I wore black and hung out in cafés in Greenwich Village and smoked cigarettes. I figured I should at least be married to a professional man. And, since Jerry had no aptitude for math or science, the only option was law."

Shargel enrolled at Brooklyn Law School in 1966. Terry, a year younger, was completing her senior year at Douglass, and Shargel lived alone in the spare room of a Manhattan brownstone. He hunkered down and, for the first time, became an A student. The professor who taught him property law, Leo Glasser, was then, as he is now, irascible, a brilliant scholar of the law, and a pedant. A quarter century later, as a federal judge, Glasser would brand Shargel a Gambino-family house counsel and disqualify him from the most recent Gotti case. "I remember he gave me an A in the course," Shargel says. "He graded me more harshly in the disqualification motion."

In July of 1968, during the summer before his final year of law school, Shargel worked as a student assistant in the Brooklyn United States Attorney's Office—the only time in his life he has sat at the government table. He had a chance to observe a number of legendary criminal defenders of the day, such as Henry Singer and Murray Edelbaum. When a prosecutor he assisted, John Leone, tried a routine truck-hijacking case against the defense attorney James LaRossa, Shargel looked longingly in LaRossa's direction. "John Leone was a good prosecutor, but in my heart I was bonding with LaRossa," he says. "I would have much preferred to be sitting at his table. The grass looked greener over there—no pun intended. I'm not talking about money. The prosecution table was drab and humorless, while the defense table seemed stylish and alive."

In January of 1969, Shargel joined LaRossa's law firm as a student clerk; he did legal research, wrote briefs, and parked LaRossa's Cadillac. By December, he had been admitted to practice law, and was made an associate. Shargel soon developed into LaRossa's law person, becoming an expert at appellate work—a desk job that involves poring over the transcript of a trial that has ended in a conviction and writing a brief

to the Court of Appeals arguing why the conviction should be overturned.

Once in a while, Shargel would get a chance to try a case—usually if
LaRossa had a scheduling conflict, or if a client couldn't afford
LaRossa's fee. Shargel's first trial involved counterfeit cashier's checks.
He lost. The second concerned a bank heist. "They showed that my guy
was almost destitute and that shortly after the robbery he went on a
trip around the world," Shargel recalls. "I got him acquitted."

In 1974, LaRossa made partners of Shargel and an older associate,
Ronald Fischetti. LaRossa was gaining in prominence, helped in part by
the prosecutor Maurice Nadjari, who had a habit of indicting judges
and public officials, then losing the cases or having the convictions
reversed. LaRossa successfully defended the judge Ross DiLorenzo and
the New York City tax-commission president Norman Levy.

By 1976, Shargel and Fischetti had grown tired of laboring in
LaRossa's shadow, and they quit to form their own partnership. The
wounds have since healed, all three men agree, but they were painful
at the time. "I guess my ego was hurt that they decided to leave
together," LaRossa says. As it turned out, Fischetti & Shargel lasted
only two and a half years; in early 1979, they split to become solo
practitioners.

Shargel was still better known as an appellate lawyer, and in June of
1979 he made national news in that capacity when the state Appellate
Division overturned the murder conviction of his client Anthony (Tony
Pro) Provenzano, and ordered a new trial. A suspect in the disappearance of Jimmy Hoffa, Tony Pro had been convicted of killing the Teamsters boss Anthony (Three Fingers) Castellito. Shargel argued
successfully that the trial judge should have dismissed a juror who had
a personal acquaintance with the prosecutor, rather than force the
defense to eliminate her by using up a peremptory challenge.

Shargel came into his own as a trial lawyer in 1981, when he
defended Nicholas Barbato, the former Republican boss of Smithtown,
New York. Barbato was accused of taking $267,500 in kickbacks from
Bowe Walsh & Associates, an engineering firm, in return for helping the

firm win a sewer contract. Shargel portrayed Barbato, whose family owned a large vegetable stand, as an honest, simple farmer—"a man with soil under his fingernails"—but a former Bowe Walsh executive, Edward Higgins, testified that he himself had withdrawn money from a slush fund and delivered part of it to Barbato personally. In a closing statement that Shargel still considers one of his finest, he ridiculed Higgins' demeanor on the stand, noted grave inconsistencies in his testimony, and, in a King-like peroration, said of his client, "This is the system that he worked for, this is the system that he believes in, and this is the system that will set him free." Barbato was acquitted.

Since Shargel's first high-profile trial was a white-collar case, he might easily have developed a practice geared toward nonviolent crime. A lot of people view LaRossa as a Mafia lawyer, and assume that Shargel became one by having worked for him. The fact is that although LaRossa has represented a number of Mafia figures—including Paul Castellano, who ran the Gambino family until December, 1985, when Gotti had him murdered—he has represented many more judges and lawyers. LaRossa is among the people who have been most critical of Shargel's visits to the Ravenite. "I can't defend Jerry's appearance in that goddam place," LaRossa says. "O.K.? I love him like a son, and I'd like to strangle him for doing it. I said, 'If you do it again, I'll come after you with a baseball bat.' And I would. Out of love. Jerry tried that case with Gotti, and he started to eat it up. He got intoxicated. It's as simple as that. Stupid. Stupid."

The man who describes himself as Shargel's other mentor, a lawyer named Michael Coiro, sees nothing wrong in such visits—he has made several himself—but Coiro is in no position to give advice. In 1989, he was convicted of acts of racketeering—obstruction of justice and helping to stash the profits of a heroin deal—on behalf of the Gambino crime family. He got fifteen years—later reduced to eleven—then nine months more for perjury. To John Gleeson, who successfully prosecuted him, Mike Coiro is the very model of a house counsel—living proof of his theory about the way the Mafia can corrupt its lawyers.

That Shargel has remained loyal to Coiro and provided him with free legal assistance has been interpreted as sinister by Gleeson.

Coiro, who is now sixty-three, is being held at the Federal Correctional Institution in Allenwood, Pennsylvania. This past fall, in a visitor's room there, dressed in a khaki uniform and sneakers, he reminisced about the days before he got into trouble—days when he was a defense attorney with a booming practice, and Jerry Shargel was a promising young man he had taken a shine to. Coiro looks a bit like the former Yankee shortstop Phil Rizzuto. As a lawyer, he was known for slapping his clients' backs and addressing everyone as "General." Jail has left him wistful but not bitter. "I'm not going to protest my innocence," he said. "I'm here."

Coiro, who grew up in the Borough Park section of Brooklyn, among several of his future Mob clients, won a remarkably high percentage of his cases. "I had a knack with jurors," he said. "They just loved me." Shargel concurs, saying, "You could be caught in the cab of a stolen tractor-trailer with two guns in your pocket, and Coiro could get you acquitted."

Shargel was twenty-five, working for LaRossa, and living on Clinton Street in Brooklyn, near the criminal courts, when he met Coiro. Though married, Coiro had no children of his own, and he could show paternal affection for young people he liked; Jerry Shargel was one of them. Because Coiro had moved to Long Island, it was often difficult for him to appear in night court for arraignments; Shargel happily stood in for him. Before long, Coiro was recommending Shargel to his clients for appellate work if they should be convicted. (Among the referrals was Jimmy Burke, of the Lucchese family—the man portrayed by Robert DeNiro in "GoodFellas.") "Mike was really my first source of business," Shargel says.

Coiro also gave Shargel his entree into the milieu of mobsters. "I said, 'Jerry, you sit in your ivory tower too much. I want you to see what the clients are really like,'" he recalled. "So we made the circuit. I brought him to Queens, and Brooklyn, and Manhattan, and opened up a whole new world for him—night clubs, supper clubs, the racetrack. There was a club on Queens Boulevard called The Suite, and I think it was the first time Jerry had been in a place like that. I introduced him around. At first, the fellas said to me, 'You know, Mike, he's an able guy, this *Mister* Shargel, but he comes on like an assistant U.S. Attorney.' I think I helped loosen him up a great deal. You have to remember, the fellas like to meet and talk with lawyers outside the office. They get a feeling of camaraderie—you're not afraid to sit in a bar and have a drink with them. 'Hey! This is Mike Coiro—he's my lawyer. This is Jerry Shargel.' The government frowns on that. They think it means you're becoming one of them."

One of the "fellas" that Shargel met was John Gotti. Gotti later employed a favorite put-down to describe Shargel in those days: "I remember Jerry when Jerry was an ambulance chaser." Gotti was not such a big shot himself at the time—he was an acting captain—but, for all the myths that have grown about him, he was certainly charismatic. And a thug. It was during this period, he later recalled, that he broke a man's legs, ankles, and jaw, then pried a gun into his mouth and taunted him: "You wanna play anymore?"

As Gotti's lawyer, Coiro had served him well. In the late sixties, Gotti was busted twice for truck hijacking, and a charge of kidnapping was thrown in the second time, but Coiro managed to work out a plea that involved no additional jail for the second case. Gotti was never long on gratitude, however. One day in 1979 or 1980, while Coiro was dining at the Villaggio d'Italiano, a Mob-owned restaurant in Queens, with Jimmy Burke, Gotti walked in, and Coiro failed to greet him. Enraged, Gotti returned to his nearby hangout, the Bergin Hunt & Fish Club, and sent for Coiro. According to the trial testimony of James Cardinali, who did menial jobs at the Bergin, Gotti threatened to "stuff" Coiro "in the fireplace," but instead assaulted him verbally: "I found you, you were a fifty-dollar ambulance chaser! You are a piece of shit! You're supposed to run when you see me! You sit there with Jimmy Burke, don't get up to say hello to me, I'll kill you!" Coiro took it meekly—"I'm sorry, Johnny"—and, Cardinali related, "that was the end of it."

Gotti's crew, which included his brother Gene, a soldier named

Angelo Ruggiero, and Ruggiero's brother Sal, trafficked in heroin. Sal had been a fugitive from three indictments since the mid-seventies, and on May 6, 1982, his chartered Learjet crashed off the coast of Georgia, killing him and his wife. Federal agents found Sal's hideout in New Jersey, and began watching Gotti's crew members more closely. It was difficult for them to sell heroin, and Angelo was worried because Sal's in-laws had been subpoenaed by a grand jury and he did not trust them.

Shortly after the plane crash, Mike Coiro was called in to help sort out these problems. He and Gotti's crewmen sat around the kitchen table of Angelo Ruggiero's home, in Cedarhurst, Long Island, never suspecting that the kitchen was being bugged by the F.B.I. Coiro managed to obtain through bribery a confidential document from the Nassau County D.A.'s office—"Forewarned is forearmed," he said—and he was prepared to coach Sal's in-laws, who, as Coiro put it, were not "people like us," on how to lie to the grand jury.

On May 12th, Gene Gotti addressed Coiro. "We don't make out . . . that you're our lawyer," he said. "You're not our lawyer. You're one of us as far as we're concerned."

"I know it, Genie, and I feel that way. That's a honor."

On May 21st, Coiro and Ruggiero once again conferred in Ruggiero's kitchen.

"I got this fucking tail on me, Mike—it's unbelievable," Ruggiero said. "I can't go no place, cause I'm being followed. . . . I might as well put heroin in my fucking hands than the money." Would Coiro hide the cash until the heat was off?

"O.K., no problem," Coiro said.

On August 23, 1983, Mike Coiro and seven Gambino soldiers, including Angelo Ruggiero and Gene Gotti, were arrested on heroin and obstruction-of-justice charges. Coiro was led, handcuffed, to his arraignment. His lawyer, Gerald Shargel, refused to accept a fee for his services.

In January of 1984, Shargel took on a partner. Judd Burstein was the very image of a law person—barely thirty years old, he had receding curly hair and a high forehead, and wore big round glasses. His mother was a judge. A scholar of the first rank, Burstein took care of writing briefs, so that Shargel could concentrate on his trial practice. In March, Shargel threw a lavish party at the Harmonie Club to commemorate the partnership.

That month, Shargel was hit with a grand-jury subpoena. Walter Mack, a prosecutor in the Manhattan United States Attorney's Office, was investigating a faction of the Gambino family which had been headed by a short, fat former butcher's apprentice named Roy DeMeo. The DeMeo crew specialized in murder; DeMeo was the Mafia's favorite general contractor for jobs in which bodies had to disappear. A Brooklyn apartment served as a slaughterhouse: dead victims were dragged into the bathroom, bled dry in the shower, stretched out on a swimming-pool liner in the living room, taken apart, and neatly packaged in cardboard boxes tied up with string. In the book "Murder Machine," authors Gene Mustain and Jerry Capeci estimate that the DeMeo gang dismembered more than two hundred victims. DeMeo disappeared on January 10, 1983, and was found a week later in the trunk of his Cadillac, shot to death. Walter Mack learned that Shargel had been the lawyer for DeMeo and several members of his crew. If DeMeo had paid Shargel's fees on behalf of those crew members— what are known as "benefactor payments"—that was evidence of the existence of DeMeo's criminal enterprise. Shargel was ordered to testify and to produce financial records. He moved unsuccessfully in district court to quash the subpoena, then appealed to the Second Circuit.

It was all too much for Judd Burstein, and within a few months he quit. Terry Shargel was furious, but Jerry, unable to carry a grudge, calculates that he has since directed over a million dollars in business to his former partner. Today, Burstein is one of the leading law persons of the New York criminal bar, and more than half of his practice is in civil litigation. He says he is baffled that Shargel's practice is so much narrower than his own. "Jerry doesn't care about being called a Mob lawyer," Burstein says. "I would. I don't want to be a Mob lawyer. I asked him once, 'You have the talent to be one of the leading lights of the bar—doesn't it upset you to be stigmatized?' He said no, because he likes what he does. It's almost paradoxical for somebody who is so great an artist—and Jerry is one of the finest trial lawyers I've ever seen—to have such relatively small horizons."

On August 13, 1984, the Second Circuit ruled against Shargel, forcing him to answer the subpoena. A week later, he appeared before the grand jury, refused on Fifth Amendment grounds to answer Walter Mack's questions, and declined to produce any records. Two days later, he returned to the witness box with immunity, and presented photocopies of check stubs—with dates and figures but no names—and three documents. One of the documents was a sales receipt for a 12-gauge shotgun—a gift from DeMeo after Shargel had mentioned feeling unsafe at night in a summer home in Quogue. (DeMeo advised him to be careful with the gun, because "if anything happened to you, I couldn't live with myself.") Shargel testified that he was almost always paid in cash by his Mafia clients, and that he kept no records of who had paid him what. As for his appointment diaries, he had destroyed them shortly before receiving the subpoena, he said, in response to a Supreme Court decision, United States v. Doe, which provided no guarantee of privilege for such diaries.

Shargel did remember that in October of 1981 DeMeo had handed him a paper bag in front of Ferrara's, a pastry shop in Little Italy.

> Q: What was in the bag?
> A.: Money.
> Q.: How much money?
> A.: I think some two thousand dollars. . . .
> Q.: What was that money received on account of?
> A.: Continued legal services in connection with . . . Mr. DeMeo.
> Q.: And it's your testimony to us that no moneys received on that occasion were . . . for any services rendered . . . to Mr. Dordal, Mr. Gaggi, or anyone else? [Paulie Pinto Dordal and Nino Gaggi were two associates of DeMeo who were

also represented by Shargel.]

A.: That's right.

This was very different from grand-jury testimony given five months earlier by Freddy DiNome, a former drag racer employed by Roy DeMeo as a chauffeur. After DeMeo's death, a police detective and an F.B.I. agent had succeeded in "flipping" DiNome—making him an informant. He remembered driving DeMeo to Little Italy and witnessing the incident with the paper bag.

> Q.: Could you tell the grand jury what you recall about
> that? . . .
> A.: We seen Jerry's car, Shargel, the lawyer. He had a . . .
> white Jaguar, four door . . . parked right in front of Ferrara's.
> Q.: And what happened?
> A.: Roy handed him a big bag of money.
> Q.: And did you hear anything said between the two?
> A.: Well, they were talking about Nino's case and they
> would also talk about Paulie Pinto's appeal. . . . He said, "I
> just gave [Shargel] a hundred and fifty thousand dollars.
> Between [Nino] and Paulie, they're breaking me."

The grand jury returned indictments against twenty-four people in the mass-murder case, and the defendant who was represented by Shargel was a crew member named Richard Mastrangelo. In a brief submitted to Abraham Sofaer, the Manhattan federal-district-court judge hearing the case, Walter Mack moved to have Shargel disqualified from the trial. He argued that Shargel had become house counsel to the DeMeo crew, that his alleged receipt of benefactor payments was evidence of a criminal enterprise and so made him a potential witness, and that he might be less than vigorous in defending Mastrangelo, because he faced possible criminal charges himself, including perjury.

Judge Sofaer issued his first opinion on March 5, 1985. He was largely sympathetic to Shargel, and called disqualification a "drastic step."

Sofaer scheduled a hearing later that month to clear up the matter. At the hearing, Judge Sofaer personally questioned DiNome, and on May 1st he issued a second opinion, disqualifying Shargel from the trial in language that can best be described as scathing. Sofaer had measured the credibility of Gerald Shargel, member of the bar and former law professor, against that of Freddy DiNome, a fourth-grade dropout and pothead who had once chopped off the head of a neighbor's dog to settle a dispute. Evidently, he found DiNome more credible.

DiNome admitted that he had never seen the money inside the bag, and he had altered his story—now the amount was only a hundred thousand dollars. "That DeMeo actually passed $100,000 in cash to Shargel in a paper bag . . . may be unlikely," Sofaer wrote. "Yet a jury may conclude that Shargel's story of having received only $2,000 at that time is also unlikely. . . . Shargel's lack of any records of his income, and the manner in which he claims he is paid and keeps track of his money, may make jurors skeptical as to his veracity in general." A jury could find that Shargel's practice of not keeping records was "adopted at the behest of his clients," he wrote, so that they "could receive legal services the value of which clearly exceeded their income from legitimate sources."

Sofaer was also troubled by a story that DiNome told about the time he was incarcerated, before he agreed to flip for the government. During an unsolicited visit, the story went, Shargel had tried to find out whether DiNome was cooperating with the government, and had said he'd arranged for a lawyer to represent DiNome at no cost. (Shargel suggested to Judge Sofaer that he had meant that DiNome's brother was going to pay the legal bills. DiNome scoffed at that: "My brother couldn't even pay attention.") Crew members were compelled to "use the lawyers that they assign to you," DiNome said. "This way, if you're doing anything wrong, they would know about it."

Sofaer wrote, "By picking a crew member's attorney, in addition to paying him, a crew leader can require him to use an attorney who will . . . seek to keep his nominal client from cooperating, or from otherwise harming the crew's interests." Moreover, Sofaer noted, a second cooperating witness had corroborated DiNome's claims about bene-factor payments to Shargel. In conclusion, he wrote, "Shargel's conduct raises a credible appearance of impropriety."

In early 1986, Freddy DiNome, who had been renamed Freddy Marino and deposited in San Antonio, Texas, as a protected witness, hanged himself.

Shargel naturally has bitter memories of the disqualification, but he recalls that Walter Mack, unlike John Gleeson, was just doing his job, and that it never got personal. Mack confirms that he and Shargel are friendly today, and that "we even joke about" the litigation. As for whether Mack ever seriously thought of prosecuting Shargel, he says simply, "It wasn't considered after Freddy died."

Shargel suggests that Judge Sofaer got taken. "That whole situation about benefactor payments turned on the word of unsavory scoundrels who sold themselves to the government and told prepos-terous stories," he says. And, no doubt reflecting on Sammy Bull Gra-vano, now in John Gleeson's hands, he adds, "One of the most dangerous aspects of this practice is that every client you ever have is a potential enemy."

Gravano was apparently a born killer, though his homicidal nature is hard to figure. His family, in Bensonhurst, Brooklyn, owned a dress business that employed fifteen people, and his early ambition was to be a hairdresser. But by the end of 1990 he had done nineteen mur-ders—ten of them for his boss, John Gotti. In 1978, he killed Nick Sci-betta, who was his brother-in-law: Scibetta's sister, Debbie, was Sammy's wife and the mother of his daughter and son. Gravano claimed that the murder was done on Mob orders, because Scibetta had become an informant, but there were persistent rumors of more personal motives. Scibetta's body was cut to pieces, and only one hand was recovered. It was buried at a funeral service attended by Gravano, who vowed to find the killer.

Gravano had first hired Shargel to defend him in a bizarre tax case that stemmed from one of his murders. In June of 1982, Frank Fiala, the boss of a Yugoslav crew, threw himself a birthday party at the Plaza Suite, a Brooklyn disco owned by Gravano, who also had title to the building and land. Fiala offered to buy the property for a million dollars, and he put down six hundred and fifty thousand; then, when he attempted to withdraw the rest from foreign bank accounts, the deal stalled. On June 27th, Sammy Bull walked into his office, in the Plaza Suite building, and found Fiala, armed with a machine gun, behind his desk. Fiala ordered Gravano to be "nice" and make sure the deal went through; he had killed Colombians, he said, and "greaseballs" like Sammy would be "easy." That night, as Fiala left the disco, Gravano's crewmen ambushed and killed him. Gravano kept the six hundred and fifty thousand dollars, and on his 1983 tax return he explained simply, "Deal was aborted by purchaser." He was indicted for defrauding the I.R.S. by failing to declare the income in 1982, and went on trial in August, 1985.

The jury was not to learn that Fiala had been killed—merely that he had died. The trial was assigned to Judge Glasser. Shargel described the late Fiala as a "nut" and a "wacko," who rode into town and offered an absurd amount of money to his unsuspecting client, for whom the deal was "a dream come true . . . like the Lotto," and he explained, "Sam Gravano is from Staten Island . . . he didn't know about foreign bank accounts." Maybe Sam made a mistake on his return, Shargel said, but he was relying on the advice of his tax attorney. The attorney's testimony supported Shargel's thesis, and Gravano was acquitted.

It may have seemed misguided to go after a man like Salvatore Gravano with a simple tax case, but the practice had a history; even Al Capone had been taken down on his taxes. In the eighties, prosecutors began to wake up to the realization that far more effective weapons against the Mafia had existed for years. In 1968 and 1970, Congress had handed prosecutors two nuclear warheads, which had largely remained unused in their silos. The first was the Omnibus Crime Control and Safe Streets Act, which gave authority for court-approved electronic surveillance. The second was the Organized Crime Control Act, which included

RICO, the Racketeer Influenced and Corrupt Organizations statute. RICO enabled the government to attack the very structure of the Mob, by linking together even petty offenses, such as gambling and loan-sharking, as "predicate acts" in a "continuing criminal enterprise."

One thing that the eighties will be remembered for is the rise of RICO and electronic eavesdropping, which began the decline of the American Mafia. Another is a dramatic worsening of relations between prosecutors and criminal lawyers, especially in New York. Perhaps there was a connection: perhaps, as prosecutors began to look at criminal organizations as a whole, instead of focussing on isolated crimes of individuals, they came to see defense attorneys as more active parts of the equation. No one knows the reason for sure, but the climate today is nasty, and it used to be collegial.

In this new, tense environment, John Gleeson, who became a prosecutor in 1985, appeared to be a man for his time, whose rise, thanks to his combination of legal talent and righteousness, could have been foretold. The criminal bar's perception of him is best summed up in five words of Jimmy LaRossa's: "You can't make him laugh." In defense circles, Gleeson's nickname is the Jesuit. Shargel says he thinks that when Gleeson went to catechism class and heard the first Psalm, "Blessed is he who has not walked in the counsel of the wicked," he misheard it as "he who has not counselled the wicked."

If John Gleeson is a devout Catholic, it is one of many things he keeps to himself. Those who get to know him discover, often to their surprise, that while he looks clean-cut—he has dark, wavy hair, and he wears V-neck sweaters under his suit jackets, and tortoiseshell glasses that seem a size too large—he talks like an Irish cop: people he prosecutes are "mopes" and "pieces-a-shit." Gleeson was born in the Bronx, the seventh and last child of an Irish-immigrant father, Patrick, who moved his family to Westchester County when John was an infant. Patrick had never finished high school, and worked as a clerk for the Metropolitan Life Insurance Company in New York. In a letter, Gleeson noted that "discrimination against the Irish was overt and at its zenith" when his father arrived in New York, in the late twenties, and added that "although it took decades," Metropolitan Life finally awoke to Patrick's "natural abilities" and moved him into management.

John Gleeson excelled in high school as a scholar and an athlete—playing basketball, soccer, and golf—while earning money as a caddie at a local country club. His fellow-students voted him "cutest." He went on to Georgetown University on an academic scholarship, majored in English, and met his future wife, Susan, a nursing student. After graduation, in 1975, Gleeson spent two years painting houses in the vicinity of Washington, D.C., and then studied for a law degree at the University of Virginia. He and Susan lived in Louisville for a year while he clerked for Judge Boyce F. Martin, Jr., of the Sixth Circuit Court of Appeals. Gleeson discovered during his clerkship that he longed to be a prosecutor, but he took an indirect route, first accepting a job as an associate at the distinguished New York law firm of Cravath, Swaine & Moore.

Gleeson applied to the Manhattan United States Attorney's Office, then headed by Rudolph Giuliani, but he had to make do with a job offer from the Brooklyn office. He joined in 1985, taking a drastic cut in pay, to something less than forty thousand a year, and moved into an apartment in Brooklyn.

He was immediately teamed up with a prosecutor named Diane Giacalone on a multi-defendant RICO case called United States v. Dellacroce. Neil Dellacroce was the underboss of the Gambino family, and one of his co-defendants was a captain, John Gotti. The case was a hodgepodge of crimes dating as far back as the sixties—mostly acts of truck hijacking, gambling, and loansharking. In December of 1985, before the case came to trial, Neil Dellacroce died of cancer, and two weeks later John Gotti had the Gambino boss Paul Castellano murdered to settle an internal dispute. The case became United States v. Gotti, and the lead defendant was the most famous criminal in America. John Gleeson was thirty-two and Diane Giacalone was thirty-five.

Giacalone liked Gleeson, although she considered him "the world's worst dresser." As she recalls it, "he owned three suits, all shiny and too small." Apart from that, he impressed her. "No one works harder than John," she says. "I worked as hard as he did, but not harder. He is absolutely committed." Laurence Shtasel, another assistant United States Attorney at the time, recalls, "Night after night, I'd leave the office, and he'd be sitting there with headphones on, going over tapes of hard-to-hear conversations until he had them memorized." The intense work took its toll. "There were times we nearly killed each other," Giacalone says.

Giacalone believed that Gleeson, who had never tried a criminal case, should acquire some experience before the Gotti trial started. Arrangements were made for him to prosecute a few smaller cases, the first of which pitted him against Gerald Shargel. Shargel's client, Giovanni Mazzola, was accused of being an intermediary in a heroin sale, but Shargel presented him as an unwitting Italian translator who believed he was involved in the sale of gold. Gleeson told Shargel that this was his first trial, and repeatedly asked how he was doing. He soon found out: Shargel won an acquittal.

Gleeson never again tried a case against Shargel, but their next encounter formed the basis of his belief that Shargel was subservient to Gotti. Shargel had been retained to represent Armond (Buddy) Dellacroce, Neil's son, in United States v. Gotti, but after his father died Buddy decided to plead guilty to one count of racketeering. Buddy was thirty years old, a drunk, and a cocaine addict; Giacalone unwisely agreed to recommend bail in return for his guilty plea, and he vanished before his sentencing date. (Three years later, he was found dead of a drug overdose.) When Giacalone gave her opening statement at the Gotti trial, on September 25, 1986, she ended by promising to offer compelling proof of the existence of the Gambino Mafia family— Buddy's guilty plea. There was an uproar at the defense table. Within days, Shargel filed an affidavit with the court, asserting that he and Giacalone had an agreement that Buddy's plea could not be used as evidence. Giacalone and Gleeson countered with affirmations calling Shargel's affidavit false. In Gleeson's view, Shargel had been brought to task by an angry John Gotti, and ordered to swear to a false statement.

Shargel calls that "preposterous," and says, "I've never submitted a false affidavit to a court in my life." Christine Yaris, a Shargel associate at the time, also insists that there was a deal, and that she was on hand when Giacalone agreed to it. There was no hearing to determine whether Giacalone or Shargel was telling the truth, because the judge, Eugene Nickerson, ruled that even if there had been a deal it had become void when Buddy jumped bail.

If Gleeson's view of Mafia lawyers was tainted by Shargel's affidavit, that was nothing compared with the experience of the trial itself. For anyone reading the transcript of the trial today, it is hard to fathom how Judge Nickerson allowed it to become what he himself called "a circus." Perhaps Nickerson believed that Gotti would be convicted anyway, and wanted to guarantee the appearance of a fair proceeding, but in fact, there was never any chance of a conviction, because, as was later learned, a juror had been bribed.

Gotti's lawyer was Bruce Cutler. He had been introduced to Gotti in 1985 by Mike Coiro, whose own legal problems made him unable to continue representing Gotti. Cutler, who is almost entirely bald and has a big, bulging, bench presser's body, once said he felt like "a candy ass" compared with his client, whom he called "a man's man," along with other rapturous praise. Cutler's style could hardly be more different from Shargel's: he does not control witnesses so much as bully them, and he seems to go out of his way to make enemies of judges and prosecutors. Cutler's antics at the Gotti trial have been well documented—slamming the indictment into a wastebasket, referring to Giacalone as a "tramp" and a "slut," and, in one of the weirdest episodes ever to occur in federal court, calling a thoroughly disreputable witness merely to humiliate Giacalone and Gleeson.

The witness was Matthew Traynor, a bank robber and self-described "liar and a dope fiend" from Ozone Park, Queens, the heart of John Gotti territory. Giacalone and Gleeson had once visited Traynor in jail, and found him in need of medical care; Gleeson then arranged for Traynor to see a doctor at Beth Israel Medical Center, where Gleeson's wife, Susan, was a nursing supervisor. Ultimately, Giacalone and

Gleeson had determined that Traynor was too awful to put on the stand as a witness against Gotti, but Cutler called him as a defense witness in February, 1987, six months into the trial. In blatantly perjured testimony, which grew odder as he went along, Traynor said that Giacalone had asked him to "frame" Gotti and the other defendants, because she, too, had grown up in Ozone Park, and Italian men from the neighborhood "had ridiculed her about being skinny." Traynor went on to say that Giacalone was keeping another of her witnesses high on heroin, and he wanted to be "blocked out" on Valium and codeine (which happened to be the medication prescribed for him at Beth Israel). He also wanted to "get laid," although Giacalone could not help him with that, instead, Traynor said, she tossed him a pair of her panties and told him to "facilitate" himself.

Throughout Traynor's testimony, Giacalone had sat quietly, scribbling notes. She asked John Gleeson to cross-examine him, and he did so with the controlled anger that is his hallmark. Traynor did his best to unnerve Gleeson, berating him for "asking stupid questions," calling him "a meek little mouse" and a "lowlife," and noting that "there are people probably got a nicer suit on than you." Gleeson unwisely brought up the panties story, and then Traynor happily heaped on more detail: "She . . . told me, sniff them and jerk yourself off in the bathroom . . . and they smelled like deep-fried scallops."

Gleeson was dealt the lowest blow when defense counsel, hoping to prove that Traynor's medication was obtained improperly, served a subpoena on Beth Israel for the job records of Susan Gleeson. Judge Nickerson immediately quashed the subpoena, pronouncing it "off the wall," but Gleeson was livid. "The subpoena on his wife—that was it," Jeffrey Hoffman, one of the defense attorneys, recalls. "I had a good relationship with Gleeson up until that point, and because of that I was designated as the guy who dealt with the prosecution. Even though the subpoena was quashed, I couldn't talk to him after that. He was just . . . gone. Nothing. Ceased."

About seven months after jury selection had begun, both sides finally rested and gave summations. The defense attorney Richard

Rehbock accused Gleeson of filing a false affidavit to obtain the medical care for Traynor, and in his rebuttal Gleeson's self-control finally cracked: "You should take that accusation," he told the jury, and "shove it down the throat of defense counsel." On March 13th, the jury announced that it had reached a verdict. As Diane Giacalone and John Gleeson stared into space, the jury foreman pronounced "Not guilty" fourteen times, freeing each defendant on each of two counts. The Brooklyn United States Attorney's Office was stunned. Giacalone soon left the legal profession for a job in the private sector; Gleeson stayed.

"I don't think John or I would ever look at the world exactly the same way," Giacalone says now. "It was a lesson for both of us—that some people are willing to do anything. You'll never be innocent again after something like that, never be innocent again."

Shargel's reputation as a trial lawyer continued to grow, and in 1988 he became the lawyer for the Bronx Democratic boss Stanley Friedman. Friedman, a thick-waisted man with a goatee and a nasal Bronx accent, had already lost a federal RICO case, and been sentenced to twelve years for improperly inducing the Parking Violations Bureau to buy handheld computers in which he had a financial interest. Now he faced a state indictment for bribing a general in the New York National Guard to recommend his computers to the Guard.

When Friedman hired Shargel, he was headed for the federal penitentiary in Springfield, Missouri, a relatively congenial setting compared with prisons in New York, such as Attica and Rikers Island. The Manhattan District Attorney made Shargel an offer: if his client pleaded guilty, he would not face any state time. Friedman mulled the offer, but he could not take it. "It would have been the only time Stanley Friedman stood up and said, 'Yes, I did it,'" Friedman says today.

Shargel tried the non-jury case in front of Judge Marie Santagata, who rejected Shargel's central thesis—that the bribe was in fact a legitimate lobbying fee—and found Friedman guilty. By now, Shargel and Friedman had grown fond of each other, and Shargel's voice cracked with emotion as he pleaded with Santagata to reject the District Attorney's demand for more jail: "Stanley Friedman is a broken man—shamed, disgraced, and humiliated. He is a man who is saying, 'I showed compassion in my life, and I am entitled to it now.' But what does he get instead? 'Hit him more! Hit him again! Give him more!'" Judge Santagata was unmoved; she sentenced Friedman to the maximum term—two and a third to seven years—to be served consecutively with his federal time. Shargel appealed. The conviction was upheld, but the consecutive sentence was vacated as "unduly harsh."

Friedman was paroled in 1992, after serving four years. "A lot of people say, 'He got twelve years and he only served four.'" Friedman says. "I shudder when I hear 'only.' Unless someone served time, they shouldn't say 'only.'"

Friedman is unstinting in his praise of Shargel: "A lot of lawyers would feel, This is not a major case—even if I win it, the client doesn't get to go home. Jerry fought for me as if my whole life was riding on it. He read every document, he knew what the law was, he summed up terrific, and we got buried. The deck was stacked against us. That judge, it was very lucky that the statute didn't provide for the death penalty—she would probably have given me that. Before the trial started, the D.A. brought me from Springfield to Rikers Island. I spent ninety-one days there, and it was more traumatic than the four years in federal prison. It's a terror camp. People walk around with razor blades under their tongues, so they can give you a quick slash if the occasion arises. The buses you ride back and forth to the courthouse are death traps ready to explode any minute. And it's degrading and torturous for visitors. Jerry would come to visit me at least once a week at Rikers, and it cost him practically the whole day. And, even though he never said this to me, he knew I was tapped out, and I know I got a tremendous break on his normal prices. We are now friends."

Like Shargel, Friedman was an attorney educated at Brooklyn Law, but he says he can understand it if Shargel is also friendly with his Mafia clients. "The government put me in with the Fat Tony Salernos of this world for four years, and I played boccie with them, and I saw

them in the hospital when they were sick and dying, and you establish a relationship, because they're human beings who cry when
they're hurting, and who have wives that visit them. Sometimes circumstances dictate your friends." Shargel's attraction to Gotti makes
particular sense to Friedman. "From the beginning of time, power is
sexy," he says.

In January, 1989, Gotti was indicted by the Manhattan District
Attorney's Office for allegedly ordering the shooting assault of John
O'Connor, a carpenters' union official. The F.B.I., which had only a
peripheral role in the case, placed a number of bugs in and around the
Ravenite Social Club. On five nights during the winter of 1989 and
1990, shortly before the assault trial began, Gotti caucused in an apartment two stories above the Ravenite with his underboss, Sammy Gravano, and his consigliere, Frank (Frankie Lo) Locascio, as the F.B.I.
listened in. There were about a dozen conversations recorded in the
private hallway behind the back door of the club, and many more
recorded in the club itself.

On November 8, 1989, a legal problem had arisen. The late Carlo
Gambino's son Tommy, a captain in the family, was about to go on
trial for perjury and obstruction of justice, and Gotti and two of his
captains, Joe Butch Corrao and George (Fat Georgie) Remini, had been
subpoenaed to testify. As far as Gotti was concerned, this was blatant
harassment. It was against his rules to testify, so the three of them
would simply have to "do a contempt" and go to jail. Gotti seemed
more upset that Bruce Cutler, Jerry Shargel, and Mike Rosen, the lawyer
for Tommy Gambino, had failed to understand that this was the only
acceptable course of action. The three lawyers had met, he said, and
determined that Tommy Gambino should plead guilty, to spare Gotti
the "aggravation."

That evening, Gotti sat in the club with a group of his men—Joe
Butch, Frankie Lo, Jackie Nose, Joe Watts, and two who were
unidentified—and expounded on a favorite theme, the perfidy of
lawyers. "I hate them," Gotti said. "You know why I hate them? They

don't give a fuck about us seriously. . . . Otherwise, they wouldn't live on Park Avenue. They'd live down on Houston Street."

Bruce Cutler—or, as Gotti called him two days later, "this imbecile"—should have known better than to suggest that Tommy plead guilty, Gotti said. (Gotti apparently sanctioned guilty pleas only for what he called "malicious mopery"—minor offenses that had nothing to do with the existence of La Cosa Nostra and did not affect other members of the family.) Gotti related that he had told Cutler, "Now, you tell Tommy to fight it. Break their fuckin' holes, like he, I know he could. And don't worry about us going to jail. Me No. 1! I like jail better than I like the streets." Later, in the hallway, he added, "Get my cell ready! Get Joe Butch's cell ready! And get Fat Georgie's cell ready! And nobody is taking the stand! Tell them to go fight!" Cutler, he said, had protested that his duty was to protect Gotti but had been told, "No, your duty is to listen!"

Gotti was also disappointed in Jerry Shargel. Fat Georgie Remini, a loan shark and numbers runner, who owned a Staten Island fruit-and-vegetable stand called the Top Tomato, was Shargel's client, and he did not want to go to jail. Gotti related a conversation in which Shargel tried to consider other options for his "friend."

Gotti claimed he had told Shargel, "*Minchia!* Show some compassion. Show some interest. Think about it before you talk. Go for a walk or something. Maybe you ain't the fastest-thinking guy in the world. Then come back. 'Listen,'" he said, mimicking Shargel, "'I wanna talk to my client, and my friend. These are my friends, and beside being my client. . . . ' Who the fuck are youse? Who you working for? Did I tell you to do this? . . . If Georgie's on the case alone, you on a case by yourself, it's a malicious mopery, drunken-driving case, you'll get sixty days, you wanna take a plea? Take a plea. You got no right and—and jeopardize other people. Who the fuck are youse?"

Three weeks later, Remini appeared in court with Shargel, refused to testify, and got sixteen months. Gotti was subsequently convicted of obstructing justice in the Remini matter, and John Gleeson clearly saw Shargel as a conspirator. Shargel, he wrote, "was in fact implementing

Gotti's desire to corruptly prevent Remini's testimony." If this was the basis of Gleeson's would-be obstruction case against Shargel, it seems weak. Remini did not need Shargel to explain to him a soldier's duty to the enterprise. On November 10, 1989, he got his instructions directly from Gotti: "Do what I tell ya." But the November 8th tape offers unequivocal proof of Gotti's state of mind. In his perception, at least, the enterprise as a whole was Shargel's client, and not George Remini, and a year and a half later Judge Glasser focussed on the damning phrase "Who you working for?"

Michael Coiro's trial began on November 14, 1989—seven years after a bug caught him scheming with John Gotti's crewmen in Angelo Ruggiero's kitchen. Coiro's case had been delayed by complex legal motions. Shargel had been his lawyer all along, but now Shargel was in the middle of another trial, and Judge Joseph McLaughlin refused to postpone Coiro's trial any further. Coiro says that he turned to Gotti for help, and that Gotti got him Bruce Cutler. (Cutler denies that Gotti was involved.)

The prosecutor was John Gleeson, but a very different John Gleeson from the hectored junior assistant in the federal Gotti case. Two and a half more years of trial experience had left him seasoned and confident. Bruce Cutler was the same Bruce Cutler. "My yelling days are over," he assured Judge McLaughlin just prior to his opening statement.

"You were doing a pretty good imitation right there," McLaughlin said angrily.

Gleeson addressed the jury: "We're here because Mike Coiro was completely and thoroughly corrupt. He became one of them." Ninety per cent of the proof in the case, he said, would come from government tapes.

The trial went badly for Cutler, who is at his best in cross-examining informant witnesses. When it came time for Cutler to put on his defense case, he handed the judge more than a hundred pages of transcript, all out of order, of tapes he wished to play. For the next four and a half hours, the jury was kept waiting as McLaughlin gave Cutler a dressing-down. Cutler's tapes were "irrelevant junk," he said, and the transcripts should have been given to him "far earlier than today."

> CUTLER: Your Honor, maybe I am missing what you are saying.
> JUDGE: You are missing a body of knowledge called the law of evidence. . . . I suggest you take a course. . . .
> CUTLER: Judge, I didn't know you wanted all of these things done beforehand. . . .
> JUDGE [booming]: Are you accustomed to keeping juries sitting out there for three or four hours?

Cutler was left with no defense case apart from two short stipulations. Gleeson, in his summation, encapsulated his theme: "Just because you're a criminal lawyer, you can't be a criminal?" Earlier, Cutler had described Coiro as having "an unusual practice, a full-service practice," and Gleeson delighted in taunting Cutler with his own words: throughout his summation, he referred to Michael Coiro as "our full-service lawyer."

On the following day, November 29th, the jury was still deliberating Mike Coiro's fate, but at the Ravenite Social Club Gotti was concerned with his own. His trial in the O'Connor shooting-assault case had not even begun, and now a corrupt police detective had passed him the news that both federal and state prosecutors wanted to try him for the murder, four years earlier, of Paul Castellano.

Gotti stood in the private hallway behind the club with Joe Butch. "Why don't you call Jerry out?" Gotti said.

"Jerry!"

From inside the Ravenite club, Shargel stepped out into the hallway.

"Say the state wanted to go after me . . . for murder," Gotti said. "But the feds want to for the same thing. Does that make sense they would do it at the same time? Do the same charge, two different places?"

"They've done it," Shargel said. "They've done it in, uh, Stanley Friedman."

The next part of the conversation was only partly audible, but Gotti apparently wondered what statute the feds might use against a hypothetical "guy like myself . . . I'm not saying me" who had killed a person for advancement.

"There's a statute called 'committing murder in furtherance of your position,'" Shargel said. Then he asked, "Who was the guy?"

"Nobody," Gotti said.

There was laughter on the tape.

"Furtherance of your position, huh?" Gotti said. "That's nice."

Shargel said he would check to see "if that statute was in effect in December '85"—the month Gotti had Paul Castellano killed.

"Yeah . . . I'm curious," Gotti said. "Not for myself."

The next day, Coiro was convicted on all counts. Although he was released pending sentencing, he did not go home after hearing the guilty verdict; instead, Cutler escorted him straight to the Ravenite club. Coiro walked upstairs to the apartment for a private meeting with John Gotti, Frankie Locascio, and Sammy Gravano, and three hours after Coiro was convicted of obstructing justice Gotti was asking him to obstruct justice again.

"Mike," Gotti said.

"Yeah, John."

"First, you know, we're sorry."

"Thank you."

"I don't have to tell ya how sorry we are."

"Oh, John."

Gravano found Coiro a seat, and Gotti said, "I think he's gonna give you ten years. And maybe look for you to do three or four."

"I'll do it, John."

"So, you know, Mike, you got no choice."

Presently, Gotti moved on to his own problems. "I've been told by a source that that pinch is coming down. It's gonna be a joint pinch"—both the feds and the state. "I think that the thing is imminent." Gotti understood that Coiro had a corrupt source of information in law enforcement—"I never once asked you who he is," he pointed out—and he hoped the source could provide the names of Gambino captains also slated for indictment.

"Can you see this guy pronto?"

"Tomorrow."

Coiro went back downstairs, leaving Gotti alone with his underboss and his consigliere.

"Fuckin' heartbreak, you know why?" Gotti said, and then he explained why: Here was a lawyer, not even a made man, facing jail more calmly than some of his captains. "Fat Georgie, did fourteen hours in jail, crying fuckin' bum!"

Gotti had underestimated Coiro's sentence by five years, and John Gleeson would see to it that Coiro got even more time. A year later, Gleeson subpoenaed Coiro to testify before a federal grand jury investigating the Gambino family. He asked Coiro repeatedly if he had ever gone upstairs to any of the apartments above the Ravenite to confer with Gotti, and Coiro denied repeatedly that he had. Confronted with the apartment tape, Coiro pleaded guilty to perjury, and got twenty-seven additional months, which was later reduced to nine months.

Gotti was a rich man, with an illegitimate yearly income running well into the millions, but on January 4, 1990, sitting in the Ravenite apartment with Sammy Gravano and Frank Locascio, all that Gotti had to say about his lawyers was that they were too greedy.

"You know, these are rats, er, Sam. And I gotta say, they all want their money up front. And then you get four guys that want sixty-five, seventy-five thousand apiece, up front. You're talking about three hundred thousand in one month, you cocksucker!"

The night before, Gotti said, he had stood in the hallway with Jerry Shargel, discussing Shargel's fee for representing Tony Lee Guerrieri—Gotti's co-defendant in the O'Connor case, which was scheduled to begin in two weeks. "You know what it felt like? You, standing there in the hallway with me last night—and you're plucking me! 'How are you?' Tony Lee's lawyer, but you're plucking me. I'm paying for it. . . . Where does it end? Gambino crime family? This is the Shargel, Cutler & Whattaya-call-it crime family!"

"They wind up with the money," Gravano said.

"They're overpriced, overpaid, and, and, underperformed," Locascio said.

His lawyers could not win cases, Gotti said, because of "a bullshit agreement" that he believed existed between them and the prosecutors: "They don't fuck with youse, and youse don't go all out in court."

"You know and I know that they know that you're taking the money under the table," Gotti said. "Every time you take a client, another one of us on, you're breaking the law. . . . If they wanna really break Bruce Cutler's balls, what did he get paid off me? . . . I paid tax on thirty-six thousand dollars. What could I have paid him?"

Gotti said he told Shargel that the least he could do was find out when he was going to be arrested for the murder of Paul Castellano.

"I say, 'Go find out information—what's going, when, when the pinch is coming, you cocksucker! We're making you an errand boy—high-priced errand boy. Bruce, worse yet!' They got a routine now, the two lawyers. Muck and Fuck, I call them. When I see Bruce: 'Hi! Jerry loves you!' he says. 'He's in your corner a hundred per cent!' When I see Jerry: 'Hi! Bruce loves you! He's in your corner a hundred per cent!' I know youse both love me." There was laughter. "Dumb fucks, you know?"

"They must really like ya," Gravano said.

"Sure, Sammy. What's not to like about us?"

Michael Cherkasky, the chief of the rackets bureau of the Manhattan District Attorney's Office, found a dramatic gesture with which to open People v. Gotti. Tall and rail thin, Cherkasky had won forty felony jury trials and lost one in his career as a prosecutor. He now explained the government's theory of the case: The carpenters' union official John O'Connor had sent vandals to wreck Bankers & Brokers, a restaurant then owned by the Gambino family and built with non-union labor. Members of the Westies, acting on behalf of the Gambino family, had shot O'Connor four times in the legs and buttocks. Cherkasky marched over to the defense table, pointed his finger, and said, "This man, John Gotti, the head of the Gambino family, ordered that assault."

To prove it, Cherkasky was going to put informants on the stand and also play tape-recorded conversations. A few of the tapes were highly incriminating but suffered from a serious drawback—poor audibility. The key tape covered a conversation between John Gotti and Tony Lee Guerrieri on February 7, 1986, at an annex to the Bergin Hunt & Fish Club. O'Connor was discussed by name, and then Gotti supposedly said, "We're gonna—gonna bust him up." But unless one had faith in the state's transcript—and it was the defense strategy to undermine that faith—there was room for doubt.

Shargel and Cutler, who remain close friends today, had never before tried a case together. But John Pollok, the law person at the defense table, had worked with Cutler, and the experience was not a pleasant one. He and Cutler were an odd couple: in contrast to Cutler, with his weight lifter's physique, Pollok was a round, jovial appellate specialist who wore polka-dot suspenders and seemed to be always munching on snacks. They had represented different defendants in United States v. Tutino, a narcotics-conspiracy case, and had nearly come to blows when Pollok filed a motion for a separate trial, on the ground that Cutler's judge-baiting had prejudiced his client. Gotti had read a transcript from the Tutino trial and now spoke to Pollok about reining Cutler in. "He made it clear that one of my roles was to make sure that Bruce didn't do that again," Pollok says. "I have come to like Bruce, I enjoy Bruce, and I think he's a nice fellow. But our strategy was to keep Bruce quiet, to keep him away from the judge."

Cutler and Judge Edward McLaughlin (not related to Joseph McLaughlin, the judge in the Coiro case) clashed anyway. A number of times, McLaughlin sustained objections and Cutler ignored him and barrelled on ahead. "Do I have to talk over you for the rest of the afternoon?" McLaughlin demanded irritably.

By the second week of the trial, Gotti, too, had lost patience with Cutler. Despite his best efforts, Gotti had been unable to rig the jury, and the Ravenite tapes revealed that he believed he could be convicted of the charges, which could bring him a sentence of twenty-five years to life. "From ten feet away," Cherkasky says, "I could hear Gotti saying something like, 'What the fuck is Brucie doing?'" And Pollok says, "As the trial wore on, Bruce became a more and more remote second to Jerry in terms of responsibility. Jerry did ninety per cent of the cross, and Bruce would mop up."

Shargel considers his cross-examination of the first witness, Vincent (Fish) Cafaro, one of his best. A slight, partly bald man in glasses who had been a captain in the Genovese family, Cafaro had originally agreed to flip after being arrested for racketeering in 1986, but then he had changed his mind, and two disappointed federal prosecutors had him sent to "the hole"—a small isolation cell at Otisville prison, in upstate New York, where conditions were abominable. Shargel proposed that after his ordeal Cafaro would say anything to please the government.

At the defense table, Shargel had thousands of pages of documents on Cafaro, including all his prior sworn statements, and he caught Cafaro in numerous inconsistencies. During the cross, Cherkasky kept rising to object, and was repeatedly overruled; finally, he stood up and was momentarily speechless. "Is he leaving?" Shargel asked. Cafaro, in his direct examination, had described his induction ceremony into the Mafia, and had mentioned that there was alcohol on the table. Shargel asked what it was for. "When they prick your finger, it bleeds, and you use the alcohol to stop the blood," Cafaro said. Shargel gave him a Jack Benny look, and said, "In other words, you were going to get into the Mafia, but you didn't want to infect your finger?"

Shargel made Cafaro revisit the torment inflicted on him by federal prosecutors, and when he was through Cafaro sounded like a broken man.

> Q: You hated those prosecutors, didn't you?
> A.:I still do.
> Q.:You wished they'd get leprosy, didn't you?
> A.:Yeah. . . . Small holes. And get bigger and bigger. . . .
> Q.:Month after month, you were in this six-by-eleven cell, right? . . . These two men, representatives of the United States government . . . were torturing you? . . . There were times in the winter when you were freezing to death? . . .

And they didn't give you proper clothes? . . . Just a jump-
suit? . . . You didn't even have socks? . . . And your feet were
cold? . . . That was in the winter, but then the summer came
. . . you're in that cell . . . and the door is closed and the
guard's saying, "Lock down! Lock down!," and you can't
breathe because there is no air?
A.: Right.

Shargel came up with several ploys for attacking the tapes, and one was
particularly effective. Edward Wright, a police investigator, had
reviewed the tape transcripts, and he had revised one of them after
repeated listening over the years, adding the name Jimmy Coonan.
Shargel set out to prove that the revision was the product of wishful
thinking. He walked over to the blackboard and wrote "Psychic." He
asked Wright to define the word, erased the board, and wrote "Sidekick." Then he sprang his trap: "Do you understand that I just pronounced 'sidekick' and 'psychic' exactly the same? . . . Is it not true,
Investigator Wright, that you may hear what you want to hear when
you're listening to that tape?"

The jury deliberated three days and acquitted Gotti and Guerrieri on
all counts. Several jurors told *Manhattan Lawyer* that they were sure the
defendants were mobsters but that the unreliability of the tape transcripts had given them reason to doubt the specific charges.

"When we were going to trial, our whole focus was on Bruce Cutler,
because he had made the previous Gotti trial into a circus," Cherkasky
says. "We succeeded in defanging Bruce, and then found we had to deal
with Jerry's brilliance and sarcasm, which we weren't prepared to do.
In retrospect, we should have tried Gotti alone and just had Cutler
there." Cherkasky shakes his head when the subject of the criminal
investigation of Shargel comes up. "It's a shame. The guy is just so
talented."

On March 29, 1990, John Gotti and Bruce Cutler spoke in the hallway
of the Ravenite Social Club. Gotti was worried. One of the backup

shooters in his murder of Paul Castellano was a soldier named Anthony (Tony Roach) Rampino, who had been arrested in 1987 for selling heroin and sentenced to twenty-five years to life. Gotti had learned that Rampino was under subpoena to appear before a federal grand jury investigating the Castellano homicide, and, while he believed that Rampino would commit contempt rather than testify, he wanted Cutler to meet with Rampino's lawyer, David DePetris, just to make sure.

"He feels he wants to take the contempt," Gotti said. "But still you— you wake him up, open his eyes. . . . "

"I understand," Cutler said.

"Tell him we don't need another phony junkie battin' against us. O.K.?"

"I understand."

The discussion turned to Raymond Patriarca, Jr., the head of the Patriarca crime family, of Rhode Island. Gotti said that if he needed to communicate with the family Cutler and Raymond's lawyer could act as intermediaries. "So I'm gonna send him a message, that if I ever wanna get a message through to them, or from them, we'll do it through you," Gotti said.

"O.K."

Five days later, Rampino refused to testify and was held in contempt.

John Gleeson was given his chance for a rematch with Gotti in late 1990, when the Justice Department awarded the Ravenite-tape case to the Brooklyn United States Attorney's Office. By then, Gleeson had been promoted to head of the office's organized crime-and-racketeering section. On December 12th, Gotti was arrested, along with Salvatore Gravano and Frank Locascio, and charged with, among other things, participating in the murder of Paul Castellano.

At that time, federal judges were usually assigned to cases at random by having their names pulled, like bingo balls, from a wheel in the clerk's office. The judge selected to hear the Gotti case was Shargel's former law professor, I. Leo Glasser. Shargel learned the news from

Gleeson in a late-night phone call. "I was elated," Shargel recalls. "Gleeson was bummed out."

There were several reasons for this. Shargel had defended Sammy Gravano in front of Judge Glasser once before, to an acquittal. It was no secret that Glasser treated Shargel like a favorite pupil in a Talmud class: whenever Shargel tried a case in his courtroom, Glasser kept him late to discuss arcane points of law. Beyond that, Glasser had a reputation as a liberal: in a civil RICO case against the Bonanno crime family, he had lashed out against the government for overzealousness.

Glasser is considered one of the most scholarly judges on the federal bench, and also one of the most cantankerous; he is constantly pulling off his glasses and forcing a pained smile to register impatience. He was appointed a federal judge in 1981, after five years as the dean of Brooklyn Law School and, earlier, eight years as a Family Court judge. Tough as he is on lawyers, he generally finds it excruciating to have to impose long prison terms.

On January 18, 1991, John Gleeson submitted to Judge Glasser the long, indignant brief in which he quoted extensively from the Ravenite tapes and moved for the disqualification of Gerald Shargel, Bruce Cutler, and John Pollok from the Gotti trial on the ground that they were all house counsel to the Mob. Glasser granted the motion, and handed down his opinion on August 1st. The language of the opinion was almost as angry as Gleeson's, and some readers thought they detected the anger of a man who felt betrayed. (Glasser insists, however, that he "intended nothing personal against Shargel," whom he calls "perhaps one of the best criminal defense lawyers I've ever seen.") Glasser wrote that "the only conclusions to be drawn are that the lawyers represent not merely an individual client, but the enterprise with which that individual is associated and receive instructions calculated to further the interests of that enterprise." The tape excerpts "reflect Gotti's resolve that the lawyers understand that their concern must be not only for their client, but that they 'got no right [to] jeopardize other people' by their representation," and Glasser quoted Gotti as asking Shargel, "Who you working for?"

Glasser found evidence that Gotti had paid all three lawyers to represent people other than himself, writing, "That benefactor payments have indeed been made to Shargel, Cutler and Pollok is a conclusion the jury can readily and justifiably reach." On January 4, 1990, Gotti spoke of paying Shargel to defend Tony Lee Guerrieri, and elsewhere on the tape he claimed he had told Shargel, "I gave youse three hundred thousand in one year. Youse didn't defend me. I wasn't even mentioned in none of these fucking things." Gotti also spoke of paying "thousands of dollars" to John Pollok—or, as he called him, "this fuckin' Pollok"—to handle the appeals for two Gambino-family members. The only evidence Glasser cited that Cutler got benefactor payments came not from the tapes but from an assertion by Michael Coiro that he had never paid Cutler to defend him.

Glasser agreed with Gleeson that Gotti's statement about paying his lawyers "under the table" was admissible evidence to support the tax-fraud charge in Gotti's indictment. He wrote, "A jury might well conclude . . . that the lawyers aided and abetted Gotti's tax fraud by not reporting the moneys he pays them. The clear implication that they, too, were committing crimes—'Every time you take a client, another one of us on, you're breaking the law'—gives rise . . . to a serious potential for conflict which justifies disqualification."

Glasser ignored a few of Gleeson's charges. Gleeson described Shargel as a "conduit of information to John Gotti," without citing any information that had been obtained illegitimately. Gleeson also alleged that Gotti and Gravano "placed" an attorney in Shargel's firm. Shargel hired Nicholas Gravante, Jr., the son of the tax lawyer who testified at Gravano's 1985 tax trial, after Gravano and Gotti mentioned that Nick, Jr., was looking for a job. Gleeson's suggestion of something sinister in Gravante's hiring seems frivolous. Gravante graduated with honors from Duke and Columbia Law School, had been offered a job as an assistant United States Attorney by Rudolph Giuliani, and, when Shargel hired him, was an associate at Cravath, Swaine & Moore—Gleeson's former law firm.

Bruce Cutler says that it would be unwise for him to discuss the disqualification—"Don't start me off, because I have strong feelings about it"—but he does contend that he was never paid by anyone to represent Coiro. "I did it because it was the right thing to do," he says.

John Pollok also denies receiving benefactor payments; regardless of what Gotti said on tape, Pollok asserts, "he never paid me for anything." He is angry for subjecting himself to the disqualification in the first place. "As the law person, I could have opted not to sit in the courtroom, but my ego got the better of me," he says. "In one short, swift affidavit by an assistant U.S. Attorney who didn't even know who I was, and one decision by a court, my reputation was destroyed."

Within three months of Shargel's disqualification as Sammy Gravano's lawyer, Gravano decided to turn informant. Gravano's defection became a source of anxiety for Shargel. One afternoon, while having a drink with the attorney Jeff Hoffman, Shargel suddenly asked, "How long do you think Gravano was in the government offices before the subject turned to me? Fifteen minutes?" Shargel had an additional reason to lament Gravano's cooperation agreement. Lawyers are not permitted to cross-examine their own former clients, so Shargel could not participate in numerous cases in which Gravano was a scheduled witness. "This guy has cost me a small fortune," he says.

Shargel admits that he expected all along to be disqualified but says he was stunned by the "tenor and tone" of Judge Glasser's decision. "I told myself, He won't do it like Judge Sofaer; he'll just gently ease me out the door. Instead, he kicked my ass down the stairs." At the time this account was first published, Shargel declined to answer the charges in the disqualification; he still faced the prospect of indictment, and said it would be foolish to give away his defense.

If Shargel had been formally charged with taking money under the table, or with some other crime suggested in the Ravenite tapes, he surely would have challenged the reliability of Gotti's pronouncements. Gotti is not always to be taken literally. To give one example, in the tape dated January 4, 1990, Gotti complained about Shargel "plucking" him the night before for his fee to defend Guerrieri. But the January 3rd conversation was also recorded, and when Shargel named his fee—seventy-five thousand dollars for the two-week trial—Gotti seemed to wonder if that was enough. "That's for the whole ball of wax?" he asked, and then added, "Win the fuckin' case, I'll buy ya a house. I got money."

Still, Shargel has never raised a credible defense against the charge of being a house counsel. Whether or not he was plucking Gotti, he was being paid by the boss of the family to represent one of his soldiers, and so was lending credence to Gotti's claim that he paid Shargel to defend other soldiers. And in return for this supply of business Gotti clearly expected Shargel to place the interests of the enterprise first. Shargel is unwilling to acknowledge the obvious conflict of interest, and his rationale is unconvincing: "If I represent the treasurer of a corporation, and he wants to do what the C.E.O. says, then I'm trying the case the way the treasurer wants." But what if the underling does not want to obey the boss? "I've never had that situation," Shargel says.

At Stub's Bar & Restaurant, in Brooklyn Heights, John Gleeson drank a mug of beer, watched a Knicks game out of the corner of his eye, and chatted—cautiously at first, then more and more animatedly—with a member of the press. After the disqualification, Gleeson had gone on to win the case against Gotti and send him to prison for life without the possibility of parole. Following the conviction, Gleeson turned down numerous requests for interviews; he does not seek publicity. He just wanted to do his job, he said, and continue the fight against the Gambinos, the Luccheses, and the Colombos—a fight that the federal government appears to be winning. "From a prosecutorial standpoint, we're slaughtering 'em," Gleeson said. "We're kickin' ass and takin' names."

After another conversation at Stub's, several weeks later, Gleeson agreed to a formal interview at his office. On the appointed day, he apologized for being late, but he had been tied up with Zachary Carter, the Brooklyn United States Attorney. He failed to mention that Carter had just promoted him to head of the entire criminal division. Gleeson's office was messier than one might have expected. "Read anything on my desk and I'll kill you," he said, in such a way that it was not quite funny. He listened to the first question, pondered it for a long time, then announced that the interview was over. He said he did not care to be dragged into a debate about house counsel, because it might "dignify" the views of those who are house counsel. He made it clear that he regretted the frankness of his conversations at Stub's, and that he would prefer to be left out of this account altogether.

Even at Stub's, Gleeson's most persistent topic had been his distrust of the news media to "get it right." He went on at some length about a newspaper column by Murray Kempton that had described John Gotti as "a statesman."

"Don't get me wrong," Gleeson said. "I don't care that much. I've got my job, and I love what I do—it's public service to the max. But, you know, I walk to sidebars"—conferences with the judge that are out of earshot of the jury—"and John Gotti is calling my wife a junkie and my mother a whore and me a faggot. I mean, I've prosecuted a lot of pieces-a-shit. And never have I prosecuted anybody with less class than John Gotti. Just a completely classless thug. And the press doesn't want to see it. When he got convicted, he was a 'statesman.' He took it nobly. I mean, he is something unique—I'm one of the first to admit that. He had a level of charisma and a way of commanding attention, not just within the Mob but within a courtroom. But he's a punk, you know?"

On a similar note, it had irritated Gleeson to read over and over again that Bruce Cutler had won an acquittal for John Gotti in the case that Gleeson had tried with Diane Giacalone. After all, he pointed out, a juror had since been convicted of taking a bribe. "Bruce is an interesting guy," Gleeson said. "He's a terrible fuckin' lawyer. Just terrible. I mean, the irony of the whole disqualification thing is that it was perceived as a tactical effort to get Bruce out of the case. All along, we thought, If tactics were the guide here, we'd be gettin' Jerry out and leaving Bruce in. The press? It's to get Bruce out. We were dyin' to get to convict Johnny with Bruce at his side. Who wouldn't be?"

Gleeson agreed that the disqualification motion had been a gamble, because of Judge Glasser's fondness for Shargel. "Oh! Jerry walked on water in that courtroom. One of the risks of that motion was that someone—it was gonna be either Jerry or me—was gonna lose a lot of capital in that courtroom once that motion was filed. And a lot of people were bettin' it was gonna be me. But the thing that nobody appreciated—and I don't mean this in a demeaning way—is what a slave Judge Glasser is to the law."

Nothing seemed to upset Gleeson more than to hear himself described as a zealot by members of the criminal-defense bar. What they really were trying to say, Gleeson claimed, was that he refused to compromise his standards in the name of collegiality. "There are prosecutors who are committed to public service, and there are prosecutors who envision themselves three years from now being a colleague of these people," Gleeson said. "I'll never be a fucking colleague of these people. I don't want to be. So I don't really give a shit what they think. Maybe it was the case five or ten or fifteen years ago, as part of some brotherhood thing, that prosecutors wouldn't apply the facts of the law and seek the relief that was appropriate. Maybe there was enough collegiality so that even though Jerry has taken a lot of money under the table, according to his client, the prosecutor would look the other way. I suppose there are prosecutors now who are gonna say, 'O.K., Jerry. Fine.' But I don't happen to be one of them. It's not that I don't like Jerry. I like him a lot. But the law's the law. And the facts are the facts."

"How did I allow this to happen to me?" Shargel says. He considers the question. "I guess it comes with the territory. You can't be in this business if you're timid or afraid. I'm not timid and I'm not afraid. Have I been willing to do things that other lawyers are unwilling to do? Absolutely. Have I been willing to go the extra yard for a client? Absolutely. And am I willing to engage in conduct that may be subject to a negative interpretation? Yeah, absolutely. Clients hire me because I'll do anything that the law will allow, without concern for how it's gonna make me look. So if you're asking me, Why has so talented and able a lawyer put himself in these compromising positions?—that's why. Because I think I'm doing what a real criminal-defense lawyer should do. I don't practice law by covering my own ass."

For his own part, Shargel insists that his notoriety has not come at too great a price. "Terry once asked me an interesting question," he says. "If someone came to me and said, 'We can turn back the clock, and you were never involved in the 1990 Gotti case, and therefore you were never on those tapes or in those headlines, and you never suffered the indignity of Judge Glasser's opinion'—would you take the offer? And, even with the luxurious benefit of hindsight, the answer is no. It was too exciting to be in that case. And I'll tell you something else. If John Gotti's conviction were reversed, and he were sitting in the Ravenite club six months from now, I'd go there again."

When asked about the price of his notoriety for his children, Shargel grows reflective. "I think about that," he says. "And when I do think about it it bothers me, because I cherish the relationship I have with my kids. I don't believe they are, at bottom, ashamed of me. Things have happened that are painful, but that's life. And, in a certain sense, I think it builds strength and character. I grew up in a bucolic New Jersey setting, in a typical fifties tract house, with a Chevrolet, and plastic on the furniture. I didn't know anyone in my entire childhood who had ever been to jail. I never even knew anyone who had been divorced. My father was as steady and conventional a man as you could ever find. He'd never do something that would embarrass me. And, to tell you the truth, I'm not sure I benefitted from all this. I don't think a Beaver Cleaver childhood is something I wanted to give to my kids. Maybe you can say I have a screw loose. Maybe it says I'm not the perfect father or the perfect husband, because I've brought some degree of grief or anxiety to my family. But I would do it again. I'd do it again."

The weekend after John Gleeson was promoted to head of the criminal division, the Shargels relaxed at their summer home in East Hampton—an airy post-and-beam construction, of unfinished wood. A Neil Young tape was playing on a boom box. Jerry Shargel was dressed in shorts and Top-Siders, and was jaunty, as usual. Terry wore a black one-piece swimsuit, and was nervous, as usual. The previous morning's *News* was lying on a side table, and a story on page 3 reported that Bruce Cutler's cancelled checks and bank records had just been subpoenaed by Gleeson's grand jury, and those of the "high-powered attorney" Gerald Shargel would not be far behind.

Shargel made light of it, and Terry did, too, but Gleeson seemed almost to hover over them, and presently they fell to talking about him. Terry said she was worried about "the way Gleeson ticks" and "what he has to prove."

Shargel tried to reassure her: "I don't think Gleeson could withstand the embarrassment of losing. If he allowed himself the possibility—"

"Gleeson is so self-righteous, can his mind accept the possibility that he might lose?" Terry said, interrupting. There was a pause, and then she touched her husband's hand and said, "You're alive."

from Boss of Bosses
by Joseph F. O'Brien
and Andris Kurins

John Gotti wanted Paul Castellano's job as head of the Gambino crime family, so he had him shot to death outside Manhattan's Sparks Steakhouse in 1985. By then, Castellano was under indictment, along with many of his colleagues, thanks largely to the work of FBI agents Joseph O'Brien and Andris Kurins. Here is the agents' account of the day they arrived to arrest the aging Don at his Staten Island mansion.

The circular driveway. The broad and gracious portico steps. The stately and imposing columns. All were as they had been on Joe O'Brien's very first visit to the Staten Island White House. The view down to the majestic Verrazano Bridge was as ever; the security cameras panned as they had always done. O'Brien rang the doorbell.

"Who is it?" The voice was unmistakably Castellano's, that breathy rumble that seemed to squeeze past a closed throat and grudgingly parted lips. He didn't sound as if he was expecting company.

"It's Joe O'Brien, Mr. Castellano. FBI. I have a warrant for your arrest."

"Ach," came the reply. The syllable seemed to hold only slight surprise and slight concern. Then there was a soft click as Big Paul broke the circuit of the intercom. O'Brien and Andy Kurins shuffled their feet and watched their breath steam in the pink glow of the Godfather's floodlights. The accompanying agents, posted as sentinels, lingered at the base of the portico stairs. Then the front door opened.

Paul Castellano appeared, his tall and rather hulking body filling most of the dim rectangle of yellow light. He was wearing gray slacks, a pale blue silk shirt, and his almost dainty slippers. His hair was neatly but not severely combed back, and he had on his lightly tinted aviator glasses. His voice was without anger. "May I ask what this is about?"

"RICO conspiracy," said O'Brien, showing the warrant. "A dozen or so of your colleagues are being arrested right now, sir."

"Really?" said the Godfather. "Right now?" He glanced out over the bay, as if he could picture his comrades being confronted all around the city. He seemed to take a connoisseur's interest in the neatness of what was, after all, law enforcement's version of a multiple hit. "Well, come in."

Silently, the Godfather led the agents through his vast entrance hall and down the long corridor, past the formal living room with its lamps like statues and the dining room like something off a cruise ship, to the kitchen. Gloria Olarte was there, her thickening body encased in designer jeans and a red cashmere sweater. With her was a distinguished-looking gentleman whom Castellano introduced as Dr. Richard Hoffman, his physician and friend.

It seemed they were just about to eat. The blond wood table at which Big Paul held his conferences was set with Lenox china and Waterford crystal, arrayed around an enormous platter full of rare roast beef, expertly sliced and oozing fatty blood. Near the head of the table, next to the high-backed chair in which the Godfather always sat, was the chrome gooseneck lamp with the dead microphone still secreted in its hollow base. The agents struggled not to look at it.

"Hello, Gloria," said O'Brien.

Castellano's maid and mistress did not answer. Her posture was rigid and her eyeballs were bulging.

"Be civil," Castellano coaxed her. "The man's only doing his job."

"Hees yob, hees yob," she hissed. "Hees yob ees only to make trouble for other people who they don't do nothing. I no like thees Meester Joe O'Brien."

Oddly, Castellano smiled. Perhaps he felt vindicated to hear his lover renounce her former fondness for the agent; perhaps that struck him as adequate compensation for the fact that he was at that moment being put out of business. He gave his massive head an indulgent shake, then absently glanced over at the roast beef. It was beautiful meat, sunburst red, and the former butcher regarded it as other men might a painting.

"I'd like to change into a suit."

"That isn't necessary," said O'Brien.

"I know it isn't," Big Paul said. "But I'd feel more comfortable. I'm asking as a favor."

Kurins and O'Brien glanced at each other. Their instructions were to bring Castellano in as quickly and smoothly as possible—no fireworks, no delays. He was going to jail, not a party; there was no particular reason to allow him time to change. But Castellano himself was being a gentleman. With his doctor, by coincidence, right on hand, he had available to him the oldest dodge in the world—the feigned heart attack or angina, the writhing, dizziness, or passing out that would earn him a nice cushy trip to the hospital. Yet he stooped to none of that.

Then, too, greatness has its prerogatives, and, to the agents standing there in his kitchen, the impression was making itself irresistibly felt that there was a greatness about Paul Castellano. This was not, God knows, a moral judgment, nor did it have to do with the man's wealth or the grandeur of his home. No, it was less rational and more primal than any of that. It was something in his bearing, some aura of pained wisdom earned through the acceptance of large responsibility. He may not have been a good man—in many ways he was an appalling one— but he had shrunk from nothing, he'd seen it all, he'd taken monstrous vows and stuck to them. You couldn't say to this man, no, you can't change into a suit, go face your accusers in a sport shirt. Certain people it is just plain wrong to embarrass. Embarrassing them is an affront to everyone, because everyone, like it or not, has a stake in their dignity. The king is allowed the royal purple even at his beheading, after all.

So Paul Castellano was allowed to change his clothes. He went up to his bedroom, accompanied by Gloria and Dr. Hoffman.

Then the doorbell rang. Joe O'Brien said hello through the intercom.

"Joe," said one of the sentinels, "there are some people here. Relatives. They wanna come in."

"Who?"

"The daughter. The son-in-law. Their baby. And the wife."

"Oh shit," said O'Brien. He glanced at his watch. Big Paul had been upstairs barely over four minutes. He must have asked Gloria to call Connie, who lived just around the corner; Nina had probably been there visiting. "Let them in."

"You sure you wanna deal with it?" asked the other agent. "They're pretty upset."

"Like screaming?"

"More like zombies."

"It's their house. Let 'em in."

A moment later, Connie Castellano marched into the kitchen, trying, as always, to look feisty and, as always, falling short. Joe O'Brien could have sworn she was wearing the same leather pants and translucent white blouse as on the first evening they had met. "Where's my father?" she demanded.

"Upstairs, changing," said O'Brien. The daughter looked like she didn't believe him. Her eyes darted wildly around the room, as if her father had for some reason been stashed in the broom closet.

Nina followed, and she seemed to be sleepwalking. She cast a quick, appraising look at the set table and the other woman's roast beef. She moved near it and sniffed the air. "On mine," she said, apropos of nothing, "I put rosemary."

Joe Catalanotti, Connie's second husband, trailed the women. He was carrying his infant daughter, and seemed somehow to be hiding behind her. For him the present scene was a no-win situation. His wife would want him to beat his chest and make some noise; that's what husbands were for. But this would irritate the FBI, and, given Cat's station in life, there was little percentage in that. On the other hand, incurring his spouse's wrath by seeming wimpy was an unappealing prospect also, especially since, for Catalanotti's predecessor, marital discord had proved fatal. So he just acted totally absorbed in handling the kid.

Big Paul returned to the kitchen, wearing a midnight-blue suit and a red silk tie, flanked by Dr. Hoffman and Gloria—the maid, the mistress, the new lady of the house. He briefly greeted his family and kissed his granddaughter with a smacking sound.

There followed a scene of such consummate awkwardness as to live in memory with the sick vividness of a bout of poisoning. Gloria started to cry. But she didn't cry like normal people, for whom tears are a release of tension; she actually got more rigid as she sobbed, her wet face crazily immobile. Castellano embraced her as his daughter looked on in rage and disgust; Nina drifted even farther off behind her tranced and vacant eyes.

Then an unmistakable odor filled the room: the Castellano granddaughter had filled her diaper. Joe Catalanotti, still playing the model dad, gently placed the infant on the dinner table, among the Lenox and the Waterford, and proceeded to change the soiled Pamper. Halfway through the job, as if unconsciously, he reached toward the platter of roast beef, picked up a slice with his fingers, and ate it.

Gloria had stopped bawling for the moment, and now it was Nina's turn to break down. She cried softly, almost silently. Then she opened her arms and started running toward her estranged husband—running slowly, with small old woman's steps that seemed to advance her hardly at all.

The Godfather's face riffled through a number of expressions as the mother of his children inexorably approached. First he looked baffled, then nonplussed, then as close to panic as the agents ever saw him. At the last possible moment, with the sure instincts of a veteran quarterback, he feinted left, ducked right, and his wife, empty-armed, ran right past him. She ended up hugging Andy Kurins.

"I think it's time," said Joe O'Brien. Dr. Hoffman handed him a small paper bag containing insulin, syringes, and medical instructions.

The Godfather, resplendent now in his immaculately tailored

mohair and silk, his supple loafers and gauzy socks, seemed almost relieved to be going. He led the procession to his own front door, and walked briskly down the portico steps to the government Plymouth.

"Thanks for not handcuffing me in front of my family." This was the first thing the Godfather said as the car door was closed behind him, and it took Kurins and O'Brien a little by surprise. They had decided with a shared glance to bend regulations and not subject Big Paul to the indignity of being manacled in his own house; they didn't think he'd notice the omission.

"I know the drill," Castellano went on. "You're supposed to cuff me. It was kind of you not to."

The agents found it difficult to respond to his gratitude, and the little two-car convoy set off in silence, the sentinels in the lead car, Andy Kurins driving the other, with Castellano and O'Brien sitting in the back. They wound down from the summit of Todt Hill, past the fences and confident houses of millionaires both legitimate and otherwise. The Godfather gave off a good smell of clove and peppermint.

At Richmond Road, the cars turned left, toward the Verrazano Bridge, and Andy Kurins put an all-news station on the radio. The speakers blared out a loud and obnoxious commercial for Crazy Eddie, the electronics dealer who claimed his prices were insane, and tried to prove the point by using a wacky announcer with the world's most irritating and maniacal voice.

"I'd like to kill that guy," said Castellano.

O'Brien couldn't help staring at him.

"Just a figure of speech," said the Godfather. "I mean, lots of people would."

Then the regular newscaster came on. *This just in,* he said. *At this moment, agents of the Federal Bureau of Investigation and the New York State Organized Crime Task Force are arresting the reputed leaders of all of New York's five Mafia families. According to U.S. Attorney Rudolph Giuliani, the*

arrests are part of the most far-reaching Mob investigation ever, an investiga-
tion aimed at convicting the entire Mafia leadership—the so-called
Commission—under federal racketeering statutes. Tonight's arrests cap a four-
year law enforcement effort, which, according to one highly placed source,
included the 1983 bugging of the Staten Island home of Paul Castellano,
alleged Boss of the Gambino family and de facto head of the Commission.

Andy Kurins watched the road.

Joe O'Brien looked straight ahead.

The Godfather leaned forward so as not to miss a word. Then he
gave a little groan. "Is that true?" he asked. "Did you guys bug my
house?"

No doubt he was using "you guys" generically. He could not have
known that the agents in the car with him were the very ones who had
planted the microphone. Still, it was not a comfortable moment.

"Yes, sir," said O'Brien. "I'm afraid it is."

"*Jesu Christo*. When? How'd ya do it?"

"I'm sorry, we can't tell you that."

"No," said the Godfather, "I suppose you can't."

His chin collapsed onto his chest, and he became totally subdued.
But with Castellano, as the agents would realize during their strange
and privileged time with him, it was hard to tell how much his
behavior had to do with frame of mind and how much with blood
sugar. His diabetes made him prey to wild swings of mood. Depression
would suddenly sweep down on him like an inky cloud; then, just as
suddenly, he might burst into ribald and sometimes bizarre humor. At
moments he seemed so weary as to be used up, defeated, sinking; then
he'd rebound as if buoyed by some saving but subversive knowledge
that nothing mattered all that much, life was almost weightless, if you
stayed calm and held your breath you would bob back to the surface.

"I feel some indigestion coming on," Big Paul said softly. "D'ya
think we could stop for some Tums. And some candy bars. I don't feel
too good."

Andy Kurins sought out Joe O'Brien's eyes in the rearview mirror.
Stopping would be highly irregular and would pose a security risk. But

the man was ill. Besides, Bruce Mouw would wince if his quarry was brought in in a diabetic coma. O'Brien nodded yes, and Kurins notified the other car on the two-way.

"Hershey bars okay?" Kurins asked, in the parking lot of a 7-Eleven.

"Snickers if they have 'em," said the Godfather.

They continued toward the bridge, and the smell of cheap chocolate in waxy wrappers made the journey seem like something out of childhood, a ride home from school. Castellano wolfed two candy bars, but seemed to take no pleasure from them; they were medicine. They brought him around incredibly fast. By midspan of the Verrazano, with the Manhattan skyline gleaming to the north, he was alert and chatty again.

"I love this bridge," he said. "It ruined Staten Island, but it's beautiful. I know a guy worked on it—he riveted his initials on the top of one of the stanchions. It's seven hundred feet up, something like that. I says to him, 'Who's ever gonna see your name up there?' He says, 'No one.' I start to ask him then why did he do it, but then I stop. I know the answer. That's what it's like for most people—somewhere they leave a tiny little mark, knowing that nobody knows or cares it's there. But they do it. That's how people are. If they believe in God, they think God sees it. They don't believe in God, they do it anyway. It's this thing about leaving some reminder you were there. You get to leave a bigger reminder, that's called being lucky. Or maybe unlucky. I go back and forth on that one."

The agents made no response, and the Godfather fell silent. But the sugar had made him hyper, and in a moment he started in again.

"Bugging a man's house," he said. "I'm sorry, fellas, I know you got your job to do, but I don't think that's right. Place of business, okay. Social club, all right. But a man's home? It's personal. No one needs to know what a man says or does when he's home. I'm sure you know all sorts of things about me that no one really has the right to know."

"There's this thing called minimization," said Joe O'Brien. "We try not to listen to personal stuff."

The Godfather gave his big head an unpersuaded shake. If he had lived in biblical times and hadn't been a criminal, he would have made a great judge, the kind who just listened, watched, and decided. You couldn't fool him. "No," he said, "you're trying to spare my feelings. But I know you know. You know all about my marriage. You know all about Gloria and me. You know all about my health. You even know about my dick."

The agents were too abashed to speak. But Castellano went on, a note of goading defiance in his voice. To Kurins and O'Brien, it did not seem that the defiance was directed against them or even against the law; it seemed, rather, to be a wider rage against all the forces that scraped away at a man's dignity, that reduced him at last to something small, fragile, quailing, ridiculous. Strip me naked, the Godfather seemed to be daring, know the worst: you can't make me ashamed.

"Come on, boys," he goaded. "Don't be squeamish. The body is just the body." He gave a dismissive glance down at his lap. "It's a bitch, this diabetes. Before the operation, I could only get a sixty percent erection."

In spite of himself, Joe O'Brien wondered what that meant, exactly. Only sixty percent as big as before? Or did it have to do with the angle? Grotesque and unwelcome images cropped up in his mind, and he looked at the skyline to banish them.

But Big Paul, his mind at full gallop now, blitzed by his runaway sugar levels, was already onto something else. "Florida?" he said. "Was the bug planted while I was in Florida?"

"I'm sorry, Mr. Castellano," said O'Brien, "we're not allowed to talk about it."

"I knew there was something there," he said. "That's what gets me. I had the house swept twice. You probably know that. You probably know a lot of things. How bad does it look for me?"

"Very bad, sir."

Instantly, Castellano seemed depressed again. He leaned back against the vinyl upholstery and rubbed his eyes. He ate more Tums and stared sullenly out the window. Then, just as Andy Kurins was pulling into the Brooklyn-Battery Tunnel toward Manhattan, he started to laugh. The laugh began as a low rumble that just slightly shook his broad shoulders, then mounted to a sort of whinny that rocked his entire frame and stretched back his lips to reveal large and equine teeth. Tears sprang to his eyes, he sniffled, and he kept right on laughing.

"Can I ask what's funny?" said O'Brien.

"Fat Tony," guffawed the Godfather. Then he was convulsed again. "Are they bringing in Fat Tony?"

"Yes, sir, I believe they are."

Castellano gave a vigorous, flubbering snort. "Fat Tony's been living on his farm. He wears overalls and flannel shirts up there. Man of the soil. He's gonna look like such a horse's ass."

The courtyard of 26 Federal Plaza could be seen from a long way off. It was lit with the biting blue white of television lights and peppered with the little shocks of strobes. All the networks were there, the famous logos emblazoned on their trucks. Newspapermen scrawled in spiral notebooks, radio reporters talked confidentially into microphones. Paparazzi lined the sidewalks, their carnivorous Nikons hungry for the shot that might make *People* magazine. From the number of government vehicles parked at curbside, it seemed clear that most if not all of the other mobsters had already been brought in. The grand entrance of Paul Castellano, the Godfather whose house had been bugged, would be the climax of the media carnival.

The lead car of the Godfather's convoy nosed in toward the curb, and immediately the newshounds began to swarm. Cameras high, microphones held like truncheons, the journalists surged toward the vehicles, their faces thrust forward in the unnatural glow like something out of a nightmare. Paul Castellano now mastered his wildly pulsating moods and composed his face into a mask of utter neutrality. But his color was bad, and as he silently presented his wrists to be cuffed he could not quite hide the tremor in his hands. Strobe flashes were already knifing off the windshield. Reporters hung over the police barricades, shoving each other like drunks at a ball game.

Andy Kurins looked over his shoulder at Joe O'Brien. "These people are vultures. I say let's duck 'em."

"Do it," said O'Brien.

Kurins floored the Plymouth and screeched away from the curb. Looking back, O'Brien relished the fallen faces in the dimming floodlights, the microphones drooping like stalks in a drought.

They drove around to the dark side of the building, where a guarded ramp led down to the employees-only garage. There they ushered the Godfather into a back elevator, to bring him to the twenty-eighth floor for processing.

"So now I owe you two," said Paul Castellano, a man who saw the just tallying of favors as the very heart of right behavior.

"You owe us nothing," said Joe O'Brien. "But give me your wrists. I've got to cuff you before we go into the office."

"Your watch. Your cash. Your tie tack."

Joe O'Brien handed the possessions back to Paul Castellano. It was late the next morning, February 26, 1985, at the interior gate of the Manhattan Correctional Center, where Big Paul had spent the night. He'd had his insulin, he'd managed to get some rest. He'd slept better, he said, knowing that his jewelry was in the safekeeping of the FBI. He didn't hold a high opinion of prison guards. "No better than Mexican customs men," he opined. "They see something they like, they take it. You protest, they laugh."

For Big Paul, as for the other Commission case defendants, this was to be a day of paperwork and technicalities, of shuttling back and forth between FBI headquarters and the courthouse, leading up to a bail hearing at three p.m. In between the bureaucratic steps, there would be pockets of dead time, and Kurins and O'Brien offered the Godfather a choice: he could stay in the cramped and bustling marshal's lockup, or he could hang around with them.

Castellano tugged at his perfectly knotted red silk tie and seemed to be considering. "Lemme ask you something," he said. "You guys hate me?"

Kurins and O'Brien hesitated, not because their answer was in doubt but because they were nonplussed to be asked the question. "No," O'Brien said, "we don't hate you."

"Good," said the Godfather. "I'm glad of that. So let's say we get to talking. The things I say—you gonna use them against me?"

"We can't promise that we won't," Andy Kurins said.

"No," said Castellano, "I guess you can't. So I gotta watch my ass. But you know, I'm so tired of doing that. The lousy health—that's where it comes from, I think. All that caution."

"You're entitled to call your lawyer," said O'Brien. "Get his advice if you want."

"Nah," said the Godfather. "The hell with it. My lawyer I can talk to anytime. For a fee. How often do I get to schmooze with the FBI? You got a quiet place we can smoke some cigars?"

With their docile prisoner properly shackled, the agents strolled through the long tunnel that connected the MCC with the courthouse, then wandered the corridors until they found a small empty office with a green metal desk, two yellow pine chairs, and a pair of smudged windows fronting on the grand staircase below. Once safely behind the frosted glass door, they removed the Godfather's handcuffs, and he produced three huge coronas from an inside pocket of his jacket.

"Partagas," intoned Kurins. Not what one usually smoked on a government salary.

Castellano gave a modest shrug. "A guy sends them to me. As a present." He leaned forward in his chair as O'Brien offered him a light. Then he laughed. "People send me the damnedest things. Sometimes people I don't even know. Gigantic crystal jars full of artichokes. This gold pinecone that it took me six months to figure out it was a cigarette lighter. And shoes. People know I like shoes. The thin leather, the workmanship. So they send me shoes, but they don't even know my size. I got a closetful that don't fit. I'm in a funny business."

The agents puffed on their cigars, wondering what exactly the Godfather would call the business he was in, if he chose to name it. But of course, he wouldn't go that far. He slightly misread the curiosity on their faces and veered off on another tack.

"Hey," he said, "I know you disapprove. That's why we're here, after all, isn't it? So the United States government can make the point that *we do not approve of how certain guineas make their living.* Okay. Fair enough. If I was the United States government, I wouldn't approve either. If I was the government, I'd put my ass in jail for a thousand years.

"But not because I'm *wrong,*" he went on. "You see, that's the part I object to—this idea that the law is right and that's the end of the story. Come on. We're not children here. The law is—how should I put it? A convenience. Or a convenience for some people, and an inconvenience for other people. Like, take the law that says you can't go into someone else's house. That's convenient for people who have houses. I have a house, so, hey, I like that law. The guy without a house—what's he think of it? *Stay out in the rain, schnook.* That's what that law means to him. Besides, the law can always change its mind. Like, the law can say you can't go into someone's house, unless it's Paul Castellano and you want to put a bug in it."

Andy Kurins flicked a glowing ash into a green metal trash can. "But you can't just have people obeying the laws that suit them," he said.

"Obviously," answered the Godfather. "But that's exactly what I'm saying. It's a practical question, nothing more. The government wants to put me away as a practical matter, hey, they can. They got the power. Me, I try not to kid myself. Some people think I'm a big man. Bullshit. What can I do? A few people, maybe I can get them jobs. They have some trouble, I can help their families. But look at this . . ." His expansive gesture took in the massive courthouse building, the huge marble steps and vast paved plaza beyond. "*This* is power. What's my little bit of influence compared to this? The government decides I'm too much trouble, they can crush me like a cockroach. I understand that. No hard feelings."

He drew deeply on his cigar and seemed, in fact, quite serene. He crossed his knees, then with unconscious fastidiousness smoothed the crease of his pants.

"Practicality," he resumed. "That's what it comes down to. I'm from Brooklyn. I grew up poor. Don't get me wrong—I'm not saying I was poor, so I didn't have to go by the rules. I hate that crybaby shit. I'm just saying I saw two choices. Practical choices. You do things one way, you got a certain set of chances. You do things the other way, you got a different set. Either way, there's pluses and minuses.

"Then, too, there's family obligations, traditions. The Castellano family was very close with the Gambino family—"

"We know that," interrupted Joe O'Brien. "In fact, we did a family tree for you that goes back five generations."

"Really?" said the Godfather. "I'd like to see that sometime." He seemed genuinely flattered, and so O'Brien didn't tell him that several of the interfamily unions legally qualified as incest, or that the inbred clans had given rise to a number of certifiable idiots.

"Well," Big Paul continued, "then you know. There are certain promises you make that are more sacred than anything that happens in a court of law, I don't care how many Bibles you put your hand on. Some of the promises, it's true, you make too young, before you really have an understanding of what they mean. But once you've made those first promises, other promises are called for. And the thing is, you can't deny the new ones without betraying the old ones. The promises get bigger, there are more people to be hurt and disappointed if you don't live up to them. Then, at some point, you're called upon to make a promise to a dying man."

"Cousin Carlo," said Andy Kurins.

For the first time since being taken into custody, the Godfather seemed close to taking offense. His eyes narrowed; he lowered the hand that held the smoked-down cigar. "Certain names," he said, "we don't use lightly."

He got up from his chair and went over to the window. The winter sun cast a feeble greenish light that threw pale shadows across the paving stones. "Isn't that Giuliani?"

The agents looked down, and sure enough, the prosecutor was standing at the base of the courthouse steps, smiling broadly and chatting affably with a gathering cluster of reporters. From above, his neatly parted hair could be seen to be thinning; his broad forehead, pointy chin, and glowing complexion made him look strangely like a walking light bulb.

"Well," said the Godfather, "if you've gotta get fucked, it may as well be by a *paisan*. Is anybody else getting hungry?"

Kurins and O'Brien realized quite suddenly that they were, and Kurins offered to fetch them some lunch from the employees' cafeteria.

Castellano groaned. "Cafeteria? That's like being in jail before you go to jail. I could really go for a good corned beef sandwich."

"From Second Avenue Deli?" asked O'Brien.

"Yeah," said the Godfather. "D'you know that's my favorite?"

"Mr. Castellano—"

"Paul," he corrected. "Enough of the mister."

"Paul," said O'Brien, strangely savoring the sound of the name, "we've been studying you for five years. You think we don't know whose corned beef you like?"

"It's the best," said the former butcher. "Lean but not too lean. Iridescent, like fish scales, the way it gets when it's cured just right. Served on that crusty rye bread with lots of caraway . . ."

Kurins and O'Brien caught each other's eyes. *Nah,* said Andy Kurins's expression. *No way,* said Joe O'Brien's gaze.

"It's only five of twelve," said the Godfather. "The bail hearing isn't till three. Of course, if you don't have the balls . . ."

Taking the Godfather to a delicatessen—this was a truly absurd idea.

The man was a federal prisoner, the central target of a vastly complex and vastly expensive law enforcement dragnet. It had taken the government half a decade to get him into the courthouse building; now two FBI agents were going to blithely let him out again to get a sandwich? No, too much could go wrong. The hovering reporters might spot him and swarm, and Kurins and O'Brien would spend the next year writing memos to justify their actions. The government Plymouth might get sideswiped by a taxi on the way uptown. Big Paul might choke on a piece of gristle and drop dead at the lunch table; this would be awkward to explain. Then, too, for all his silk and mohair, for all the seeming calm of his conversation, the fact remained that the man could be not unjustly characterized as a desperado. The seriousness of the Commission indictment seemed to be getting through to him hour by hour; he must have felt cornered, and he was not accustomed to losing. His sense of right conduct notwithstanding, his mood swings made him unpredictable and his actions, like his conversation, were at moments bizarre. It was by no means out of the question that the Godfather had some escape plan in mind. No, taking him to a delicatessen was out of the question.

"We'll take the cuffs off when we get to the car," said Joe O'Brien.

"Good," said Castellano. "I'd have a tough time eating otherwise."

"Now we'll walk through the hallways like we own the place," said Andy Kurins.

"Is there any other way?" the Godfather asked.

With Castellano between them, the two agents, stone-faced, strolled through the busy courthouse corridors. Clerks seemed to be fighting the temptation to stare; secretaries whispered to each other behind their hands. A robed judge walked by, appearing not to have the faintest idea who the manacled fellow was. Avoiding the main bank of elevators, the threesome descended a dimly lit stairwell to the underground garage, encountering no one but a young paralegal who was blowing a chestful of marijuana out an airshaft window.

They got into the Plymouth, Kurins driving, O'Brien and the now unshackled Godfather again in back. At the head of the ramp, out in the greenish sunlight, the television crews had already parked their trucks. Spiked antennas poked at the sky; technicians milled, waiting for the action promised later that afternoon. Producers strolled around with clipboards; women reporters raised the collars of their furs and sipped tea from cardboard cups.

"Paul," said Joe O'Brien, "you might want to duck your head as we go by."

"I'm sorry," said the Godfather. "I don't do that."

But since the media people weren't expecting news, they didn't seem to notice that news was going by. The Plymouth wheeled onto Chambers Street and headed uptown at Centre.

"I'm starting to fade," Big Paul announced, as they crossed Canal Street. "Fucking blood sugar. The way it comes on, there's a moment you can notice it happening, the wooziness, the field of vision closes in. If you don't notice it right then, you lose track of what's going on. Then you got a problem."

He smiled, a far-off smile like you sometimes see on the faces of old immigrants when they talk about the Old Country—except that Paul was talking about the house from which he'd been exiled only since yesterday. "At home," he said, "I have this trail of food. Over here I have a bowl of raisins. Over there, a dish of almonds. Somewhere else, I got some pignolia cookies stashed. Gloria, she always makes sure the dishes are full. She checks. She says, 'Meester Paul, you almost finish all the feegs; Gloria, she get some more.' She takes good care of me, that girl."

Andy Kurins turned east on Houston Street and drove on in embarrassed silence; Joe O'Brien looked pointedly out the window. Oddly, it did not make them particularly uneasy to be going out for lunch with a man who could sentence people to death with a lift of his eyebrow. They didn't avert their gazes from Big Paul because he bribed cops, corrupted politicians, made a travesty of labor unions, or stuck his meaty fingers in the city's food supply. But when he started gushing like a teenager about his girlfriend, they simply couldn't look him in the eye.

"I know you don't like her," he blurted out. "You think I don't know that? I mean, you'd like her fine if she was just the maid. You'd find her funny, gutsy, entertaining—just like I did. But then you'd draw the line, right? The hired help. The spick. My friends feel the same way. They wouldn't say it to me, of course, but I feel it. I don't really give a shit, but yeah, it disappoints me. Lack of imagination is what it is. They have this image of the mistress—piled-up hair, long nails, big boobs. I ask you: Does this have anything to do with what really happens between a man and a woman? No. It's just a certain style, it goes with the watch and the car."

Eager to cut short the Godfather's defense of his girlfriend, Andy Kurins slipped through an amber light at Second Avenue and Tenth Street, and parked in front of a fire hydrant alongside the deli's awning. Castellano pointed up at its peculiar lettering as they moved briskly across the sidewalk. "That sign always cracks me up," he said. "If you don't look closely, you'd really think it was Hebrew."

Inside the noisy restaurant, the harried-looking maître d' started to give them a perfunctory hello, then did a double take. His wide eyes made it clear that for Paul Castellano a lifetime of discretion and self-effacement had largely gone by the board in the past twenty-four hours; of all the things Big Paul was fated to lose, his cherished privacy was the first to go. Anyone who read a newspaper, watched television, or listened to the radio now knew that he was the Godfather and that he had been arrested. People who had never heard of him until yesterday now spoke of him familiarly, and as for those already acquainted with his name and face, if not his job title, he now appeared as someone larger than life and back from the dead. The maître d', in fact, bore the terrified expression of someone either looking at a ghost or expecting to be taken hostage.

"Mr. Castellano," he mumbled, "I thought you were—"

"I was," the Godfather cut in, forestalling any indiscreet remarks. "These are friends of mine, Max. Mr. Kurins and Mr. O'Brien."

The flustered little man smoothed down his hair and tried to recapture his composure. "Ah yes, I believe I've seen you gentlemen in here before."

"You have," said O'Brien. "But you've never talked to us."

Max blinked.

"Put us way in the back," Castellano ordered. "And forget that we were here."

He led them through the maze of close-packed tables. If Kurins and O'Brien had been worrying about Castellano being swarmed at the restaurant, they needn't have: at Second Avenue Deli, no one looked up from his food.

Seated, the Godfather dug into the stainless steel bucket of sours that was placed on the table between the napkin dispenser and the pot of mustard. "Dill pickles on an empty stomach," he said. "Best thing for my indigestion."

He polished off the gherkin, grabbed another, and continued. "Can you believe there are people who don't love to eat? I don't trust people like that. Something's missing in 'em. It's like they don't really love the world, they don't really feel that life is wonderful. Hello, Sadie."

The waitress had come over. She was around sixty, had blond hair like straw from too much bleaching, and she combed only the parts that she could see. Nor did she have the gift of quiet speech. "Mr. Castellano," she bellowed.

The Godfather put a finger to his lips, a gesture that even in this incongruous setting seemed to crystallize the Mafia dictum of *omertà*: silence. "Corned beef, Sadie. Rye. And a Cel-Ray."

"Three," said Joe O'Brien.

"That bug," said the Godfather, when the waitress had retreated. "I been thinking about it."

He wagged a finger at the agents. The prospect of food seemed to have perked him up, and his tone was probing, almost playful. But Big Paul had so many tones. With his subordinates, as the tapes amply displayed, he could be gruffer than gruff and cruder than crude, not just matching his boys' obscenities but topping them in profane ingenuity. With associates from the legitimate business world, be could mouth the expected executive platitudes that sounded solid and revealed nothing. With law enforcement, he was faultlessly polite, yet imbued his words with a certain edge that kept it clear where the lines were drawn. When he hoped to extract information, he might use the disarmingly direct question, or the slyly oblique one, or a kind of schoolyard humor.

"Yeah," he resumed. "I can't get that bug off my mind. And I think I finally figured out where you put it. I started feeling irritable, see? Little things, they bothered me. I got short-tempered, moody. Then I finally figured out why. You put the bug up my ass, didn't you? Yeah, you put that bug right up Big Paul's ass!"

The corned beef arrived, and Kurins and O'Brien hid behind the mountainous sandwiches. They were not about to get drawn into a discussion of where the surveillance microphone had or had not been placed. Undaunted, the Godfather switched gears and went on chatting.

"Jesus, that's good," he said, having removed a prodigious bite from his sandwich. "Exactly what I shouldn't be eating, but what the hell."

Then, much to the agents' chagrin, he brought the conversation back to his paramour. "It's amazing," he said, "how Gloria makes the stuff I'm supposed to eat taste like real food. She uses these Spanish herbs and spices—stuff I've never heard of."

Kurins and O'Brien silently munched their corned beef and sipped their Cel-Rays, yet their disapproval seemed to be loud in the Godfather's ears. Carefully, almost daintily, he put the rest of his sandwich back on his plate.

"Listen," he began, "there's something I'd like you guys to know. I don't know why I give a damn, but I do. I want you to know I was never a womanizer. The occasional encounter, okay, it happens. But I was never one to keep a mistress. I didn't need a young babe at my elbow like a lotta these guys. I was too busy, I didn't see the point. Besides— laugh if you want—I loved my wife. And my kids. And it seemed to me, you cheat, you're not just cheating on the woman, you're cheating on the whole family. That didn't seem right to me.

"All right, so now you say I'm an old fart, an old hypocrite, my body's all messed up, I've got this young girlfriend, and I've been a bastard to my poor dear wife. But it isn't quite that simple. I'm old, yeah. I'm sick. But desire remains. Maybe it would he better if it didn't, but it does. And what the hell is a man supposed to do when desire remains and he simply cannot bring himself to touch his wife ever again?

"You guys are young. I'm sure your wives are pretty, and I hope to God you enjoy each other. And I hope that what happened to me never happens to you. It happened in the morning. That's when it always happens, I think—never at night, but when you first crack an eye, you wanna look at the new day and see some hope. You wake up, you look over at your wife, who's still asleep. And you see an old lady. Gray hair. Papery skin. Loose flesh. You're still fond of her. In a way, maybe you even still love her. And you know she's no older or more beat-up than you are. But you also know in that moment you will never touch her again. You can't. Touching her would be like making love with death."

The Godfather wiped his lips on a paper napkin and pushed his plate away from him. Fastidiously, he smoothed his tie. Then, with a harshness that surprised the agents, he called for Sadie to clear away his half-eaten lunch.

"Didn't ya like it today?" she asked him.

The Don Is Done

by Jeffrey Goldberg

When Jeffrey Goldberg made the rounds of var-

ious mobsters' children in 1999, he found many

of them in sad disarray. Some persisted in crime

against mounting odds, while others tried to

succeed in more legitimate operations—but all

of them suffered for the sins of their fathers.

John J. Gotti, the bloody-minded truck hijacker who led the Gambino crime family to ruination, has a friend in Joseph Castellano, whose father Gotti murdered.

The murder took place in midtown Manhattan on a December evening in 1985, in front of Sparks Steak House, which, owing to the death of Paul Castellano at its threshold, is now a popular tourist destination. John Gotti did not actually shoot Joseph Castellano's father, but he arranged the killing and handpicked the assassins—"button men" is the archaic term for their profession—who did the job. A jury found Gotti guilty in Castellano's murder, and other murders, in 1992.

There is no one associated with organized crime who doesn't believe that Gotti ordered Castellano's death. Joseph Castellano, whose life was turned inside out by the murder, says he doesn't believe it. "I know they say that Mr. Gotti"—he is careful to employ the honorific—"was the one who murdered our father," he told me recently. "But I don't know. I have no proof of this. The Government says this is true, but what do you want from the Government? My father was watched by the Government for 40 years, and then on the day he gets killed, what happened? Where was the F.B.I.?"

Don't get him started.

"I don't believe anything," he said, convincingly. "It's like 'Star Trek,' fiction. Clinton, Nixon, Gotti, it's all the same." His doubts, he said, have led him to question the existence of the crime family the Government says his father led. "What is a Gambino crime family?" he asked. "Does this Gambino crime family have an office? Does the office have a plaque on the door that says, 'Gambino crime family'?"

Joseph Castellano is a 60-year-old pizza-maker with heart trouble and a fierce desire to live out his days in peace, which might explain why he defends his father's killer. We were talking about Gotti while seated at a corner table in Big Louie's Pizzeria on Sunrise Boulevard in Fort Lauderdale. Castellano is ordinary in appearance. He was wearing a white windbreaker and tinted glasses, which made him look very much like the retirees who line up each afternoon in restaurants across South Florida in search of the earliest early-bird special.

Except for his nose. The nose is extraordinary—a giant, kingly nose. It is his father's nose, the nose that prompted Gotti and other traitors inside the Gambino family to refer to their boss—behind his back, of course—as "Nasabeak."

Like his father before him, Joseph Castellano is a wealthy man. Along with his brother, Paul Jr., he owns the Big Louie's on Sunrise, along with five other Big Louies in Fort Lauderdale. They also own a chain of popular and affordable rib restaurants called Bobby Rubino's, as well as a poultry wholesale business and a pasta concern.

Like his father before him, too, Joseph lives in splendor, in a million-dollar home behind a tall gate near the ocean. The Castellanos have always favored extravagant homes. When his father served as boss of the Gambino crime family, he lived in a Staten Island mansion so regal it was known as the White House. It was not the sort of house Carlo Gambino, Castellano's cousin and predecessor and a hater of flamboyance, would have liked. "It was a hell of a nice house,"

Castellano's cousin, Peter Castellano, a reputed Gambino family soldier, once told me. "Not my idea of a home. I like a ranch-type, five, six
rooms, a nice den, end of story. But Paul liked the big houses."

Despite his wealth and surname, Joseph Castellano never appears in
the Florida newspapers, and law-enforcement officials in Fort Lauderdale have no photographs of him. He lives a life of near-complete
anonymity. But he made no attempt to hide his identity when, after
surveilling the nose, I approached his table. He was initially reluctant
to talk about his life, but he became animated when I turned the subject to Paul Castellano's revenge.

"What do you mean, revenge?" he asked.

I offered up a theory proposed to me by a one-time Castellano par-
tisan: that the woes of the Gotti family—John Gotti's imprisonment for
life and his cancer and his son's coming trial on racketeering charges,
charges that could land him in jail for 20 years—can be seen as a kind
of payback for the grief Gotti visited on the Castellanos.

To accept this theory, Castellano must accept Gotti's guilt, which,
publicly at least, he doesn't, and he must accept an unorthodox definition of revenge. "I don't know of any revenge," he said, and in fact,
his father's murder was never avenged in the traditional Sicilian
manner. By rights, John Gotti should have been killed for violating a
basic tenet of mob life, which is, Never kill a boss without permission
of the other bosses.

It is true that the history of the Gambino family is laced with regi-
cide. The first boss, Vincent Mangano, was killed by the second, Albert
Anastasia, who was himself betrayed by the third, Carlo Gambino. But
traditionally, most boss hits have been sanctioned. It is said that Vincent (Chin) Gigante, the recently jailed boss of the Genovese family
and the last great mafioso of the century, tried to have Gotti killed for
breaking the rules. But he didn't succeed.

The Gambino family accepted Gotti as the new boss at virtually the
same moment John Cardinal O'Connor denied Paul Castellano, the
slain boss, a public funeral mass. Further humiliation was to follow.
The Castellano brothers, who were running their father's food whole-

sale company, Dial Poultry, were soon visited by their cousin, Tommy Gambino, a captain in the family and Carlo's son. Tommy Gambino, like most everyone else in the family's "white collar" faction, was frightened cold by the louche and murderous Gotti, and he carried a message from his new boss to the Castellanos: "He told them that what happened happened, let it go, and start paying tribute to Gotti," says J. Bruce Mouw, who until last year ran the Federal Bureau of Investigation's Gambino squad and is the Federal agent most responsible for the Gambino family's downfall. "This was their blood cousin telling them this."

So they did the logical thing, and fled to Florida. And in their move was the seed of revenge, because revenge, to paraphrase—liberally—an old Sicilian expression, is a dish best eaten at Big Louie's on Sunrise Boulevard in Fort Lauderdale.

Paul Castellano had a vision for his children: he did not want them to be like him. He wanted them to be entirely legitimate, upstanding members of their community. He shielded them from the mob, and he set them up in businesses that could earn them money legally. And it worked. The Castellano brothers are not mobsters.

Or to put it another way, no one has proved that they are mobsters. When I mentioned the Castellanos to the former sheriff of Broward County, Nick Navarro, who has arrested in Florida such eminent persons as Carmine Galante and Meyer Lansky, he threw up his hands: "What can I say? They're in the restaurant business. We don't know anything about them." He added: "Have you tried their ribs? They have very good ribs."

There are whiffs and intimations of mob influence in the Castellanos' business empire—Bobby Rubino, the man for whom the restaurant chain is named, was a reputed mob front man—and the money used to build the Castellano business empire may not have been pristine. But the brothers have had no trouble with the law.

"My family went through hell," Joseph Castellano said. "But maybe it's all been a blessing in disguise. Having this name, the past, we lead a very clean life. We pay our taxes. For a lot of businessmen, paying taxes is a curse. I like paying taxes."

The Castellano story is not unusual. Among the hundreds of "made men" who make up the membership of New York's Five Families, many among them surely hope their sons will follow them into their peculiar profession. But many more among them don't: more and more frequently, sons of the mob are graduating from law school and medical school or playing by the rules in the world of legitimate business.

"Only a real gavone wants for his kids what we got," a former captain in the Colombo crime family, Salvatore (Big Sal) Miciotta, once told me. A gavone is a lowlife. Big Sal, who weighs 350 pounds and has killed five men ("I'm feeling tremendous amounts of remorse," he said), argued that the Five Families are headed for dissolution because of what might be called a crisis of human-resource management. "Idiots and wannabes are who's attracted to this life now," he said.

In other words, even if RICO, the Racketeering Influenced Corrupt Organization statute, didn't exist; even if Rudolph Giuliani hadn't appeared on the scene 15 years ago to lead his war against the mob; even if the Government hadn't won to its side so many turncoats that, today, defectors—"rats," if you come from certain neighborhoods in South Brooklyn and Queens—could form their own family, the mob might be in a state of collapse simply because the smartest gangsters want nothing so much as to protect their sons from the life they had chosen. The story of the Mafia's decline, then, might be the story of the choices fathers make for their sons.

Paul Castellano made the right choices for his sons, and, in this regard, he has got his revenge. When his sons die, they will almost certainly die as old men in their own beds, the kind of death that eludes most mobsters. And that certainly might elude John Gotti Jr.

"You know, you have choices," Victoria Gotti was saying in her smoked-oyster voice. I had just suggested that perhaps her brother, John Jr., would have been better served by following the lead of such men as Joseph Castellano—that maybe he should have escaped to a place where his name would bring him less trouble.

"Yeah, you can pick up and move to, say, Albuquerque, New

Mexico," she continued. "It's like the old 'Cheers' thing, except that no one knows your name there—and you can become another person, step into someone else's shoes." She paused for a second, and her face hardened. "But it's the coward's way out."

John Gotti's daughter, a Nancy Sinatra song come to life, was dressed in black velvet—Armani—and her thick hair, once black, now blond, hung low down her back. She was sitting in her living room, and under the Christmas tree was a framed portrait of her father, looking fearsome and resolute, the type of man who credibly threatened to "sever" people from their heads. When I mentioned that the portrait seemed designed to intimidate, she said: "My dad was a people person. He loves people."

Her shelves hold the complete works of Sidney Sheldon, as well as two copies of "How to Help Your Man Lose Weight." She is a successful writer of throat-gripping, romance-tinged mysteries, and her talents are reported to be Sheldonian in scope. She is taken by romance: her mansion in Old Westbury, on Long Island, is built to look like Tara, which it does, more or less, except for the rusty cars parked by the side. Her husband, Carmine Agnello, has for many years been a leading figure in the New York City auto-salvage business.

Victoria is 35, a year older than her brother John, who is known to everyone except his family and friends as Junior and who is reputedly the acting boss of the Gambino family. It is Victoria, though, who is generally held to be the smartest of John Gotti's four children, the most eloquent interpreter and guardian of the family tradition.

"The way we were taught is that if you feel strongly enough to fight for something, then you fight," she said. "Rising up from the streets under the circumstances my dad was raised in, you don't throw in the towel and say, 'Come and get me.' How do you say to your children: 'Yeah, gee, we ran like bats out of hell. We ran because we were afraid.' I won't do that. My brother won't do that. Will he ever run and hide? No."

Junior, an ardent collector of Native American memorabilia, told me two weeks ago that he looks to Indian history for strength and for lessons about the abuse of government power.

"If you look at the history of the Indians, you see that they were oppressed by the Government," he told me during a brief conversation in an elevator at the White Plains Federal Courthouse in Westchester County, where he is to stand trial. "It's just the same with Italian-Americans. We're oppressed just like the Indians. It's history repeating itself."

In person, without benefit of tabloid magnification, Junior is a reasonably sized human being. He is not tall at all, and, after adhering religiously to the Atkins Diet—a lot of meat, no pasta—he is merely bulky. He is dressed for court in a black polo shirt buttoned to the collar and a black-and-white checked jacket.

He was especially keen that day to talk about the exploits of Chief Joseph of the Nez Perce Indians, who were the target of a particularly vicious Government campaign overseen by Gen. William Tecumseh Sherman. "Chief Joseph was an extremely dignified, intelligent leader," Junior said. The elevator, which was carrying us to a courtroom where prosecutors would soon ask a judge to revoke his bail, was stuck on the bottom floor, but Junior, lost in his reverie, didn't notice. "Chief Joseph was the main strategist for the Nez Perce," he said, the autodidact in him impossible to suppress. "But his brother was the field general. A lot of people don't know that."

We talked for a moment longer, about a book of Nez Perce history called "I Will Fight No More Forever," and he said, his voice full of enthusiasm, "I'm reading a book about Crazy Horse right now that's really—" Just then the elevator door opened. Standing there were the Ruggiero brothers, Angelo and John, sons of his father's closest mob ally, the late Angelo (Quack-Quack) Ruggiero. The Ruggieros were joined by several other friends, a few of whom, according to the text on their jackets, were affiliated with auto-salvage firms in Queens. As soon as Junior saw them watching us, he turned cold and mumbled, "We'll talk about this later."

He seemed to have much more to say, and he did. The next day, Gotti Jr. wrote me a letter in which he gives the distinct impression that he thinks of himself as an Indian chief and of the Mafia as a vanishing tribe of honorable men, the outer-borough equivalent of the Sioux

Nation. The letter came inside a greeting card whose cover featured a drawing of a Lakota warrior raising his peace pipe to the sky.

"When I think of the American Indian," Junior's handwritten letter read, "I think of their courage, strength, pride, their respect and their loyalty toward their brothers. I honor the reverence they share for tradition and life. These traits are hungered for in a society that is unfortunately plagued by those whose only values are self-centered and directed at others' expense. A society which seems to be forced to embrace the Judas, and liars." Given his world, which is riddled with traitors, it is not hard to understand his interest in Judas. Inside the greeting card, Junior, who is under house arrest, wrote a saying he attributes to Chief Joseph: "Any man who was born a free man should not be contented when penned up, and denied liberty to go where he pleases."

There are perhaps reasons less rooted in myth that explain why John Gotti Jr. never left to build a life independent of his father's.

A family friend, Joseph Corozzo Jr., a lawyer who is the son of a Gambino family soldier and the nephew of a captain, says that one reason Gotti didn't tell his son to run was that he couldn't envision a place to run to.

"My family, John's family, are very parochial," Corozzo says. "It always makes me laugh when these guys, these so-called high-ranking organized-crime members, go for bail hearings, and the judge asks, 'Will your clients surrender their passports?' Half of these guys don't even have passports. Some of them go to New Jersey and think it's like a great journey. So where's he gonna go? The Castellanos, they've been wealthy for generations. They're big businessmen. We're not talking about Castellanos or Gambinos here."

From where Victoria sits, there's no reason to run. Her family is innocent, and she will fight for justice on her own turf. Her brother is no boss of bosses, but a legitimate businessman. She maintains that tapes of conversations between her brother and father held during prison visits show that her brother is living clean. "On the tapes," she said, "my father is saying, 'John, you've got to be 100 percent legitimate,' and he gives him fatherly advice, 'You know, John, with the Government, come tax time, if you owe them $10, pay $12!'" (Prosecutors say conversations like these are scripted by father and son to be ostentatiously exculpatory, to which Gotti's lawyers say, Of course that's what prosecutors are going to say.)

Legitimate, too, Victoria said, is her husband, a reputed Gambino soldier: "He's this big made guy, right? I laugh when I read the stories, because my husband couldn't be a bigger pussycat."

Victoria made a game effort to convey innocence, but it's a difficult thing to do when so many of your relatives are neck-deep in the rackets. She is directly related to at least 6 of the 200 or so made men of the Gambino family. Her father has not relinquished the title of boss, despite having no chance of ever returning to the streets of Ozone Park. Three of her father's brothers are Gambino captains or soldiers. One of them, Gene Gotti, is serving a 50-year sentence for heroin trafficking. Her brother, awaiting trial, has been the target so far of several grand juries. And then there's her husband. Victoria is fatalistic.

"My dad always said, 'Save your tears for when you really need them, and now is not the time,'" she said. "God is not going to give us more than we can handle."

The great draw of gangster life—for the actual gangster and for the law-abiding citizen who fantasizes, Mitty-like, about waking at noon, whacking people and wearing diamond-encrusted Rolexes—is that the burdens and petty humiliations of responsible citizenship needn't be borne.

Now consider the life of John Gotti Jr., 34, reputed mob boss, in the twilight time of the Mafia. He faces trial shortly on extortion and racketeering charges that could keep him in jail until he is in his 50's. When he visits his father in prison, he gets yelled at. His mother had to tell him to stiffen his spine and reject a plea deal he was jumping to take. His sister had to help bail him out of jail. Law-enforcement officials say his brother-in-law, Agnello, is better at organized crime than he is. Every legitimate business he has opened has tanked. He has a weight problem. He dresses badly. He drives a minivan. The tabloids say he's stupid. And no one in the Mafia likes him.

A single letter Gotti received several years ago from the Pacific Employers Insurance Company captures vividly the petty insults a junior Don faces these days.

"Dear John A. Gotti," the letter begins, "Perhaps you've forgotten? We have no record of receiving payment of the premium for your Homeowners Insurance policy. We value your business and would like to continue to provide your insurance protection. Unfortunately, this letter must serve as notice that your policy is canceled."

Gotti Jr. isn't the only reputed mobster who is having a terrible time these days: Most bosses are imprisoned, and fearing Federal decapitation, few men want to rise to head the leaderless families.

"If our efforts are sustained over time, we will reduce the L.C.N. to the level of a street gang," says Lewis Schiliro, the assistant director in charge of the F.B.I.'s New York office, using the F.B.I. abbreviation for La Cosa Nostra.

The mob is weak and growing weaker, law-enforcement officials say; the debridement of Mafia-riddled industries—construction, concrete, waste hauling—is nearly complete, and the total membership of all Five Families in New York does not exceed 750.

Each family is unhappy in its own way, but no family has fallen further, faster, than the Gambinos. When he killed Castellano, Junior's father inherited 21 crews—groups of soldiers led by captains and supplemented by mob associates. Today, the family is down to about 11 crews. The Gambino influence, once felt in the garment center and in the Teamsters, in construction and in garbage hauling, is waning. The Gambino collapse is striking in its suddenness.

The Gambino collapse, however, does not mean that Gotti Jr. is through just yet. He might very well win the case against him. The indictment against him is a goulash of circumstantial extortion charges, a strange robbery charge, a minor telephone-card scam and, most prominently, the allegation that Junior was the secret power behind the yuppie strip club Scores. Prosecutors, in their fashion, have cut deals with some of the most violent, reprehensible players in this drama. One of the Government's key witnesses, a self-professed "two-bit leg-breaker" named Willie Marshall, is supposed to link Gotti Jr. directly to the extortion of Scores. The Government may have a difficult time selling Marshall's credibility to a jury, and, if the indictment is any indication, prosecutors may have a tough time selling Junior as a mob boss.

"The Government's campaign reminds me of something that Gregory Scarpa"—a now-dead member of the Colombo crime family—"once was heard to say," says Gerald Shargel, who, with Bruce Cutler, represented the senior Gotti and now represents the junior. "After he killed a particular person, he was heard saying that he hated the guy so much that he wanted to dig him up and kill him again. The Government hates John Gotti the father so much that they're trying him again, through his son."

The Gotti family, so aggrieved, has reconciled itself to the notion that even if Junior beats the case, he still might come out the loser. "He can't win," Victoria Gotti said, suggesting that the Government's war on her family is without end. "I can't win, no matter what I've done in life. The difference with me is, I don't care. Even if he wins this case, they will make him something he doesn't want to be—larger than life, a public figure. The headlines will go on and on. He doesn't want it. John never wanted it."

Though he is said to be the acting boss, it is perhaps more accurate to describe Junior's main role as protector of his father's business interests. This is, of course, a distinction without a difference in the minds of law enforcement. The minds of prosecutors go foggy with ambition when the name Gotti appears before them, and the father's decision to involve his son in his life has made Junior a fat and permanent target of prosecutorial zeal.

Salvatore (Sammy the Bull) Gravano, the underboss who turned coat on John Gotti, once told a story that explains exactly how things went wrong for the boss's son. During a meeting with Gigante, the Genovese family boss, the senior Gotti, filled with pride, told Gigante that he had just "made" his son; that is, inducted him into the Gambino family. Gigante, who would not induct his own sons into the Genovese family, replied, "Jeez, I'm sorry to hear that."

John Gotti was a good family man, his daughter Victoria told me. "Absentee father?" she said, referring to the common perception that her father was a club-hopping, family-ignoring playboy. "I wish."

She recalled her father's overprotective hand on the night of her prom. "My dad would have me call from each stop, and there were a lot of stops," she said. "I remember calling once, and he says, 'You know what time it is?' And I say, 'Yeah, about 3.' He says, 'Let me tell you exactly what time it is—3:40.' He says I gotta come home. I said: 'Dad, I really can't do that. There's a whole limousine with other couples.' And he said, 'I could send someone to pick you up.'"

It is embarrassing enough when a father intervenes on prom night, but it is a different matter entirely—for his daughter, and especially for her date—when the father is John Gotti.

"I said, 'Dad, really, can I stay, Dad, really.' You know what? He caught on. He said, 'We'll talk about this when you get in.' Well, he was waiting in his favorite chair when I got in. And I thought: 'Well, this is it, I'm punished for life. Was it really worth it?' I mean, I hated the guy anyway. But an hour later, we were laughing about it."

His relationship with his son John is described by friends as more distant, but equally protective. One of Junior's oldest friends, Steven Kaplan, remembers their relationship as "normal father-son stuff."

"If we were going out to the Boulevard"—Cross Bay Boulevard in Howard Beach—"for something to eat, he would say, 'Be careful, don't get in any trouble,'" Kaplan, a 250-pound weightlifting partner of Junior's, explained recently. "When you're with the father, most of the time you just listened to his stories. He told good stories."

By high school, Junior had left local public schools for the New York Military Academy. It was there, his sister remembers, that he fell in love with weightlifting. "They were always working out," she said. "There was an emphasis on discipline."

Junior was away at school when the greatest catastrophe to befall the

Gotti family occurred—the 1980 traffic accident that killed Junior's younger brother, Frank. "They sent someone to get John at school," Victoria remembered, "but the driver wouldn't tell him what happened. I remember watching from my window my father, whose eyes were bloodshot, walking John up the street, and I remember John just buckling when he heard."

The accident was a tragedy for another family on the street; the driver of the van, a neighbor, that mistakenly ran over young Frank later disappeared, his body never found. Law-enforcement officials believe that members of Gotti's crew cut the unfortunate man in two with a chainsaw.

After graduation, Gotti Jr., who is described by his friends as an avid reader, went straight to work. "College wasn't talked about much," according to Michael McLaughlin, another longtime friend, who grew up in neighboring Ozone Park.

Through his 20's, Junior, whose father was by then boss of the family, would periodically show up on the media radar, usually after a bar fight, creating the impression that he and his posse were roughnecks. Kaplan and Michael McLaughlin recently sought to dissuade me from this view. The two men, both in their 30's, are Gotti Jr. stalwarts. Kaplan's parents even put up their house as bail collateral for young Gotti. McLaughlin is described by law-enforcement officials as Junior's principal business associate; Kaplan is often said to be his bodyguard, which Kaplan denies. Bruce Mouw describes him, more colorfully, as "the guy who holds guys down so Junior can beat them."

McLaughlin, though rough, is friendly; Kaplan is more threatening. One evening earlier this month, while debating the strengths of various mob movies, Kaplan lavishly praised "The Godfather." I countered that "The Godfather," while hugely entertaining, kept alive destructive myths, and suggested "Donnie Brasco" as a compelling depiction of hard-luck mob life. It is for this reason that "Donnie Brasco" is not popular in certain circles. Kaplan's eyes grew beady, and he said, very slowly, in a manner meant to preclude further dissent, "'The Godfather' is a better movie." Two broken thumbs up, as it were.

McLaughlin and Kaplan, as well as Victoria Gotti, make the case that young Gotti is a homebody who loves his family and would like nothing more than to be left alone with his friends, his legitimate business interests and his four children.

"We're regular guys who did regular things," McLaughlin explained. "We went through our racquetball phase, our football phase, our bowling phase." He said there was never any attempt by Gotti to capitalize on his father's name. "We go to a bowling alley, he's not going to jump the line to get a lane," McLaughlin said. He went on to say: "If we hung out on street corners, we'd be street-corner punks. But because we hung out in social clubs at one point in our lives, now they say that the whole thing is organized crime."

They—that is, law-enforcement officials—also say it's organized crime because in the late 1980's, Junior's father inducted him into the Gambino family. This fact his friends deny, obviously. To know Junior, they say, is to know that he is more the lighthearted jokester than a ham-fisted gangster.

"Once, we were driving past Anthony Amoruso's house—he's another friend—and he's a real neat freak," Kaplan recalled. "There were these five-gallon jugs of Deer Park water out front, and John says, Go by Petco, the pet store. We buy a dozen goldfish, and John puts the fish in the jugs. When we come back from the weekend, the fish are still there, so John says, Go by Petco, and he buys food and he feeds the fish. Amoruso wouldn't give John the satisfaction for a month."

John Gotti Jr., merry prankster.

His friends say the father's raffish profile and manner of dress are not for the son, though there have been moments of flash. There was the big wedding at the Helmsley Palace in 1990, when he married Kim Albanese, of the Valley Stream Albaneses. Every wiseguy in the tristate area seemed to be there, and Leona Helmsley even hung an Italian flag outside the hotel in Gotti's honor. It was not publicly discussed that the bride was very pregnant at the time.

By the time his father was convicted on murder and racketeering charges in 1992, Junior was poised for greatness. His father, who promoted him to captain shortly after the wedding, made him acting boss, law-enforcement officials say, because he knew only relatives would be allowed to visit him in prison.

"John Gotti has done some horrible things in his lifetime, he made a lot of widows, but one of the worst things I ever saw him do was make his son acting boss," Mouw, the former F.B.I. Gambino specialist, said. "That was sealing the son's fate."

Junior's mother knew this, which is why, sources say, she became enraged when she learned her husband had made her son his successor.

Though he was said to be acting in his father's place, Junior was described, as he entered his mid-30's, as a man with far more plebeian tastes than a self-respecting mob boss should admit to. He drives a minivan, a Chrysler Town & Country, "which is the Cadillac of mini-vans," Victoria Gotti says, echoing "Get Shorty." It is in this minivan, apparently, that he ferries his children to school and once, it is said, ferried cupcakes to a P.T.A. bake sale.

His taste in clothing runs to mock turtlenecks, track suits and brushed Filas. And his taste in food is similarly dubious, at least for a Gotti.

"Once, when we were driving down from the Marion prison to St. Louis after visiting my father, I couldn't wait to eat," Victoria Gotti recalled. "I was thinking Ruth's Chris Steak House, or some Italian food, but John says, Cracker Barrel. I said, 'What's Cracker Barrel?' He said I'd love it. So we get there, and all the furniture and everything is wood. Then he said the chicken and biscuits are really good. Chicken and biscuits? I said I was hoping for a steak. He said they had a country-fried steak that was excellent. I said, 'Country-fried steak?' I had the chicken and biscuits. I was glad there was dinner on the flight back home."

As he built for himself the life style of a typical Long Island commuter father, Junior Gotti, in the minds of law enforcement—and many mobsters—did not stop acting to protect his father's interests in legal and illegal businesses across New York. The soft-focus details of Junior's life may very well be true, Mouw said, but "he's still a green-eyed monster," F.B.I. shorthand for an especially greedy mobster. "He only cares about the money coming in."

Mouw does not believe that Junior is stupid, the "dumbfella" of tabloid fame, but he is convinced that young Gotti does a poor job of overseeing what's left of his father's empire, which includes loan-sharking and gambling operations.

"He's a laughingstock," he said. "The Genovese family won't even meet with him. A lot of the family's earnings are gone. They've lost their construction interests, and Junior has done nothing to try and reclaim them. They lose in sitdowns with other families over loan-sharking and extortion beefs—the family is in ruins."

According to people familiar with the prison-visit conversations between father and son, the son consistently glosses over the parlous state of the Gambino family's affairs. The videotapes are said to be spectacles, Gotti Sr. in full opera buffa mode. He yells, he screams, he rants at the cosmic injustice of it all, while his son sits and absorbs the anger. Those who have seen the tapes say it is a wonder that Junior can summon up the courage to say anything bad at all to his father. They say it appears that he's a trapped man, that he's already in jail himself.

"I occasionally meet guys from this life style," Peter Castellana Jr. told me when I visited him at his office one day. "I spoke to one once, and he said he wasn't making any money. What's the point anymore? The Government is too strong. I tell these guys, 'Think with your brain.' What's the long-term benefit? Ninety-nine out of a hundred of these guys end up dead or in jail. It doesn't pay. The whole life style is disappearing."

Peter Castellana Jr. is the devoutly Catholic son of the reputed Gambino soldier Peter Castellana, founder of the Western Beef Corporation of Ridgewood, Queens. Peter Jr. and his three brothers now run Western Beef. They run it cleanly, legally, they say, and therefore Dad—well, Dad isn't really welcome anymore.

"I'm not saying he's banned or anything," Peter Jr. said. "I love my dad. But he's always looking for ways to connive himself back into the business. He could come here if he wants. But he knows better."

Castellana sighed and slumped in his chair. Behind him, on the wall, hung a silver crucifix. On another wall was the sword he carried when he was a cadet at the LaSalle Military Academy, where Carlo Gambino and Paul Castellano also sent their sons.

First things first, though: the name. "You see," Joseph Castellana, one of the brothers, told me once, "Castellano ends with an 'o,' but Castellana ends with an 'a.' Castellano, Castellana. It's different."

Not as different as the Brothers Castellana would like. They claim— and no one has yet proven otherwise—that they are far removed from organized crime. But the Castellanas, the Castellanos and the Gambinos are all related, and this makes things difficult for Peter Jr., who is trying, he says, to lead his family to the promised land of total business legitimacy. The most intractable problem for Peter Jr., however, is Peter Sr.

The Western Beef story is another story of fathers and sons: Like the Castellanos, the Gambinos and others, the father wants legitimacy for his sons. But the price, he is learning, is his own exile.

Western Beef, with headquarters in an orange-painted complex in a gray and threatening section of Ridgewood, Queens, runs 21 supermarkets and a food-wholesaling operation. It is the Castellana brothers who bought the assets of Dial Poultry from the Castellano brothers when they left New York in a hurry.

Peter Castellana Jr., who is 38 years old but whose eyes carry great big bags and whose shoulders slump under the weight of his name, wants nothing more than to be accepted as a legitimate businessman. "It's my opinion that there shouldn't be African-Americans, Italian-Americans, Jewish-Americans," he said. "We should all have the last name 'American.' Forget about my last name. I'm Peter American.

"I get it coming and going," he continued. "I'm not in the Mafia, so I don't get any of the benefits of being in the Mafia, but everybody thinks badly of me because they think I'm in the Mafia anyway. Coming and going."

As he talked, in walked the man law enforcement calls Frankie Meats.

"We still got that problem in East New York," Frankie Meats said, cryptically. "It's a rat's nest." The saturnine Castellana just nodded and looked expectantly at Frankie Meats.

"If I was in the Mafia, would I have Frank here?" he asked. Frank

O'Hara—he was christened Frankie Meats by his onetime colleagues at New York State's Organized Crime Task Force when he went to work for Castellana—just laughed. A former cop, he is now director of security for Western Beef. He was recommended to Castellana by a private-investigations firm Castellana hired to investigate his own company. The investigation he paid for cleared him of any mob associations. "At first, having Frank here was kind of like buying protection," Castellana said. "But then it turned out he's really good at his job."

The senior Castellana, a taciturn ex-felon—he spent time in jail for bankruptcy fraud—denies any involvement in organized crime. "What am I doing that's organized in a crime way?" he asked when I spoke with him once. "They're always saying that there's rackets in the meat business, but I never seen rackets. Do you see rackets? If I'm in the rackets, then what was I doing working six, seven days a week for 40 years?" The answer could be that he was making illegitimate money the legitimate way. There is no rule that says mobsters must spend their days in social clubs, drinking espresso and playing cards. Castellana's cousin Paul Castellano was the model of the hard-working, white-collar mobster. The blue-collar mob is exemplified by the Gotti family: the senior Gotti was incapable of running a complex business operation like a garment-center trucking concern—or a wholesale food company. The white-collar side tolerated the blue-collar side because it was from those ranks that the real muscle was drawn.

By going to an office, by appearing to be an upstanding citizen, Castellana, late in his life, can still maintain the appearance of legitimacy. Peter Jr. walks a thin line in protecting the fiction. When he grows frustrated, he accuses his father of all sorts of nefarious, though abstract, deeds: "My father knows meat, don't get me wrong, but he's always looking for an angle." He professes no knowledge, however, of actual criminality on his father's part, organized or otherwise. "I don't know if he's a Mafia guy," Peter Jr. said. "He's always denied it. I never ask."

Peter Jr. bleeds sincerity, but some in law enforcement see the cleaning-up of Western Beef as a charade. "No son of a made guy is going to fire his father without everyone being in on the joke," Bruce Mouw said.

Castellana the son says he is weary of explaining himself. "My father is my father and I'm me," he told me. "I'm just tired of this. Twenty years ago, I wanted to change my name. Pete Castle. But you can't escape your name. A lot of Italian-Americans have to go through this."

He knows, he said, that "God loves me for who I am."

"Hey, check out those guys," Goumba Johnny was saying, nodding in the direction of four knuckle-scrapers in leather jackets who had just made it past the bouncer at Club Enigma, a Bay Ridge discotheque that appears to have been flash-frozen in 1977. "They've definitely got their Up-to-No-Good Italian evening wear on. Must be mobsters. Gotta be."

Goumba Johnny smiled when he said this. He introduced me to the disco's owners, two middle-aged men from Bensonhurst who told me their club is clean, but they get hassled anyway, because of their "Brooklyn problem."

What Brooklyn problem?

"You know," one of them said, "everybody thinking we must be with somebody from that life."

Goumba Johnny explained it this way: in a chain of neighborhoods that stretch from Bay Ridge in the west, through South Brooklyn and on to Ozone Park and Howard Beach in Queens, "everybody knows a guy who is a guy or who is with a guy or is related to a guy or who thinks he's a guy." A guy being a wiseguy.

We drove to a restaurant on Brooklyn's Third Avenue, a "yuppie Italian" bar. Goumba Johnny sat down. "Are you waiting for Sal?" a middle-aged man asked Johnny, to which he answers negatively.

"Now you could interpret that two ways," he explained to me. "Maybe it's somebody just looking for his friend, or maybe it's some-body looking for a wiseguy to go commit a crime with. Since we're Ital-ians here, let's just assume it's criminal." Goumba Johnny pulls out his knot—a wad of cash that, as they say in Bensonhurst, could choke a horse—and leaves a 20 on the bar. "You know the difference between a Jewish knot and an Italian knot?" he asked. "A Jewish knot has ones on the outside and the insides filled with hundreds. An Italian knot is a hundred-dollar bill on the outside, and the rest inside are ones."

Goumba Johnny—John Sialiano is his given name—is a comedian, a local radio personality, a former vice president of the strip club Scores and someone whose fate is tied to that of Gotti Jr.

"Would you believe I never even met the guy until we were all arrested?" Sialiano said.

Sialiano was picked up in last January's sweep of Junior's alleged associates. He was charged with income-tax evasion and extortion—extortion, for allegedly shaking down a former owner of Scores, Michael Blutrich. Blutrich today is a denizen of the Federal witness security program, but he is not scheduled to testify at either Gotti's trial or at Sialiano's, because he has admitted to downloading child pornography from the Internet, and because he himself pleaded guilty to extorting Scores employees.

"That's the funny thing about this whole case—even if it's true that I was extorting him, I was extorting an extorter," Sialiano told me. "I'm the antihero. I'm the Holden Caulfield of Scores. I'm Goumba in the Rye!"

Scores, to Sialiano, was providing a service to businessmen and professional athletes. Sure, there were mobsters present: "Saying that you notice mob guys in a strip club is like going to Sylvia's in Harlem and saying, 'I detect the presence of black people here.'" But Scores, he claims, was clean. "It was a great place that served a purpose," he said. "I would say that between '94 and '96 were great years. The place really took off. I was running 115 girls a night, and without a doubt I had the best-looking group of girls in the entire topless industry in those years." When he saw Junior brought into the arrest center in White Plains last January, he knew that his life had taken a turn toward oblivion: "When he walked in, I thought, 'Man, this is deep.'"

Sialiano is not accused of being a mobster, but he says he has sympathy for Italian-Americans who are. "The Italian-American male is to the Federal Government what the black male is to a Southern police force," he said. "It's guilty until proven innocent."

His position is self-serving, of course, but it resonates nonetheless. Peter Castellana would certainly agree.

The charges against Sialiano don't amount to very much; he was arrested, most everyone says, in the hope that he would flip and become a witness against the junior Gotti, who, the Government maintains, was the puppet master at Scores.

Scores is at the center of the Government's case against Junior, and it is symbolic of the reduced reach of the mob. A single count from the massive RICO indictment illustrates the almost comic smallness of the case against the fearsome Junior Gotti and his Gambino family. The count concerns the activities of Stephen Sergio, a reputed Gotti associate who will be better remembered by mob historians for his nickname, Sigmund the Sea Monster, than for his criminal exploits: "Stephen Sergio testified that he did not receive proceeds from the coat room at Scores, whereas, as he then and there well knew and believed, he did receive proceeds from that coat room, in violation of Title 18, United States Code, section 1503." In other words, the United States Attorney's Office for the Southern District, whose prosecutors are leading the worldwide fight against Islamic terror, is also fighting to make sure that strip-club coat rooms are run free of mob taint. (The Justice Department won the battle against Sigmund the Sea Monster, who pleaded guilty to racketeering charges related to the coat room.)

Of course, you might ask yourself: Are strip-club coat rooms all that's left for the mob to control?

Ten or 15 years ago, a good Mafia wiretap was a line into a world of mayhem and blood and betrayal. Now, a good Mafia wiretap is a line into a world of malfunctioning prostates and sciatica.

Here is a brief excerpt from a conversation taped recently in Florida between two reputed Genovese family mobsters, Vincent Romano and John Cerrella, who is known as Sideburns.

> CERRELLA: "How are you, buddy?"
> ROMANO: "O.K., pal. Would you believe I just got up?"
> CERRELLA: "Did you really?"

ROMANO: "When I spoke to you—."

CERRELLA: "Did you, you laid down, how you feel?"

ROMANO: "Yeah, all right, the leg feels much better, much better, much, much better. I took a couple of glasses of tomato juice, you know, for potassium."

CERRELLA: "Right, right."

ROMANO: "I took a potassium pill. I took and uh, I was sitting up, I said let me expletive go lay down. Feel better when I lay down. You know, and I conked out."

It is not merely a figure of speech to say that the Mafia is dying. Geriatric gangsters are just one of the problems besetting Italian-American organized crime: There's the RICO problem, there's the recruitment problem, there's the defector problem, there's the sons-who-don't-want-to-go-into-the-business problem, and there's the fathers-who-won't-let-their-sons-go-into-the-business problem.

"The shrinking of Italian-American neighborhoods results in a lack of gangs, which means that there are no minor leagues to supply the majors anymore," according to Ronald Goldstock, the former chief of the state Organized Crime Task Force. "And it used to be that some children of mobsters would go legitimate, but now most of them are going legitimate."

Certainly, the sustained pressure of the Federal Government over the past 15 years has caused many would-be gangsters to realize that a life in organized crime could lead directly to jail. But the mob might be weakened now, even if the RICO statute had never been written. "The whole theory of our life was for it to be a steppingstone for our children," Big Sal Miciotta, the Colombo captain, once told me. By this light, the Gotti family is pushing against the flow of history.

Joseph Castellano, the son of a boss, says as much. While ceding nothing about his father—and casting no aspersions on the Gottis—he suggests all the same that Paul Castellano's great advantage was that he knew the way things should work.

"Whatever they said my father did, I don't do," he told me as we sat in his pizzeria, the Florida sun baking the street outside. "This is the way it works. It's evolution. The first generation comes up rough, and in the second generation, things should be fine and quiet and clean. That's the way it should work."

Castellano said he doesn't believe that such a thing as the Gambino crime family exists. In 10 years, he might be right.

acknowledgments

Many people made this anthology.

At Thunder's Mouth Press and Avalon Publishing Group:
Neil Ortenberg and Susan Reich offered vital guidance and support.
Dan O'Connor, and Ghadah Alrawi also were indispensible
Tom Dyja and f-stop Fitzgerald lent intellectual and moral support.
Maria Fernandez oversaw production with scrupulous care and attention, with help from Paul Paddock.

At the Portland Public Library in Portland, Maine:
The librarians cheerfully worked to locate and borrow books from across the country.

At Shawneric.com:
Shawneric Hachey deftly handled permissions and found just the right photographs.

At The Writing Company:
Nate Hardcastle helped find the selections for this book and kept things moving. Taylor Smith, Mark Klimek and March Truedsson took up slack on other projects.

Among friends and family:
Will Balliett made it fun. Jennifer Willis gave me good advice. Harper Willis and Abner Willis made me smile.

Finally, I am grateful to the writers whose work appears in this book.

b i b l i o g r a p h y

The selections used in this anthology were taken from the editions listed below. In some cases, other editions may be easier to find. Hard-to-find or out-of-print titles often are available through inter-library loan services or through Internet booksellers.

Arlacchi, Pino. *Mafia Business*. London: Verso, 1986.

Dannen, Fredric. "Defending the Mafia". Originally appeared in *The New Yorker*, February 21, 1994.

Dannen, Fredric. "The G-man and the Hit Man". Originally appeared in *The New Yorker*, December 16, 1996.

Eppolito, Lou and Bob Drury. *Mafia Cop*. New York: Simon & Schuster, 1992.

Goldberg, Jeffrey. "The Don is Done". Originally appeared in *The New York Times Magazine*, January 31, 1999.

Joey with Dave Fisher. *Killer*. Chicago: Playboy Press, 1973.

Kennedy, William. *Legs*. New York: Penguin Books, 1984.

Maas, Peter. *Underboss*. New York: HarperCollins Publishers, 1997.

McCall, Bruce. "Gangland Style: The Transcript". Originally appeared in *The New Yorker*, February 7, 1994.

O'Brien, Joseph F. and Andris Kurins. *Boss of Bosses*. New York: Simon & Schuster, 1991.

Pileggi, Nicholas. *Casino*. New York: Simon & Schuster, 1995.

Pistone, Joseph D. and Richard Woodley. *Donnie Brasco*. New York: Penguin Books, 1987.

Puzo, Mario. *The Godfather*. New York: Simon & Schuster, 1969.

Exciting titles from Adrenaline Books

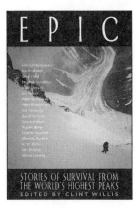

EPIC: Stories of Survival from the World's Highest Peaks

Edited by Clint Willis
A collection of 15 gripping accounts of legend-making expeditions to the world's most challenging mountains, including selections by Greg Child, David Roberts and Maurice Herzog.
$16.95 ($26 Canada), 352 pages

HIGH: Stories of Survival from Everest and K2

Edited by Clint Willis
The first anthology ever to focus exclusively on the two highest, most formidable mountains in the world. Includes accounts by Chris Bonington, Robert Bates, Charles Houston and Matt Dickinson.
$16.95 ($26 Canada), 336 pages

CLIMB: Stories of Survival from Rock, Snow and Ice

Edited by Clint Willis
This collection focuses on the most exciting descriptions of the hardest climbing in the world. From the cliffs of Yosemite to the windswept towers of Patagonia to the high peaks of Alaska and the Himalaya, *Climb* offers more than a dozen classic accounts.
$16.95 ($26 Canada), 272 pages

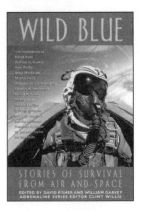